George Frederick Emery

Handy Guide to Patent Law and Practice

George Frederick Emery

Handy Guide to Patent Law and Practice

ISBN/EAN: 9783337232764

Printed in Europe, USA, Canada, Australia, Japan

Cover: Foto ©Suzi / pixelio.de

More available books at **www.hansebooks.com**

HANDY GUIDE

TO

PATENT LAW AND PRACTICE.

BY

GEORGE FREDERICK EMERY, LL.M.,

*Of the Inner Temple, Esq., Barrister-at-Law, formerly Abbott Scholar
in the University of Cambridge, and late Scholar
of Trinity College.*

AUTHOR OF 'PEOPLE'S GUIDE TO THE PARISH COUNCILS ACT FOR
RURAL DISTRICTS,' ETC.

London:
EFFINGHAM WILSON, ROYAL EXCHANGE.
1896.

DEDICATED

(*with permission*)

TO

THE RIGHT HONOURABLE
SIR RICHARD WEBSTER, Q.C., M.P., G.C.M.G.,
HER MAJESTY'S ATTORNEY-GENERAL.

CONTENTS.

	PAGE
PREFACE	vii
TABLE OF CASES	ix
LIST OF ABBREVIATIONS USED	xx
STATUTES	xxi
CHAP. I. INTRODUCTION	1
,, II. SUBJECT MATTER OF LETTERS PATENT	13
,, III. WHO MAY APPLY FOR A PATENT .	35
,, IV. HOW TO OBTAIN A PATENT . . .	43
,, V. SPECIFICATIONS	60
,, VI. OPPOSITION TO THE GRANT OF A PATENT	77
,, VII. KEEPING UP A PATENT	87
,, VIII. RIGHTS OF PATENTEE	91
,, IX. LICENSES	99
,, X. AMENDMENT OF SPECIFICATIONS .	106
,, XI. PROCEEDINGS BEFORE LAW OFFICERS	115
,, XII. PROFESSIONAL ASSISTANCE IN PATENT MATTERS	121
,, XIII. INFRINGEMENT	125
,, XIV. ACTIONS FOR INFRINGEMENT . .	135
,, XV. REVOCATION OF LETTERS PATENT .	153
,, XVI. THREATS	160
,, XVII. PARTICULARS OF OBJECTIONS . .	171
,, XVIII. TRIAL OF A PATENT ACTION . .	177
,, XIX. JUDGMENT IN INFRINGEMENT ACTION	188

CONTENTS.

		PAGE
Chap. XX.	Certificate of Validity	193
„ XXI.	Costs	196
„ XXII.	Extension of Term of Letters Patent	201
„ XXIII.	Offences	214
„ XXIV.	Register of Patents	216
„ XXV.	Miscellaneous	223
„ XXVI.	International and Colonial Arrangements	233
	List of Fees	239
	Patent Forms and Fees	242
	Patent Agents Rules	278
	Index	289

PREFACE.

The matters dealt with in this volume may be divided roughly under two heads, one comprising everything relating to the Patent Office, and those matters in which a solicitor is not usually employed; and the other dealing with the various forms of legal proceedings connected with patents in which the services of a solicitor are but rarely dispensed with.

In dealing with non-litigious matters my endeavour has been not to omit anything which is of practical value, and I believe that, so far as these are concerned, this book contains sufficient information to enable any capable person (if he deems such a course advisable) to dispense with professional assistance.

In the chapters which deal with litigation attention is confined to those points in which proceedings connected with patents differ from other legal proceedings, and on these I have tried to give in as concise a manner as possible sufficient information to enable a solicitor, without further assistance from books, to conduct any kind of patent action.

An adequate treatment of Patent Conveyancing would have unduly enlarged the book, and it has been thought better to omit any mention of it.

My best thanks are due to J. H. Taylor, Esq., of Trinity College, Cambridge, and Queen's College, Oxford, for his kindness in verifying the references and correcting the proofs. I am also indebted to the kindness of the Comptroller General for information on a few points of practice not clearly provided for by the Rules.

G. F. EMERY.

2, Harcourt Buildings, Temple;
1st January, 1896.

TABLE OF CASES.

			PAGE
Adie v. Clarke	1877	2 App. Cas. 426; Clarke v. Adie (No. 2)	144
Re Ainsworth	1885	Gr. 269	117
Allan's Patent	1867	L.R. 1 P.C. 507	210
Allen v. Rawson	1845	1 C. B. 566	41
Alliance Pure White Lead Syndicate v. MacIvor's Patents, Ltd.	1891	8 R.P.C. 321	175
American Braided Wire Co. v. Thomson & Co.	1888	C.A., 5 R.P.C. 120, 696, 7 R.P.C. 152	40, 189
Amos v. Chadwick	1877	4 Ch. D. 869	150
Re Anderson and McKinnell	1887	Gr. A.P.C. 23	115, 116
Andrew & Co., Ltd. v. Crossley Brothers, Ltd.	1891	C.A., 9 R.P.C. 165	114
Anglo-American Brush Corporation v. Crompton	1887	C.A., 4 R.P.C. 27	174
Re Arnold	1887	Gr. A.P.C. 5	113
Automatic Weighing Machine Co. v. Knight	1889	C.A., 6 R.P.C. 304	20
Automatic Weighing v. International Hygienic Society	1889	6 R.P.C. 480	194
Avery's Patent	1887	4 R.P.C. 152, C.A. 322, 36 Ch. D. 307	155, 157
Badham v. Bird	1888	5 R.P.C. 238	186
Badische Anilin Fabrik v. Levinstein	1885	24 Ch. D. 156; C.A., 2 R.P.C. 143, 29 Ch. D. 366	196

b

			PAGE
Badische Anilin v. Levinstein	1887	H.L., 4 R.P.C. 449; 12 App. Cas. 710	18, 72
Bailey v. Roberton	1878	3 App. Cas. 1075	66, 67
Bainbridge v. Wigley	1810	Parl. Rep. 197, 1 Goodeve P.C. 30	61
Re Bairstow	1888	5 R.P.C. 289	78, 116
Bakewell's Patent	1852	15 Moo. P.C.C. 385	210
Barlow v. Baylis	1870	Griff. 45	30
Barrett v. Day	1890	7 R.P.C. 54	166
Beanland's Patent	1887	4 R.P.C. 489	209
Beard v. Egerton	1846	19 L.J. 39; 3 C.B. 123; 8 C.B. 206	63, 71, 72
Re Beck and Justice	1886	Gr. A.P.C. 10	107
Bennett v. Lord Bury	1880	5 C.P.D. 339	151
Benno Jaffé v. John Richardson & Co., Ltd.	1893	10 R.P.C. 136	150
Benno Jaffé Fabrik v. Richardson	1894	11 R.P.C. 102	176
Bergmann v. Macmillan	1881	17 Ch. D. 423	94
Betts v. De Vitre	1864	11 Jur., N.S. 9	138
Betts v. Willmot	1871	6 Ch. 239	133
Blakey v. Latham	1889	C.A., 6 R.P.C. 190	165, 196
Bloxam v. Elsee	1827	6 B. & C. 178; 3 L.J. (O.S.), Q.B. 93	61
Bodmer's Patent	1849	6 Moo. P.C.C. 468	212
Bodmer's Patent	1853	8 Moo. P.C.C. 282	202
Boulton v. Bull	1795	Dav. P.C. 196, 2 H.Bl.P. 463	17
Bovill v. Ainscough	1867	Lawson, 'Pat. Pract.,' 2nd edit., 495	151
Bovill v. Moore	1816	Dav. P.C. 361, Carpmael Rep. 348	62
Boyd v. Horrocks	1889	C.A. 6 R.P.C. 159	129
Boyd v. The Tootal Broadhurst Lee Co., Ltd.	1894	11 R.P.C. 175 (Lanc. Court Case)	189, 193
Brandon's Patent	1884	1 R.P.C. 154	202
Bray v. Gardner	1887	C.A., 4 R.P.C. 40	108
The British Tanning Co. v. Groth			236
Briton, &c., Life Assurance v. Jones	1889	60 L.T. 637	151

TABLE OF CASES. xi

			PAGE
Brook v. Aston	1857	8 E. & B. 485	23
Brown v. Jackson	1895	A.C. 446	129
Brunton v. Hawkes	1821	4 B. & A. 550	76
Campion v. Benyon	1821	3 B. & B. 10	74
Cannington v. Nuttall	1871	L.R., 5 H.L., 216	25
Carpenter v. Smith	1841	1 W.P.C. 534	28
Carr's Patent	1873	L.R., 4 P.C. 539	208
Challender v. Royle	1887	C.A., 4 R.P.C. 363, 36 Ch. D. 425	163, 165, 169
Chambers v. Chrichley	1864	33 Beav. 374	145
Re Chandler	1886	Gr. 270	116
Chanter v. Dewhurst	1844	12 M. & W. 823	99
Chanter v. Leese	1839	5 M. & W. 701	103
Cheavin v. Walker	1876	5 Ch. D. 850	214
Cheetham v. Nuthall	1893	10 R.P.C. 321	146
Cheetham v. Oldham	1891	8 R.P.C. 168	13
Chollet v. Hoffman	1857	7 E. & B. 686	137
Church's Patents	1886	3 R.P.C. 95	203
Claridge's Patent	1851	7 Moo. P.C.C. 394	212
Clarke v. Adie	1875	L.R., 10 Ch. 675	129
Clarke v. Adie	1877	2 App. Cas. 320	24
Clarke v. Nichols	1895	12 R.P.C. 310	140
Clark's Patent	1870	L.R., 3 P.C. 421	203
Cockling's Patent	1885	2 R.P.C. 151	211
Cochrane v. Smethurst	1816	1 Stark 205	62
Re Codd	1884	Griff. 305	110
Cole v. Saqui	1889	C.A., 6 R.P.C. 41; 40 Ch. D. 132	199
Colley v. Hart	1890	7 R.P.C. 111	165
Colley v. Hart	1890	7 R.P.C. 101	166, 168, 182
Combined Weighing Machine Co. v. Automatic Weighing Machine Co.	1889	6 R.P.C. 502	166
Cook v. Pearce	1843	8 Q.B. 1063	62
Cornish v. Keene	1835	1 W.P.C. 08	29, 41
Crampton v. Patents Investment	1888	5 R.P.C. 404	170, 193
Crane v. Price	1842	1 W.P.C. 409	26

xii TABLE OF CASES.

			PAGE
Crompton v. Anglo-American Brush Corporation	1887	C.A., 4 R.P.C. 197; 35 Ch. D. 283	174
Cropper v. Smith	1884	28 Ch. D. 151	108
Cropper v. Smith	1885	H.L., 2 R.P.C. 17	147
Crossley v. Beverley	1829	1 R. & M. 166 n., 1 W.P.C. 106	132, 188
Crossley v. Dixon	1863	10 H.L.C. 293	101, 102, 144, 146
Crossthwaite v. Steel	1889	6 R.P.C. 190	145
Dangerfield v. Jones	1865	13 L.T.N.S. 142	22
Darby's Patent	1891	8 R.P.C. 380	208, 211
Re Dart		Gr. P.C. 307	50
Day v. Foster	1890	7 R.P.C. 54	166
Deacon's Patents	1887	4 R.P.C. 119	207
Deeley's Patent	1894	11 R.P.C. 72	159
Deeley's Patent	1895	C.A., 12 R.P.C. 199	157, 159
Delta Metal v. Maxim-Nordenfelt Co.	1891	8 R.P.C. 247	194
Derosne's Patent	1844	2 W.P.C. 1	209
Re Dietz	1889	6 R.P.C. 297	117
Dowson Taylor & Co. Ltd. v. The Drosophore Co., Ltd.	1894	11 R.P.C., Lanc. Court Case	169
Dowson Taylor & Co., Ltd. v. The Drosophore Co., Ltd.	1895	C.A., 12 R.P.C. 95	169, 170
Dollond's Case	1758	2 H. Bl. 470; 1 W.P.C. 42	42
Drake v. Muntz's Metal Co.	1886	3 R.P.C. 43	142
Drummond's Patent	1889	43 Ch. D. 80, 6 R.P.C. 576, 59 L.J. Ch. 576	158
Dudgeon v. Thompson	1877	3 App. Cas. 44	131
Duncan & Wilson's Patents	1884	1 R.P.C. 257	207
Duncan Steward's Patent	1885	3 R.P.C. 7	209
Re Eadie		Griff. 279	79
Edge v. Harrison	1891	8 R.P.C. 74	158
Edgeberry v. Stephens	1691	2 Salk 447; 1 W.P.C. 35	37
Edison Bell Phonograph v. Edison Phonograph	1894	11 R.P.C. 33	194
Edison Bell Phonograph Corporation, Limited v. Smith	1894	C.A., 11 R.P.C. 400	170, 179, 181
Edison Bell Phonograph Cor-	1894	C.A., 11 R.P.C. 389	192

TABLE OF CASES. xiii

			PAGE
poration, Ltd. v. Smith and Young			
Edison United Phonograph Co. & The Edison Bell Phonograph Co., Ltd. v. T. Lewis Young	1894	11 R.P.C. 489	152
Edison and Swan Electric Light Co. v. Holland	1889	C.A., 6 R.P.C. 243	71
Edison and Swan United Electric Light Co. v. Woodhouse & Rawson	1887	C.A., 4 R.P.C. 93	25
Edlin v. Pneumatic Tyre, &c.	1893	10 R.P.C. 311	167
Re Edmunds	1888	Griff. 281	78
Ehrlich v. Ihlee	1887	4 R.P.C. 115	148
Elmslie v. Boursier	1869	L.R., 9 Eq. 217	37
English & American v. Gare Machine	1894	11 R.P.C. 627	168
English & American Machinery Co.,Ltd. v. Union Boot & Shoe Machine Co., Ltd.	1894	C.A., 11 R.P.C. 367	176
Fairburn v. Household	1884	1 R.P.C. 109	170
Fairburn v. Household	1885	C.A., 2 R.P.C. 195	177
Fenner v. Wilson	1893	C.A., 10 R.P.C. 283	167
Fletcher's Patent	1893	10 R.P.C. 252	216
Foxwell v. Bostock	1861	4 De G. J. & S. 313	74
Franklin Hocking & Co., Ltd. v. Franklin Hocking	1887	C.A., 4 R.P.C. 442	131
Frearson v. Loe	1878	9 Ch. D. 58	30
Frearson v. Loe	1878	9 Ch. D. 65	95, 126, 137
Fusee Vesta v. Bryant & May	1887	4 R.P.C. 71	109
Gadd v. Mayor of Manchester	1892	9 R.P.C. 516, C.A., 67 L.T. 569	28, 30, 199
Galloway's Patent	1843	1 W.P.C. 725	202, 207
Gerrard v. Edge	1889	C.A., 6 R.P.C. 372	175
Gaulard & Gibbs' Patent	1887	34 Ch. D. 386	158
Gaulard & Gibbs' Patent	1888	5 R.P.C. 526, C.A., 6 R.P.C. 215	157

			PAGE
Gibson & Campbell v. Brand	1841	1 W.P.C. 628	39
Gibson v. Brand	1842-4	Scott, N.R. 890, 4 M & G. 179	74
Gibson v. Brand	1842-4	Scott, N.R. 844, 1 W.P.C. 631	74
Gillett v. Wilby	1839	1 W.P.C. 270	76
Görz & Högh's Patent	1895	W.N. 105	158
Goucher's Patent	1865	2 Moo. P.C.C., N.S. 532	203
Goucher v. Clayton	1864	11 Jur., N.S. 107	145, 146
Graham v. Fanta	1892	Div. Ct., 9 R.P.C. 164	122, 215
Re Grenfell & McEvoy's Patent	1890	7 R.P.C. 151	56
Guilbert Martin v. Kerr	1887	4 R.P.C. 18	196
Guyot v. Thomson	1894	11 R.P.C. 541	101
Haddan's Patent	1885	Griff. 108, 54, L.J. Ch. 126	158
Re Hall	1888	21 Q.B.D. 137	108
Hancock v. Somervell	1851	39 'Newton's Lond. Journal,' 158	29
Hardy's Patent	1849	6 Moo. P.C.C. 441	212
Harris v. Rothwell	1887	C.A., 4 R.P.C. 225	32
Harrison v. The Anderston Foundry Co.	1876	1 App. Cas. 574	23, 75
Harwood v. Great Northern Railway Co.	1865	11 H.L.C. 682	23
Haslam v. Hall	1887	4 R.P.C. 203	142
Haslam v. Hall	1888	5 R.P.C. 27, C.A. 144	194
Hassall v. Wright, &c.	1870	L.R. 10, Eq. 509	137
Hastings v. Brown	1853	1 E. & B., 454	72
Haydock v. Bradbury	1887	4 R.P.C. 74	194
Hazeland's Patent	1894	11 R.P.C. 467	208
Heald's Application	1891	8 R.P.C. 429	41
Heap v. Hartley	1889	C.A., 6 R.P.C. 495; 42 Ch. D. 461; C.A., 6 R.P.C. 495	103, 137
Heath's Patent	1853	2 W.P.C. 247	209
Re Heath and Frost	1886	Griff. 285	80
Heath v. Unwin	1855	H.L. 2 W.P.C. 314	128
Heathfield v. Greenway	1894	11 R.P.C. 17	174
Henser v. Hardie	1894	11 R.P.C. 421	142
Herbert's Patent	1867	L.R. 1 P.C. 399	212
Herrburger v. Squire	1888	5 R.P.C. 581	167
Heugh v. Chamberlain	1877	25 W.R. 742	145

TABLE OF CASES.   XV

			PAGE
Higgs v. Godwin	1858	E.B. & E. 529 ; 27 L.J.Q B. 421	18
Hill's Patent	1863	1 Moo. P.C.C. N.S. 258	209
Re Hill	1888	5 R.P.C. 599	81, 116
Hills v. Evans	1861	31 L.J. N.S. Ch. 460 ; 4 De G. F. & J. 288	31, 179
Hill v. Thompson and Forman	1817	1 W.P.C. 237	23
Hills v. Laming	1853	9 Ex. R. 256	101, 146
Hills v. London Gas Light Co.	1860	5 H. & N. 336	29
Hinks and Son v. The Safety Lighting Co.	1876	4 Ch. D. 607	25
Hocking v. Hocking	1887	C.A., 4 R.P.C. 412	131
Holliday v. Heppenstall	1889	C.A, 6 R.P.C. 320	175, 176
Holmes v. L. & N.W.R.Co.	1852	12 C.B. 831	74
Horsey's Patent	1884	1 R.P.C. 225	203
Horton v. Mabon	1862	16 C.B. N.S. 141 ; 31 L.J.C.P. 255	22
Houghton's Patent	1871	L.R. 3 P.C. 461	202, 209
Houschill Co. v. Neilson	1843	H.L. 1 W.P.C. 673	17
Howes v. Webber	1894	11 R.P.C. 586	140
Incandescent Gas Light Co. v. Cantelo	1895	12 R.P.C. 262	93, 133
Johnasson v. Palgrave	1880	Lawson, 'Pat. Pract.,' 2nd edit. 497	151
Johnson's Patent	1871	L.R., 4 P.C. 75	208
Johnson v. Edge	1892	C.A., 9 R.P.C. 142	164
Re Jones		Griff. 313	109
Jones' Patent	1840	1 W.P.C. 579	202
Joy's Patent	1893	10 R.P.C. 89	208
Jupe v. Pratt	1837	1 W.P.C. 146	20
Kelly v. Batchelar	1893	10 R.P.C. 289	134
Kensington Electric, &c. v. Lane Fox Electrical	1891	8 R.P.C. 277	165
King, Brown & Co. v. Anglo-American Brush Co.	1889	6 R.P.C. 424	27, 29
Re Knight	1887	Gr. A.P.C. 35	117
Kurtz v. Spence	1887	C.A., 4 R.P.C. 427	169
Re Lake	1887	Gr. A.P.C. 16	52, 107
Lake's Patent	1889	6 R.P.C. 550	85

TABLE OF CASES.

			PAGE
Lake's Patent	1891	8 R.P.C. 227	208
Re Lancaster	1884	Griff. 293	80
Lane Fox's Patent	1892	9 R.P.C. 411	209
Law *v.* Ashworth	1890	7 R.P.C. 86 Lanc. Court	169
The Leather Cloth Co. *v.* The American Cloth Co.	1865	11 H. L.C. 523	214
Lee's Patent	1856	10 Moo. P.C.C. 226	202
Leonhardt *v.* Kalle	1895	12 R.P.C. 103	72
Lister *v.* Norton	1885	2 R.P.C. 68	150
Livett's Patent	1892	9 R.P.C. 332	208
Lowe's Patent	1852	8 Moo. P.C.C. 1	206
Re Luke	1886	Griff. 294	79
Lyon's Patent	1894	11 R.P.C. 537	212
Lyon *v.* Goddard	1893	C.A., 10 R.P.C. 344	206
Lyon *v.* Mayor, &c., Newcastle-upon-Tyne	1894	11 R.P.C. 218	141
Re Macevoy	1888	5 R.P.C. 285	80
Re Main's Patent	1890	7 R.P.C. 13	235, 237
Mullet's Patent	1866	L.R. 1 P.C. 308	212
Mandleberg *v.* Morley	1894	11 R.P.C. 1	198
Mandleberg *v.* Morley	1895	12 R.P.C. 35	198
Marsden *v.* Saville Street Foundry and Engineering Co.	1878	L.R., 3 Ex.D. 203	36, 39
Mathers *v.* Green	1865	L. R., 1 Ch. 29	94, 100
Middleton *v.* Bradley	1895	W.N. 123(7)	198
Miller's Patent	1894	11 R.P.C. 55	158
Mills *v.* Carson	1892	9 R.P.C. 338, C.A., 10 R.P.C. 9	102
Montforts *v.* Marsden	1895	C.A., 12 R.P.C. 270	92, 101, 124
Moore *v.* Thomson	1890	H.L., 7 R.P.C. 325	145
Morgan Brown's Patent	1886	3 R.P.C. 212	213
Morgan *v.* Seaward	1836	1 W.P.C. 174	18, 29, 71
Moseley *v.* The Victoria Rubber Co.	1887	4 R.P.C. 252; see IV De Gex F. & J., p. 299	31
Moser *v.* Marsden	1892	C.A., 9 R.P.C. 214	139
Moser *v.* Marsden	1893	C.A., 10 R.P.C. 350	38
Myers *v.* Baker	1858	3 H & N. 802	214

TABLE OF CASES　　　　　　　　　xvii

			PAGE
Muirhead v. The Commercial Cable Co.	1895	C.A., 12 R.P.C. 39	102, 144
Muntz's Patents	1846	2 W.P.C. 121	207
Murray v. Clayton	1872	L.R., 15 Eq. 115	191
Napier's Patent	1861	13 Moo. P.C.C. 543	210
Napier's Patent	1881	L.R., 6 App. Cas. 174	202
Neilson v. Harford	1841	1 W.P.C. 355	21
Newsum v. Mann	1890	7 R.P.C. 310	197
Newton's Patents	1884	9 App. Cas. 592; 1 R.P.C. 177	208
Nobel's Explosive Co. v. Anderson	1894	11 R.P.C. 115	97
Nobel's Explosive Co. v. Jones	1882	8 App. Cas. 1	138
Normandy's Patent	1885	9 Moo., P.C.C. 452	212
North British Rubber Co., Ltd. v. The Gormully & Jeffry Mfg. Co.	1895	12 R.P.C. 17	141
Nuttall v. Hargreaves	1891	C.A., 8 R.P.C. 450	65
Otto v. Linford	1881	C.A. 46, L.T.N.S. 35	20, 180
Otto v. Singer	1890	7 R.P.C. 7	100
Otto v. Steel	1886	3 R.P.C. 120	194
Otto v. Steel	1886	C.A., 3 R.P.C. 109	32
Parkinson v. Simon	1894	C.A., 11 R.P.C. 493	186
Peckover v. Rowland	1893	C.A., 10 R.P.C. 234	130
Peckover v. Rowland	1893	10 R.P.C. 118	176
Penn v. Bibby	1866	L.R. 1 Eq. 548	175
Penn v. Bibby	1866	L.R. 2 Ch. 132	63
Penn v. Bibby	1866	L.R. 3 Eq. 308	190
Penn v. Jack	1867	L.R. 5 Eq. 81	190
Perkin's Patent	1845	2 W.P.C. 17	208
Pettit Smith's Patent	1880	7 Moo., P.C.C. 133; 1 Goodeve P.C. 533	211
Pickard & Co. v Prescott	1892	H.L., 9 P.R.C. 195	32
Plating Co. v. Farquharson	1879-83	Griff 187	149
Plimpton v. Malcolmson	1876	3 Ch. D. 568	70
Plimpton v. Spiller	1876	Lawson, 'Pat. Pract.' 497	151
Post Card Automatic Supply Co. v. Samuel	1889	6 R.P.C. 560	100, 146
Proctor v. Bailey	1889	C.A., 6 R.P.C. 538	138

TABLE OF CASES.

			PAGE
Proctor v. Bennis	1887	36 Ch. D. 740	75, 139
Ralston v. Smith	1865	11 H.L.C. 223	15, 23
Redges v. Mulliner	1893	10 R.P.C. 21	102, 146
Reg. v. Judge of C. Ct. of Halifax	1891	C.A., 8 R.P.C. 338	135
Rendell's Patent	1894	Lanc. Ct. 11 R.P.C. 277	157
Rex v. Arkwright	1785	1 W.P.C. 66	69
Richardson v. Castrey	1887	4 R.P.C. 265	185
Rolls v. Isaacs	1881	19 Ch. D. 268	18
Roper's Patent	1887	4 R.P.C. 201	210
Rothwell v. King	1887	4 R.P.C. 397 (Lanc. Ct. Case)	198
Russell v. Cowley	1834	1 W.P.C. 459	23
Re Rylands	1888	5 R.P.C. 665	107
Ryland's v. Ashley's Patent Bottle Co.	1890	C.A., 7 R.P.C. 175	150
Saxby's Patent	1870	L.R., 3 P.C. 292	207, 211
Semet and Solway's Patent	1895	[1895] A.C., 78 12 R.P.C. 10	210, 211
Re Serrell	1889	6 R.P.C. 101	107
Shallenberger's Application	1889	6 R.P.C. 550	236
Shaw v. Jones	1889	6 R.P.C. 328	190
Sheehan v. G.E.R.Co.	1880	16 Ch. D. 59	136
Shone's Patent	1892	9 R.P.C. 438	211
Siddell v. Vickers	1889	6 R.P.C. 464	191
Siddell v. Vickers	1892	C.A., 9 R.P.C. 152	188, 191
Siemens v. Taylor	1892	9 R.P.C. 393	103
Simister's Patent	1842	1 W.P.C. 723	210
Simpson v. Holliday	1866	5 N.R. 340; L.R. 1 H.L. 315	73
Skinner v. Perry	1894	11 R.P.C. 406	170
Skinner v. Perry	1893	C.A., 10 R.P.C. 1	164
Sleight's Patent	1893	10 R.P.C. 447	158
Smith v. Cropper	1885	10 App. Cas. 249	115
Smith v. Lang	1890	C.A., 7 R.P.C. 148	175
Société Anonyme de Glaces v. Tilghman's Sand Blast Co.	1883	C. A., 25 Ch. D. 1	93, 133
Southby's Patent	1891	8 R.P.C. 433	210
Speckhart v. Campbell	1894	C.A., "Times," March 13th	136
Steedman v. Marsh	1856	2 Jur. N.S. 391	18
Steers v. Rogers	1893	H.L. 10 R.P.C. 245	93

			PAGE
Stewart v. Casey	1892	C.A., 9 R.P.C. 9	217
Stoney's Patent	1888	5 R.P.C. 518	210
Stuart's Application	1892	9 R.P.C. 452	85
Taylor v. Hare	1805	1 W.P.C. 292	101
Thomas's Patents	1892	9 R.P.C. 367	207
Thompson v. American Braided Wire Co.	1889	H.L. 6 R.P.C. 528	26
Thompson v. Macdonald & Co.	1891	8 R.P.C. 9	173
Turner v. Winter	1787	1 W.P.C. 80	71
Tweedale v. Ashworth	1892	H.L., 9 R.P.C. 121.	197
Ungar v. Sugg	1891	8 R.P.C. 385; C.A., 9 R.P.C. 114	164, 170
Union Electrical Power Co. v. Electrical Power Storage	1888	C.A., 5 R.P.C. 329; 38 Ch. D. 325	168, 169
United Horse Nail Co. v. Stewart and Co.	1887	4 R.P.C. 130; 13 App. Cas. 401	189
United Telephone Co. v. Dale	1884	25 Ch. D. 778	132
United Telephone Co. v. Donohoe	1886	31 Ch. D. 399	143
United Telephone Co. v. Mottishead	1886	3 R.P.C. 213	185
United Telephone Co. v. Patterson	1889	6 R.P.C. 140	194
United Telephone Co. v. Walker	1887	4 R.P.C. 63	189, 190, 192
Vaisey's Patent	1894	11 R.P.C. 592	154
Van Gelder's Patent	1889	6 R.P.C. 28	115
Van Gelder v. Sowerby Bridge Flour Co.	1890	C.A., 7 R.P.C. 41	137
Vickers v. Siddell	1890	H.L. 7 R.P.C. 303; XV App. Cas. 496	23, 65, 74
De Vitre v. Betts	1873	L.R., 6 H.L. 319; 21 W.R. 705	188
Von Heyden v. Neustadt	1880	50 L.J. Ch. 128; 14 Ch. D. 230	33, 40, 133
Vorwerk & Son v. Evans & Co.	1890	7 R.P.C. 174	184
Walton v. Lavater	1860	8 C.B., N.S. 162	133, 145
Walton v. Potter	1841	1 W.P.C. 586	131
Washburn and Moen Mfg. Co. v. Q.	1889	6 R.P.C. 398	138

			PAGE
Watling v. Stevens	1886	C.A., 3 R.P.C. 147	66
Watson v. Holliday	1882	20 Ch. D. 780	192
Wegmann v. Corcoran	1879	13 Ch. D. 65	72
Wenham Co. v. Champion Co.	1891	8 R.P.C. 22	143
Westinghouse v. Lancashire Rail. Co.	1884	1 R.P.C. 253	192
Wirth's Patent	1879	12 Ch. D. 303	38
Wright's Patent	1839	1 W.P.C. 576	210
Wright v. Hitchcock	1870	L.R. 5, Ex. 37	133
Wood v. Zimmer	1815	1 W.P.C. 82 n; Holt N.P., 60	29
Woodcroft's Patent	1846	2 W.P.C. 31	209
Woodward v. Sansum & Co.	1887	C.A., 4 R.P.C. 166	64, 66
Yates & Kellett's Patent	1887	4 R.P.C. 150	208

ABBREVIATIONS USED IN TABLE OF CASES.

A.C. & App. Cas.	Law Reports, Appeal Cases.
B. & A.	Barnewall and Alderson's Reports.
B. & B.	Broderip and Bingham's Reports.
B. & C.	Barnewall and Cresswell's Reports.
Beav.	Beavan's Reports.
C.B.	Common Bench Reports.
C.B. N.S.	Common Bench Reports, New Series.
Ch. or L.R. Ch.	Law Reports, Chancery Appeal Cases.
Ch. D.	Law Reports, Chancery Division.
C.P.D.	Law Reports, Common Pleas Division.
Dav. P.C.	Davis's Reports.
De G. F. & J.	De Gex, Fisher, and Jones' Reports.
De G. J. & S.	De Gex, Jones, and Smith's Reports.
E. & B.	Ellis and Blackburn's Reports.
E.B. & E.	Ellis, Blackburn, and Ellis's Reports.
Ex. R.	Welsby, Hurlstone, and Gordon's Reports.
Gr. or Griff.	Griffin's Patent Cases.
Gr. A.P.C.	Griffin's Additional Patent Cases.
H. Bl.	Henry Blackstone's Reports.
H.L.C.	Clark's H. of L. Reports.
H. & N.	Hurlstone and Norman's Reports.
Holt N.P.	Holt's Nisi Prius Reports.
Jur. N.S.	Jurist, New Series.
L. J.	Law Journal.
L.R. Ch.	Law Reports, Chancery Appeals.
L.R. C.P.	Law Reports, Common Pleas.
L.R. H.L.	Law Reports, House of Lords, English.
L.R. P.C.	Law Reports, Privy Council.
L.R. Ex.D.	Law Reports, Exchequer Division.
L.R. Eq.	Law Reports, Equity Cases.
L.T.	Law Times Reports.
L.T. N.S.	Law Times Reports, New Series.
M. & G.	Manning and Granger's Reports.
Moo. P.C.C.	Moore's Privy Council Cases.
M. & W.	Meeson and Welsby's Reports.
N.R.	New Reports, Bosanquet and Pullen.
Q.B.	Queen's Bench Reports.
Q.B.D.	Law Reports, Queen's Bench Division.
R. & M.	Russell and Mylne's Reports.
R.P.C.	Reports of Patent Cases or Patent Office Reports.
Salk.	Salkeld's Reports.
Scott N.R.	Scott's New Reports.
Stark.	Starkie's Reports.
W.N.	Weekly Notes.
W.P.C.	Webster's Patent Cases.
W.R.	Weekly Reporter.

STATUTES.

	PAGE
STATUTE OF MONOPOLIES, 21 Jas. I, c. 3	2
STATUTE OF LIMITATIONS	201
5 & 6 Will. II, c. 83 (1835), Letters Patent	204
PATENTS, DESIGNS, AND TRADE MARKS ACT, 1883	
[46 & 47 Vict. c. 57]—	2
Sect. 4	12, 35, 77
,, 5	35, 68, 73
,, 5 (3)	46, 63
,, 5 (4)	46, 65
,, 5 (5)	46, 60
,, 6	11, 50
,, 7 (1)	50
,, 7 (5)	53
,, 8	54
,, 9	56
,, 9 (3)	117
,, 9 (5), 10	57
,, 11	11, 77
,, 11 (3)	117
,, 11 (4)	118
,, 12	11, 58, 59
,, 12 (3 b)	59
,, 13	50, 52, 58, 136
,, 14	53
,, 15	58
,, 16	91
,, 17 (1) (2)	87

PATENTS, DESIGNS, AND TRADE MARKS ACT, 1883
[46 & 47 Vict. c. 57]—*continued*—

	PAGE
Sect. 17 (3) (4)	89
,, 17 (4)	89
,, 18 (1)	107
,, 18 (2)	110
,, 18 (3)	111
,, 18 (4)	112, 117
,, 18 (5)	112
,, 18 (6)	113
,, 18 (7)	113, 117
,, 18 (8)	107
,, 18 (9)	113
,, 19	108, 159
,, 20	114
,, 22	104
,, 23	216
,, 24	88
,, 25 (1)	202
,, 25 (2)—(4)	206
,, 25 (5)	212
,, 25 (6)	203
,, 25 (7)	213
,, 26 (1)	153
,, 26 (3) (4)	154
,, 26 (5) (6)	157
,, 26 (7)	158
,, 26 (8)	155
,, 27	96
,, 28 (1) (3)	182
,, 28 (2) (3)	212
,, 29 (1)	141
,, 29 (2) (3)	147
,, 29 (4) (5)	148
,, 29 (6)	197
,, 30	139

STATUTES. xxiii

PAGE

PATENTS, DESIGNS, AND TRADE MARKS ACT, 1883
[46 & 47 Vict. c. 57]—*continued*—

Sect.	Page
31	194
32	163
33	76
34	3, 36
35	226
36	91
37	58
38	118—120
39	33
40	6
42	228
43	98
44	223
44 (9)	153
45	225
46	2, 87
82	3
83 (2)	182
84	4
85	217
86	11, 43
87	217
88	219
89	220
90	221
93	214, 222
94	112, 227
95	227
96	220
97	49, 88, 225
98	55, 88, 226
99	226
100	228
101	4

PAGE

PATENTS, DESIGNS, AND TRADE MARKS ACT, 1883
[46 & 47 Vict. c. 57]—*continued*—

Sect. 102	. . . .	227
,, 103, 104	. . . .	233
,, 104 (1)	. . . .	233
,, 105	. . . .	214
,, 107	. . . .	183
,, 108	. . . .	215
,, 109	. . . .	153
,, 110	. . . .	227
,, 111 (1)	. . . .	135
,, 111 (2)	. . . .	219
,, 112 (*a*)	. . . .	227
,, 112 (*b*) (*c*)	. . . .	215
,, 116	. . . .	10
,, 117	. . .	215, 233
Sched. I	. . .	7, 92

PATENTS, DESIGNS, AND TRADE MARKS ACT, 1885
[48 & 49 Vict. c. 63]—

	. . . .	2
Sect. 3	. . .	56, 58
,, 4	. . . .	31

PATENTS, DESIGNS, AND TRADE MARKS ACT, 1886
[49 & 50 Vict. c. 37]—

	. . . .	2
Sect. 2	. . . .	46
,, 3	. . . .	34

PATENTS, DESIGNS, AND TRADE MARKS ACT, 1888
[51 & 52 Vict. c. 50]—

	. . . .	2
,, 1 (1)	. . .	122, 214
,, 1 (4)	. . .	122, 215
,, 2 (2)—(5)	. . . .	52
,, 4	. . . .	77
,, 5	. . . .	108
,, 26	. . . .	135

CHAPTER I.

INTRODUCTION.

From an early period in history the Crown appears to have possessed the power of granting to the inventor or introducer of a new industry the sole right or monopoly of carrying on that industry for a limited time. In this way the inventor had an opportunity of obtaining the reward of his labour by being enabled to prevent for some years the competition of those who had merely to copy his processes; at the same time the monopoly might not be for an unlimited time, for then those who had learned the new trade would have been restrained from earning a livelihood by its practice. *Monopolies in ancient times.*

The grant of a monopoly for a new industry was entirely an act of grace on the part of the Crown, and it was usually made a condition of the grant that full information as to the mode of carrying on the trade should be given at any rate to those engaged in it; so that they might after the expiration of the monopoly period continue to carry on the industry on their own account. *Grant of a monopoly was an act of grace.*

The powerful Queen Elizabeth greatly abused this right of granting monopolies; and, to prevent *Abuses of monopolies.*

a recurrence of such abuses, Parliament passed, in the reign of her feebler successor, the famous Statute of Monopolies,* which clearly defines the power of the Crown in this respect, and upon which our present Law of Patents for inventions is based.

<small>Statute of Monopolies.</small>

The most important section of this Act is the sixth, which declares and enacts that the previous declaration as to the illegality of monopolies

<small>Statute of Monopolies, sect. 6.</small>

"shall not extend to any letters patent and grants of privilege for the term of fourteen years or under, hereafter to be made for the sole working or making of any manner of new manufactures within this realm, to the true and first inventor or inventors of such manufactures, which others at the time of making such letters patent and grants shall not use, so as they shall not be contrary to law, nor mischievous to the state, by raising prices of commodities at home, or hurt of trade, or generally inconvenient. The said fourteen years to be accompted from the date of the first letters patent or grant of such privilege hereafter to be made, but that the same shall be of such force as they should be if this Act had never been made, and of none other."

The grant of letters patent for inventions is now regulated by the Patents, Designs, and Trade Marks Acts, 1883,† amended by Acts passed in 1885,‡ 1886,§ and 1888.‖

<small>Act 1883, sect. 46. Invention defined.</small>

The Act of 1883 defines an invention, for which alone a patent can be granted, to mean any manner of new manufacture the subject of letters patent, and grant of privilege within the above section

---

* 21 Jac. I, c. 3.   † 46 & 47 Vict., c. 57.
‡ 48 & 49 Vict., c. 63.   § 49 & 50 Vict., c. 37.
‖ 51 & 52 Vict., c. 50.

of the Statute of Monopolies, and to include an alleged invention.

The interpretation of this important section has frequently been the subject of judicial decision, so that it is now pretty accurately determined. In the course of time its scope has been somewhat enlarged by the decisions of judges; manufactures have been held to include processes, and inventors have been held to include importers, so that the first importer of an invention known only abroad is entitled to apply for letters patent for the same, and to describe himself as the first and true inventor. *Interpretation of Statute of Monopolies. Manufacture includes process. Inventor includes importer.*

The Statute of Monopolies provided for the grant of letters patent to the first and true inventor only; and, until 1883, if he died without applying for a patent, his successors could not obtain a valid patent for his invention. It is now provided that the legal representatives, that is the executors or administrators of a deceased inventor, may within six months of his death apply for letters patent for any invention of which he died possessed; and if he should die after applying, but before the patent is sealed, it may be granted to his legal representatives, and so not be lost to his estate. *When inventor dies before taking out patent, patent granted to legal representatives. Act 1883, sect. 34.*

Patent Office.

The Act provided for the establishment of a Patent Office; this is situated in Southampton Buildings, Chancery Lane, W.C., and is under the immediate control of an officer, called the Comptroller-General of Patents, Designs, and Trade *Act 1883, sect. 82. The Comptroller.*

Marks, who acts under the superintendence and direction of the Board of Trade. This official will be frequently referred to hereafter as the Comptroller. The Act also provided that any act or thing directed to be done by or to the Comptroller might, in his absence, be done by or to any officer for the time being in that behalf authorised by the Board of Trade.

<small>When Comptroller is absent.</small>

The Act also provides for a seal for the Patent Office, with which letters patent are sealed, and this takes the place of the Great Seal formerly used for that purpose.

<small>Seal of Patent Office. Sect. 84.</small>

The Act of 1883 also provides that—

<small>Sect 101. Power for Board of Trade to make general rules for regulating business of Patent Office.</small>

"(1) The Board of Trade may from time to time make such general rules and do such things as they think expedient, subject to the provisions of this Act—

"(c.) For making or requiring duplicates of specifications, amendment, drawings, and other documents:

"(d.) For securing and regulating the publishing and selling of copies, at such prices and in such manner as the Board of Trade think fit, of specifications, drawings, amendments, and other documents:

"(e.) For securing and regulating the making, printing, publishing, and selling of indexes to, and abridgments of, specifications and other documents in the Patent Office; and providing for the inspection of indexes and abridgments and other documents:

"(f.) For regulating (with the approval of the Treasury) the presentation of copies of Patent Office publications to patentees and to public authorities, bodies, and institutions at home and abroad:

"(g.) Generally for regulating the business of the Patent Office, and all things by this Act placed under the direction or control of the Comptroller, or of the Board of Trade.

"(2) Any of the forms in the first schedule to this Act may be altered or amended by rules made by the Board as aforesaid. [Altering forms.]

"(3) General rules may be made under this section at any time after the passing of this Act, but not so as to take effect before the commencement of this Act, and shall (subject as hereinafter mentioned) be of the same effect as if they were contained in this Act, and shall be judicially noticed. [Effect of rules.]

"(4) Any rules made in pursuance of this section shall be laid before both Houses of Parliament, if Parliament be in session at the time of making thereof, or if not, then as soon as practicable after the beginning of the then next session of Parliament, and they shall also be advertised twice in the official journal to be issued by the Comptroller. [Rules to be laid before Parliament.]

"(5) If either House of Parliament, within the next forty days after any rules have been so laid before such House, resolve that such rules or any of them ought to be annulled, the same shall after the date of such resolution be of no effect, without prejudice to the validity of anything done in the meantime under such rules or rule, or to the making of any new rules or rule." [Rules may be annulled by Parliament.]

The Board of Trade have issued several sets of rules under this section, and the rules at present in force are those of 1890 and a few added in 1892. These will be referred to as Patent Rules, and may be treated as if contained in the Act itself.

The Patent Office is open to the public every week-day between the hours of ten and four, except on the days and times following: [When Patent Office is open. Patent Rules 7.]

Christmas Day.
Good Friday.
The day observed as Her Majesty's birthday.
The days observed as public fast or thanksgiving or as holidays at the Bank of England.

There is at the Patent Office an excellent Public Free Library, which is open daily from 10 a.m. to 10 p.m., except on Sundays, Christmas [Patent Office library.]

Day, Good Friday, and Bank Holidays; and except also on Christmas Eve, Easter Eve, and the day observed as Her Majesty's birthday, when the library closes at 4 p.m.

The library contains all the printed Specifications, Indexes, and other publications of the Patent Office, and also a collection of the leading British and foreign scientific journals, Transactions of the learned societies, and text-books of science and art.

The Act also provided that—

<small>Act 1883, sect. 40. Official journal</small>
"(1) The Comptroller shall cause to be issued periodically an illustrated journal of patented inventions, as well as reports of patent cases decided by courts of law, and any other information that the Comptroller may deem generally useful or important.

<small>Sale branch.</small>
"(2) Provisions shall be made by the Comptroller for keeping on sale copies of such journal, and also of all complete specifications of patents for the time being in force, with their accompanying drawings (if any).

<small>Publications.</small>
"(3) The Comptroller shall continue, in such form as he may deem expedient, the indexes and abridgments of specifications hitherto published, and shall from time to time prepare and publish such other indexes, abridgments of specifications, catalogues, and other works relating to inventions, as he may see fit."

Several volumes of these have been published, and with current specifications may be obtained at the sale office of the Patent Office.

<small>Applicant for patent must make full disclosure of his invention</small>
Before a patent can be granted the inventor or applicant for the patent must disclose to the public full information as to the mode of carrying out his invention, so that at the expiration of the term for which the patent is

granted the trade may be open to all. This disclosure is made by means of the complete specification, which will be described later, and which must be filed at the Patent Office, and be open to public inspection before the patent can be granted. *in his complete specification.*

Form of Grant of Letters Patent.

The following form of a grant of Letters Patent to a single inventor will hereinafter be the subject of frequent reference.

VICTORIA, by the grace of God of the United Kingdom of Great Britain and Ireland Queen, Defender of the Faith: To all to whom these presents shall come greeting: *Act 1883, Sched. 1.*

Whereas *John Smith, of* 29, *Perry Street, Birmingham,* in the county of *Warwick, engineer,* hath represented unto us that he is in possession of an invention for "*Improvements in Sewing Machines,*" that he is the true and first inventor thereof, and that the same is not in use by any other person to the best of his knowledge and belief : *Recitals.*

And whereas the said inventor hath humbly prayed that we would be graciously pleased to grant unto him (hereinafter together with his executors, administrators, and assigns, or any of them, referred to as the said patentee) our Royal Letters Patent for the sole use and advantage of his said invention :

And whereas the said inventor hath by and in his complete specification particularly described the nature of his invention :

And whereas we, being willing to encourage all inventions which may be for the public good, are graciously pleased to condescend to his request :

KNOW YE, therefore, that we, of our especial grace, certain knowledge, and mere motion do by these presents, for us, our heirs and successors, give and grant unto the said patentee our especial license, full power, sole privilege, and authority, that the said patentee by himself, his agents, or licensees, and no others, may at all times hereafter during the terms of years *Grant.*

herein mentioned, make, use, exercise, and vend the said invention within our United Kingdom of Great Britain and Ireland, and Isle of Man, in such manner as to him or them may seem meet, and that the said patentee shall have and enjoy the whole profit and advantage from time to time accruing by reason of the said invention, during the term of fourteen years from the date hereunder written of these presents: And to the end that the said patentee may have and enjoy the sole use and exercise and the full benefit of the said invention, We do by these presents for us our heirs and successors, strictly command all our subjects whatsoever within our United Kingdom of Great Britain and Ireland, and the Isle of Man, that they do not at any time during the continuance of the said term of fourteen years either directly or indirectly make use of or put in practice the said invention, or any part of the same, nor in anywise imitate the same, nor make or cause to be made any addition thereto or subtraction therefrom, whereby to pretend themselves the inventors thereof, without the consent, license, or agreement of the said patentee in writing under his hand and seal, on pain of incurring such penalties as may be justly inflicted on such offenders for the contempt of this our Royal command, and of being answerable to the patentee according to law for his damages thereby occasioned: Provided that these our letters patent are on this condition, that if at any time during the said term it be made to appear to us, our heirs, or successors, or any six or more of our Privy Council, that this our grant is contrary to law, or prejudicial or inconvenient to our subjects in general, or that the said invention is not a new invention as to the public use and exercise thereof within our United Kingdom of Great Britain and Ireland, and Isle of Man, or that the said patentee is not the first and true inventor thereof within this realm as aforesaid, these our letters patent shall forthwith determine, and be void to all intents and purposes, notwithstanding anything hereinbefore contained: Provided also, that if the said patentee shall not pay all fees by law required to be paid in respect of the grant of these letters patent, or in respect of any matter relating thereto at the time or times, and in manner for the time being by law

Prohibition to others.

How grant may become void.

Patentee to pay fees.

provided; and also if the said patentee shall not supply or cause to be supplied for our service all such articles of the said invention as may be required by the officers or commissioners administering any department of our service in such manner, at such times, and at and upon such reasonable prices and terms as shall be settled in manner for the time being by law provided, then and in any of the said cases, these our letters patent, and all privileges and advantages whatever hereby granted shall determine and become void, notwithstanding anything hereinbefore contained: Provided also that nothing herein contained shall prevent the granting of licenses in such manner and for such considerations as they may by law be granted: and lastly, we do by these presents for us, our heirs and successors, grant unto the said patentee that these our letters patent shall be construed in the most beneficial sense for the advantage of the said patentee. In witness whereof we have caused these our letters to be made patent this   One thousand eight hundred and   and to be sealed as of the
One thousand eight hundred and

To supply goods for the service of the Crown.

(SEAL OF PATENT OFFICE.)

Discussion of Grant of Letters Patent.

In this form of grant of letters patent to a single inventor they are expressed to be granted on the request or application of the inventor made in the prescribed form, in which he represents to the Crown that he is possessed of an invention, of which he gives the title, that he is the true and first inventor thereof, and that the same is not in use by any other person or persons to the best of his knowledge and belief; and that

Representations of applicant to the Crown

being the case, he humbly prays that a patent may be granted to him for the said invention.

are recited in the grant.
It will be noticed that in the grant all these representations are recited.

Effect of recital.
This recital has the effect of making the applicant warrant the truth of all his representations; and the grant is made simply on the strength of these representations being supposed to be true.

Crown takes no responsibility for truth of recitals.
The Crown on its part takes no responsibility for the truth or otherwise of any of the representations, and it is provided that if the invention is not new, or if the patentee is not the first and true inventor, the letters patent shall determine, and be entirely void.

Grant is voluntary on part of the Crown.
The grant is stated to be made "of our especial grace, certain knowledge, and mere motion," and it is recited that "we, being willing to encourage all inventions which may be for the public good, are graciously pleased to condescend to his request." This affirms the principle that there is no right on the part of the inventor to demand the grant of the letters patent, but that the grant is a voluntary act of favour on the part of the Crown.

Crown cannot be compelled to grant a patent.
There are no means for compelling the Crown to grant letters patent for any invention; the acts and rules only govern the forms which must be complied with in making the grant; and the Act of 1883 specially provides that—

Sect. 116.
"nothing in this Act shall take away, abridge, or prejudicially affect the prerogative of the Crown in relation to the granting of any letters patent, or to the withholding of a grant thereof."

There is, therefore, no doubt that the Crown might step in and prevent the grant of a patent on any application; but this power is rather a matter of historic interest, and in the ordinary course if an application for a patent be made in proper form, and the examiner to whom it is referred report that— *But is unlikely to interfere.*

"the nature of the invention has been fairly described, and the application, specification, and drawings (if any) have been prepared in the prescribed manner, and that the title sufficiently indicates the subject-matter of the invention," *Act 1883, sect. 6.*

the Act provides that—

"if there is no opposition, or, in case of opposition, if the determination is in favour of the grant of a patent, the Comptroller shall cause a patent to be sealed with the seal of the Patent Office." *Act 1883, sect. 12. As a rule patent will be granted.*

The Comptroller has the power of refusing to grant a patent for any invention of which the use would, in his opinion, be contrary to law or morality; but with this exception he does not appear to have any power of refusing the grant if the examiner gives a favourable report on the formal points which alone are referred to him, unless an opposition be decided in favour of the opponent. *Act 1883, sect. 86. Except for illegal or immoral purpose, Comptroller has no discretion as to grant in ordinary cases.*

Now the grant of a patent can be opposed only on one of three grounds, namely:

"(i) That the applicant had obtained the invention within the United Kingdom from the opponent, or from a person of whom he is the legal representative; or *Act 1883, sect. 11. Grounds on which patent can be opposed.*

"(ii) That the invention has been patented in this country on an application of prior date; or

Act 1883, sect. 4.

"(iii) That the complete specification describes or claims an invention other than that described in the provisional specification, and that such other invention forms the subject of an application made by the opponent in the interval between the leaving of the provisional specification and the leaving of the complete specification."

Unless opposed, patent is granted.

Unless, therefore, the patent applied for can be brought within the range of one of these objections there is nothing to prevent any person obtaining a patent for anything he pleases, even though the patent when obtained will be clearly bad.

Patentee can bring actions

As soon as a person has obtained a patent he is, as we shall see later, in a position to bring actions against any persons who may infringe his

and threaten.

patent, and also to threaten to bring such actions against infringers; and even though he utterly fail to establish the validity of his patent, he may still be enabled by such means to injure the business of his rivals in trade, and to reap considerable profits.

Bad patent often valuable.

If a patent is of doubtful validity, but not clearly bad, it may, nevertheless, be a very valuable property, since those desiring to use the invention will often prefer to accept a license and pay royalties under such a patent rather than incur the cost and risk of a patent action.

An action enhances value of patent.

The value of such a patent will be greatly enhanced if it be made the subject of an action for infringement, and a certificate be obtained that its validity has been called in question, since in that case any subsequent infringer may be compelled, if unsuccessful in an action for infringement, to pay the patentee's costs as between solicitor and client, a risk which few are willing to incur.

The certificate is only that the validity was called in question, and not that it was established, so that even when the patent is held bad a certificate of validity may be obtained. A certificate may be given even when the action is settled upon terms arranged between the parties, so that the certificate may be obtained without there being any actual decision on the question of validity. *Certificate of validity.*

Even if at the trial the patent is held bad, the patentee need not always lose hope, for he may be successful on an appeal; or, if he can arrange matters with his opponents, he can in the Court of Appeal get the judgment against his patent reversed, and an injunction granted upon the terms which he has arranged without his being obliged to disclose those terms.* *Judgment against patent may be reversed on appeal, even by arrangement.*

It need hardly be said that in order to make a bad patent valuable it is necessary to have very skilful management; and, to avoid running risks, an intimate knowledge of the law of threats is also needful; but with these conditions a bad patent backed up by sufficient capital may sometimes be worked so as to give the patentee a monopoly nearly as perfect as if the patent were good. *Skilful management required to work bad patent.*

It must always be remembered that the profit arising from an invention is not proportionate to the difficulty of making it; many patents of great value protect only very slight improvements on existing machines or processes. Provided an in- *Slight invention often valuable.*

* Cheetham v. Oldham, 1891, 8 R.P.C. 168.

vention is useful and shows some ingenuity, the amount of ingenuity is of little consequence, and as a general rule it may be said that the smaller the scope of a patent the less is the chance of its being upset. The cost of obtaining a patent is now so low that if the inventor be in a position to get the invention worked at all, a very small royalty will soon repay his outlay and yield him a profit, which may be out of all proportion to the amount of time and thought which he has bestowed on the invention.

Cost of patent is small.

On the other hand, it very often happens that a useful invention of great ingenuity, which the inventor is not in a position to get taken up, never repays him the fees expended in applying for a patent. There can be no doubt that it is often far easier to make an invention than to make it a commercial success; and an inventor who cannot work his own patent will, as a rule, be wise if he be content to accept a small profit for himself, and leave the rest to those who undertake the more difficult and risky task of introducing it to the public.

Difficulty of getting an invention taken up.

CHAPTER II.

SUBJECT-MATTER OF LETTERS PATENT.

LETTERS patent can be granted only for an invention that is for "*a new manufacture within this realm which others, at the time of making such letters patent and grants, shall not use;*" it must, therefore, in every case be determined whether the subject-matter of a proposed patent is a manufacture, and if so whether it be a new manufacture within this realm.

What is a Manufacture?

The first question, What is a manufacture? is one comparatively simple to answer; it is a matter of law, and the whole law of the subject was summed up in 1865 by Lord Westbury in the House of Lords; he said:

"Your Lordships are well aware that by the large interpretation given to the word 'manufacture,' it not only comprehends productions, but it also comprehends the means of producing them. Therefore, in addition to the thing produced, it will comprehend a new machine or a new combination of machinery; it will comprehend a new process or an improvement of an old process."[*]

---

[*] Ralston v. Smith, 1865, 11 H.L.C. 223.

A subject for copyright is not an invention.

The term manufacture does not extend to those things which are the proper subjects of copyright, such as books, pictures, carvings, and designs, where what are protected are really only new forms produced by the exercise of a known art or manufacture, and cannot be looked upon as being themselves new manufactures. For instance, a new design of lace made by a novel arrangement of well-known machinery would not be the subject of a patent; while a patent might be granted for a new combination of machinery for producing an old design of lace.

A discovery may not be an invention.

It is not enough that a person should make a discovery. A man may discover a law of nature which has never before been suspected, and yet he cannot take out a patent, so as to prevent others from using the result of his discovery.

Effect of drug not an invention.

He may discover that a known drug can produce new and valuable effects, but this is not subject-matter for a patent, because it is merely a new application of an old substance which anyone might make, not in any sense a new manufacture; while the discovery that a new mixture of drugs is useful will entitle the discoverer to a patent for the manufacture of such a mixture.

No patent for a principle.

The law of nature or the effect of a drug are what may be termed principles, and a patent cannot be granted for a principle. This was very clearly stated by Justice Butler, who said:

"The very statement of what a principle is proves it not to be ground for a patent. It is a first ground and rule for arts and sciences, or, in other words, the elements and rudiments of them. A patent must be for some new production from those elements, and not for the elements themselves."*

It has, however, been laid down that—

"A patent will be good, though the subject of the patent consists in the discovery of a just, general, and most comprehensive principle in evidence or law of nature if that principle is by the specification applied to any special purpose, so as thereby to effectuate a practical result and benefit not previously attained."†

In some cases a patent may go very near to covering a principle, and it may be difficult to tell whether it is really for a principle or only for the product obtained by applying a principle. *Patent may nearly cover principle.*

It is also necessary that the subject of a patent should be useful, since, if it were not, the explanation of how to carry it into effect would be of no value, and the patent would fail because the consideration on which it was granted had failed. *Invention must be useful.*

The question as to how much utility is necessary is a somewhat difficult one to answer, but it is certain that a very small amount is sufficient: this seems reasonable, since, if there is the smallest utility in the invention, the consideration for the grant cannot be said to have wholly failed, and as long as there is any consideration it is sufficient to support the grant. In one case Baron Alderson, in addressing the jury, said : *How much utility must there be?*

" A question in this case will be whether you think the steam-engine was a useful invention ; if it was of any use. I think

* Boulton v. Bull, 1795, Dav. P.C. 196.
† Househill Co. v. Neilson, 1843, 1 W.P.C. 673.

if it was of different construction from any other steam-engine, and of any use to the public, then that is sufficient."*

It has been judicially stated that " the intention to produce a profitable matter is of the essence of a patent ;" † and with this no fault can be found. But the question, Has the patent proved profitable or not ? is quite another matter. The House of Lords have clearly laid down that—

<small>Commercial success has no relation to utility.</small>

" The element of commercial pecuniary success has no relation to the question of utility in patent law generally, though of course, where the question is of improvement by reason of cheaper production, such a consideration is of the very essence of the patent itself, and the thing claimed has not really been invented unless that condition is fulfilled." ‡

Thus in only one class of case can the question of commercial success or failure be properly taken into account.

<small>Utility is question of fact.</small>

The question of utility is one purely of fact, and must, like other questions of fact, be treated entirely by itself without reference to other cases.

What is a " New Manufacture " ?

To entitle it to the protection of a patent a manufacture must be new within this realm—that is, within the United Kingdom and the Isle of Man. It is no objection to an invention that it has been used in a foreign country, or even within a British colony.§

* Morgan v. Seaward, 1835, 1 W.P.C. 176.
† Higgs v. Godwin, 1858, E.B. & E. 529 ; 27 L.J.Q.B. 421.
‡ The Badische Anilin v. Levinstein, 1887, 4 R.P.C. 462.
§ Rolls v. Isaacs, 1881, 19 Ch. D. 268.

SUBJECT-MATTER OF LETTERS PATENT.

It will perhaps assist us in considering what is a new manufacture, or, to put it more shortly, what is an invention, if we consider all inventions as divided into two classes:

1. Master or pioneer inventions—that is, inventions which open up new industries.
2. Improvement inventions.

Master Inventions.

A man makes a master invention when he does something of a new kind which nobody else has ever done. In such a case it is very probable that when once the result has been obtained it becomes easy to invent ways in which that result may be attained, and to improve on the method of attaining it, and very possibly on the result itself; the real invention consists of the idea of doing a certain thing, and not so much in the means for doing it.

A patent for such an invention is usually spoken of as a master patent.

The specification of a master patent needs to be very carefully drawn, so as to make it claim as much as possible without claiming too much, so as to run the risk of being held bad for claiming a principle. An inventor may be rightly entitled to a master patent, yet through the bad drafting of his specification he may find himself only entitled to an amount of protection so small as to be practically valueless, since it only enables him to prevent the use of a few out of many ways of attaining the same result. An invention of this

_{Claim of a principle must be avoided.}

kind certainly seems to deserve the most considerate treatment, though the following statement of Baron Anderson, made in 1837, has been considered to be rather strong:

Master patent is liberally construed.

"You cannot take out a patent for a principle. You may take out a patent for a principle coupled with a mode of carrying the principle into effect, provided you have not only discovered the principle, but invented some mode of carrying it into effect. But then you must start with having invented some mode of carrying the principle into effect; if you have done that, then you are entitled to protect yourself from all other modes of carrying the same principle into effect, that being treated by the jury as a piracy of your original invention."*

This must be somewhat modified, and the Court of Appeal have laid down that where a patent has been granted for a method of applying a new principle—

"you can prevent anyone from using the same method of carrying that principle into effect, and you can prevent anyone from using only the same thing with a colourable difference."†

Patent must be for practical application.

The great point to remember is that the patent cannot be granted for the principle, but only for the practical application of the principle, the carrying of it into practice. Thus it has been said that—

"If you have a new principle or a new idea as regards any art or manufacture, and then show a mode of carrying that into practice, you may patent that, though you could not patent the idea alone, and very likely could not patent the machine alone, because the machine alone would not be new."‡

---

* Jupe v. Pratt, 1837, 1 W.P.C. 146.
† Automatic Weighing Machine Co. v. Knight, C.A., 1889, 6 R.P.C. 304.
‡ Otto v. Linford, C.A., 1881, 46 L.T.N.S. 35.

SUBJECT-MATTER OF LETTERS PATENT.

In the case of a master patent we may put it shortly that though every method of carrying out an invention cannot be claimed, for that would be claiming a principle,* still the claim can be made in such a way that any method used for carrying out the invention infringes it; and, even though the method itself may be new in all its more important details, and may be rightly the subject of another patent, such patent will be in reality only for an improvement on the invention of the original inventor, and will be tributary to his master patent.

Every method cannot be claimed.

Patent for improvement tributary to master patent.

If this were not the case it would be almost impossible, when introducing a new industry, to prevent others from imitating it with small differences, so as to appear not to infringe the rights of the original inventor.

Improvement Inventions.

Naturally the number of master patents is very limited, and by far the greater number of applications are for patents for improvements in established industries.

In the case of a master patent the fact that ingenuity has been displayed is hardly open to doubt, but in the case of other inventions there must be proof that some inventive genius has been displayed.

There must be some invention.

This question of whether there is any invention in the subject-matter of a patent is very closely connected with the question of whether there is

* Neilson v. Harford, 1841, 1 W.P.C. 355.

sufficient novelty in an invention to support a patent.

There may be novelty without invention.

There is, of course, novelty in doing anything which has never been done before, but the means of doing it, though novel, may be so obvious to anyone skilled in the subject, that the discovery of it cannot be said to require any such exercise of inventive genius as could rightly entitle the man who first happened to do it to a patent for preventing others pursuing a like course.

Public knowledge must be considered.

Before deciding whether anything is really an invention or not, regard must be had to what is called the state of public knowledge at the time. It is not a question of what the inventor himself actually knew about the subject, but of what an ordinary skilled person would be expected to know. Thus if one thing is known to be the mechanical or chemical equivalent of another, the mere substitution of one for the other, even if it gives the same result in a cheaper way, is not an invention for which a patent can be granted; but the discovery that they are equivalents and the substitution of one for the other in the manufacture, provided such substitution is useful, may well be the subject of a patent.*

Substitution of equivalent not invention,

but discovery of equivalent may be.

New application of a general principle may be invention.

"If with a particular purpose in view you take the general principles of mechanics, and apply one or other of them to a manufacture to which it has never before been applied, that is sufficient ground for taking out a patent." † There must, however, be some novelty in the applica-

* Horton v. Mabon, 1862, 16 C.B.N.S. 141; 31 L.J.C.P. 255.
† Dangerfield v. Jones, 1865, 13 L.T.N.S. 142.

tion;* "you cannot have a patent for a well-known mechanical contrivance merely when it is applied in a manner or to a purpose which is not quite the same, but is analogous to the manner or purpose in or to which it has been hitherto notoriously applied."† But application must not be analogous to old.

"A patent cannot be granted merely for a new use of an old machine."‡ nor new use of old machine.

The invention may consist in a new process for obtaining a known result, as for the manufacture of a well-known substance; and it may none the less be a good invention because it consists only in the omission of a step in the old process of manufacture, since this may effect a considerable saving in the cost of the process.§ New process for old result. Omission of step in process.

Again, an invention may consist in a new combination of old materials previously in use for the same purpose, or for a new method of applying such materials;‖ or in a new combination of old parts to produce a new result, or to produce a known result in a more useful and beneficial way,¶ or in a combination which may consist not entirely of old parts, but may contain some parts which are entirely novel; and in such a case the patent may be made to protect not only the whole combination, but also these novel parts, or subordinate integers, as they are called. Combination of old parts may be invention. Combination of old and new parts. Subordinate integers may be protected.

* Brook v. Aston, 1857, 8 E. & B. 485.
† Harwood v. Great Northern Railway Co., 1865, 11 H.L.C. 682.
‡ Ralston v. Smith, 1865, 11 H.L.C. 223.
§ Russell v. Cowley, 1834, 1 W.P.C. 459.
‖ Hill v. Thompson & Forman, 1817, 1 W.P.C. 237.
¶ Harrison v. The Anderston Foundry Co., 1876, 1 App. Cas. 577.

The law on the subject of subordinate integers was stated by Lord Cairns in the House of Lords in the following language:

Subordinate integers.

"Inside the whole invention there may be that which itself is a minor invention, and which does not extend to the whole, but forms only a subordinate part or integer of the whole. Now, again, that subordinate integer may be a step or a number of steps in the whole, which is or are perfectly new, or the subordinate integer may not consist of new steps, but may consist of a certain number of steps so arranged as to form a new combination within the meaning which is attached by the Patent Law to the term 'combination.' Suppose that in a patent you have a patentee claiming protection for an invention consisting of parts which I will designate as A, B, C, and D; he may at the same time claim that as to one of those parts, D, it is in itself a new thing, and that as to another of those parts, C, it is itself a combination of things which were possibly old in themselves, but which, put together and used as he puts them together and uses them, produce a result so new that he is entitled to protection for it as a new invention. In a patent of that kind the monopoly would or might be held to be granted not only for the whole and complete thing described, but to those subordinate integers entering into the whole which I have described. But then the invention must be described in that way; it must be made plain to ordinary apprehension, upon the ordinary rules of construction, that the patentee has had in his mind and has intended to claim protection for those subordinate integers."*

When invention is only combination of old parts.

In the case of a combination consisting entirely of old parts, so that the whole invention consisted in combining well-known things, the House of Lords pointed out how the novelty and incidentally the invention could be tested in the following language:

* Clark v. Adie, 1877, 2 App. Cas. 320.

"The test of novelty is this:—Is the product which is the result of the apparatus for which an inventor claims letters patent effectively obtained by means of your new apparatus, whereas it had never been effectively obtained by any of the separate portions of the apparatus which you have now combined into one valuable whole for the purpose of effecting the object you have in view?"*

The new combination may differ only to a very small extent from an old one, it may be merely a slight addition or modification in one part of a machine, which when made looks as if it ought to have been obvious; but, as Jessel, Master of the Rolls, said— *[Small addition may be invention.]*

"Where a slight alteration in a combination turns that which was practically useless before into that which is very useful and very important, judges have considered that, though the invention was small, yet the result was so great as fairly to be a subject of a patent; and, as far as a rough test goes, I know of no better."†

Even—

"the introduction into an old combination of a new shape of one of the old elements of that combination, which involves a law of nature otherwise left on one side, may be good subject-matter for a patent."‡

And in dealing with the case of a combination patent, Chief Justice Tindal in 1840, in giving judgment, said:

"We are of opinion that if the result produced by such a com- *[New or better article.]*

---

* Cannington v. Nuttall, 1871, L.R., 5 H.L. 216.

† Hinks and Son v. The Safety Lighting Co., 1876, 4 Ch. D. 607.

‡ Edison and Swan United Electric Light Co. v. Woodhouse and Rawson, 1887, C.A., 4 R.P.C. 93.

New or better article.
bination is either a new article, or a better article, or a cheaper article to the public than that produced before by the old method, such combination is an invention or manufacture intended by the statute, and may well become the subject of a patent."*

This judgment has been frequently followed,† and in a well-known case on wire bustles where the fact of invention was hotly disputed, as bustles were well-known articles, and the materials used by the patentee were also well known, the House of Lords held that the patent was good on the following ground :

Complete article.
"The result is a complete article, light, effective, not likely to get out of order, and capable of being manufactured, and therefore sold cheaply, and I am unable to say that to produce a new thing combining those qualities required no invention."‡

One case no authority in another.
Although decided cases are of considerable value in helping us to deal with the questions of novelty and invention, it must always be remembered that the question of invention is one of fact in each case depending on the circumstances, and a decision in another case is no authority."§

Anticipation.

Hitherto we have treated the question of novelty from the point of view of general public

---

* Crane v. Price, 1842, 1 W.P.C. 409.

† Vickers v. Siddell, 1890, H.L., 7 R.P.C. 306; Lyon v. Goddard, 1893, 10 R.P.C. 338.

‡ Thompson v. American Braided Wire Co., 1889, H.L., 6 R.P.C. 528.

§ Lyon v. Goddard, 1893, C.A., 10 R.P.C. 344; H.L., 11 R.P.C. 353.

knowledge, and it has been assumed that the thing claimed by the patent was in the widest sense of the word novel, that is, the actual thing had never before been done, or if done it had only been done in some way different from that pointed out in the specification of the patent. The question which we have now to deal with is one of less difficulty. A patent may be bad because what is claimed in it has been anticipated by something done, or proposed to be done, before the date of the patent. Letters patent must be for a manufacture which others at the time of making such letters patent and grant do not use. And this has been extended to mean not only that the invention must not be in use at the date of the patent, but it must not have been in use at any time before the date of the patent,* unless such use was merely experimental and was not published. Again, the invention must not have been published within the realm, since the knowledge of how to use the invention is equivalent to the actual user; and people must not be prevented from doing that which they are assumed to have known how to do before the grant of the patent. *[margin: Patent may be anticipated]* *[margin: by prior user.]* *[margin: By prior publication]*

Thus the invention may have been anticipated by prior user or by prior publication. We have now to see what ought to be reckoned as sufficient prior user or publication to invalidate a patent.

Perhaps the simplest kind of anticipation is by prior public user of the invention. *[margin: What is prior user.]*

* King, Brown, and Co. v. Anglo-American Brush Co., 1889 6 R.P.C. 424.

The user must be public,—that is, known to others besides the inventor, and known to them without their being bound to secrecy,* so that they might be at liberty to use it themselves. Again, it is not enough that the invention has been put in use by some person other than the inventor who applies for a patent, if such use was only by way of trial or experiment, and was not of a commercial character or openly practised. As Lord Abinger has said :

Prior user must be commercial.

" The meaning of 'public use' is this :—that a man shall not by his own private invention, which he keeps locked up in his own breast, or in his own desk, and never communicates it, take away the right that another man has to a patent for the same invention.†

" The public use and exercise of an invention means a use and exercise in public, and not by the public."

Public use means use in public, not by the public.

And in the same case Baron Alderson explained that—

" Public use means a use in public so as to come to the knowledge of others than the inventor, as contradistinguished from the use of it by himself in his chamber."‡

In a case in which the defendants to an action for infringement pleaded that they had used the invention before the date of the patent, Chief Justice Tindal, in instructing the jury, said :

" If it was generally known and practised, and not merely as a matter of experiment, and that kept secret by the party, and thrown away as the result of that which was of no use to the

---

* Gadd v. Mayor of Manchester, 1892, C.A. 9 R.P.C. 516.
† Carpenter v. Smith, 1841, 1 W.P.C. 534.
‡ Ibid., p. 542.

public, the patent is gone; or if the defendants have shown that they practised it and produced the same result in their factory before the time the patent was obtained, they cannot be prevented by the subsequent patent from going on with that which they have done."*

A patent may probably be anticipated by the public sale of a finished article or exposing for sale of a finished article produced by the use of the patented invention, even though a mere examination of such product would not disclose the details of the invention, or enable others to use the invention; for it has been laid down that— *Sale of finished article may anticipate process.*

"The public sale of that which is afterwards made the subject of a patent, though sold by the inventor only, makes the patent void."†

But the cases on this question are not quite consistent. Again, such prior public user need not extend to the date of the patent; it has been held that— *User need not extend to date of patent.*

"If it is proved distinctly that a machine of the same kind was in existence, and was in public use,—that is, if use or if trials had been made of it in the eye and in the presence of the public, it is not necessary that it should come down to the time when the patent was granted."‡

In a case of prior user it is necessary that the user should have been a user of the actual inven- *The actual invention must have been used.*

* Cornish and Sieven v. Keene, 1835, 1 W.P.C. 510.
† Wood v. Zimmer, 1815, 1 W.P.C. 82n; Holt, N.P., 60; cf. Hancock v. Somervell, 1851, 39 Newton's Lond. Journ. 158; Morgan v. Seaward, 1837, 1 W.P.C. 195; Hills v. London Gas Light Co., 1860, 5 H. & N. 336.
‡ King, Brown, and Co. v. Anglo-American Brush Co., 1889, 6 R.P.C. 424.

tion which is the subject of the patent: it is not enough that a machine somewhat resembling the patented machine, but inferior to it, should have been used even though it produced a similar result, for it has been clearly laid down that—

"A machine which would do the work of the patent machine more or less badly is not an anticipation of the patent."*

Even if such a machine contains some of the parts which the inventor believed to be new, his patent may still be good for an improvement on such prior machine; for, as Jessel, Master of the Rolls, stated—

"It does not follow that because an inventor thinks he has invented more than he has in fact, and describes the advantages of his invention, and some of these advantages arise from an old portion of the invention, it may not still be a good patent, provided that the invention as claimed is so limited as to fail to cover the actual thing in use, while it covers some of the advantages mentioned; in such a case it may still, no doubt, be a good patent."†

<small>What is prior publication.</small> Lastly, an invention may be anticipated by prior publication. This means publication without any reservation, for the communication of an invention to a person who is aware that it is not intended to be published does not amount to a publication.‡

"The antecedent statement must be such that a person of ordinary knowledge on the subject would be able practically to

---

* Barlow v. Baylis, 1870, 45 Griff.

† Frearson v. Loe, 1878, 9 Ch. D. 58.

‡ Gadd and Mason v. Mayor, &c., of Manchester, C.A., 1892, 9 R.P.C. 516 ; 67 L.T. 569.

apply the discovery without the necessity of making further experiments and gaining further information before the invention can be made useful. The information as to the alleged invention given by the prior publication must, for the purposes of practical utility, be equal to that given by the subsequent patent."*

The law on the question of prior public user and prior public knowledge was in 1861 summed up by Lord Chancellor Eldon in these words: *Anticipation must be complete.*

"Whatever is essential to the invention must be read out of the prior publication. If specific details are necessary for the practical working and real utility of the alleged invention, they must be found substantially in the prior publication. Apparent generality, or a proposition not true to its full extent, will not prejudice a subsequent statement which is limited, accurate, and gives a specific rule of practical application. The reason is manifest, because much further information, and therefore much further discovery, are required before the full truth can be extricated and embodied in a form to serve the uses of mankind. It is the difference between the ore and the refined and pure metal which is extracted from it. .... Upon principle, therefore, I conclude that the prior knowledge of an invention to avoid a patent must be a knowledge equal to that required to be given by a patent, viz. such a knowledge as will enable the public to perceive the very discovery, and to carry the invention into public use."†

The most usual way in which an invention gets published is in the specification of a patent (provisional specifications were all published prior to 1885, but now a provisional specification is not published unless it is followed up by a complete specification) or in some book or periodical. *Publication may be by specification, Act 1885, sect. 4,*

---

* Moseley v. The Victoria Rubber Co., 1887, 4 R.P.C. 252; see 4 De Gex F. & J., p. 299.

† Hills v. Evans, 1861, 31 L.J. Ch. 463.

In the case of a book or periodical published in England it is not necessary to prove anything beyond the date of publication, but an invention may be published in any well-known foreign language, such as French or German, and in the case of a foreign publication it is necessary to show that at least one copy was published in England.

[margin: or by book or periodical, whether published in England]
[margin: or abroad.]

It is not necessary to prove that anyone in this country read the account of the invention; it is enough that they were in the position of being able to do so.

Thus the deposition of a German specification in the library at the Patent Office,* or presumably the deposition of the anticipation at any public library, where it would be notified in the catalogue and open to inspection without any record being kept of such inspection, or the sale in this country of a foreign periodical containing a description of the patented article,† before the date of the patent, is a prior publication of the invention.

[margin: Book in public library.]

But, on the other hand, the mere fact that a foreign book containing a description of the invention is in an inner room of the British Museum is not of itself evidence of publication; it would be necessary to show that some one had looked into it.‡

The prior publication must be complete in itself, it is not enough for an anticipation to be

[margin: Publication must be complete in itself, and]

---

* Harris v. Rothwell, C.A., 1887, 4 R.P.C. 225.
† Pickard and Co. v. Prescott, H.L., 1892, 9 R.P.C. 195.
‡ Otto v. Steel, C.A., 1886, 3 R.P.C. 109.

contained in several independent documents; this *it must not be collected from different places.* is evidence of public knowledge, and may be used to show that there is no sufficient subject-matter for invention; but the fact that by comparing a number of documents it is possible to get sufficient information to enable one to do that which is described in the specification is not an anticipation of the patent.*

Publication at an Exhibition before Application for Patent.

Before leaving the consideration of what prior user or publication will defeat a patent, one case must be mentioned in which the exhibition of the invention before application for a patent is made will not affect the subsequent application, provided all the necessary formalities are complied with.

It is provided that—

"The exhibition of an invention at an industrial or international exhibition, certified as such by the Board of Trade, or the publication of any description of the invention during the period of the holding of the exhibition, or the use of the invention for the purpose of the exhibition in the place where the exhibition is held, or the use of the invention during the period of the holding of the exhibition by any person elsewhere, without the privity or consent of the inventor, shall not prejudice the right of the inventor or his legal personal representative to apply for and obtain provisional protection and a patent in respect of the invention, or the validity of any patent granted on the application, provided that both the following conditions are complied with, namely: *Act 1883, sect. 39, protection of patents exhibited at industrial exhibitions.*

"(*a*) The exhibitor must, before exhibiting the invention, give

---

* Von Heyden v. Neustadt, 1880, 50 L.J. Ch. 128.

the Comptroller the prescribed notice of his intention to do so ; and

"(b) The application for a patent must be made before or within six months from the date of the opening of the exhibition.

Act 1886, sect. 3.

"Whereas it is expedient to provide for the extension of this section to industrial and international exhibitions held out of the United Kingdom, be it therefore enacted as follows :

Protection of patents exhibited at international exhibitions.

"It shall be lawful for Her Majesty, by Order in Council, from time to time to declare that sections thirty-nine and fifty-seven of the Patents, Designs, and Trade Marks Act, 1883, or either of those sections, shall apply to any exhibitions mentioned in the Order in like manner as if it were an industrial or international exhibition certified by the Board of Trade, and to provide that the exhibitor shall be relieved from the conditions, specified in such sections, of giving notice to the Comptroller of his intention to exhibit, and shall be so relieved either absolutely, or upon such terms and conditions as to Her Majesty in Council may seem fit."

For these cases the Patent Rules, 1890, provide that—

Patent Rule 15. Notice to Comptroller of intended exhibition.

"Any person desirous of exhibiting an invention at an industrial or international exhibition, or of publishing any description of the invention during the period of the holding of the exhibition or of using the invention for the purpose of the exhibition in the place where the exhibition is held, shall, after the Board of Trade have issued a certificate that the exhibition is an industrial or international one, give to the Comptroller notice of his intention to exhibit, publish, or use the invention, as the case may be.

"For the purpose of identifying the invention in the event of an application for a patent being subsequently made, the applicant shall furnish to the Comptroller a brief description of his invention, accompanied, if necessary, by drawings, and such other information as the Comptroller may in each case require."

P. 264.

This notice to the Comptroller must be given on Patent Form O, which must bear a stamp for 10s.

CHAPTER III.

WHO MAY APPLY FOR A PATENT.

Under the Statute of Monopolies a patent could be granted to the true and first inventor or inventors of a manufacture; and this has been but slightly modified by later statutes. It is still true that a valid patent can only be granted to the true and first inventor or inventors (if living), either alone or in conjunction with others who are not inventors, but the words have been frequently subject to judicial consideration, and their scope has been materially widened from what they at first sight might seem to include.

Later statutes have also affected the class to whom patents may be granted by making provision for cases in which, by the untimely death of an inventor, his estate would have formerly been deprived of the benefit of his invention.

It is now provided that—

"(1) Any person, whether a British subject or not, may make an application for a patent.

"(2) Two or more persons may make a joint application for a patent, and a patent may be granted to them jointly." Who may apply for a patent, Act 1883, sect. 4.

The Act of 1885 declares that—

"Whereas doubts have arisen whether under the principal Act a patent may lawfully be granted to several persons jointly, some or one of whom only are or is the true and first inventors or Sect. 5.

inventor; be it therefore enacted and declared that it has been and is lawful, under the principal Act, to grant such a patent."

Thus a patent may be applied for by any person or group of persons, whether British subjects or aliens; and since person includes corporation, there is nothing to prevent a patent being applied for by a joint-stock company, either alone or in conjunction with other corporations or persons.

Corporation may apply.

It is obvious that a corporation cannot invent anything, but, as we shall see later, the inventor may be only an importer; so that a corporation might, as the importer of an invention, be able to apply for a patent, and to describe itself as the true and first inventor.

Corporation may be true and first inventor.

A case having arisen which showed that there might be hardship when an inventor died without having applied for letters patent,* it was provided that—

"(1) If a person possessed of an invention dies without making application for a patent for the invention, application may be made by, and a patent for the invention granted to, his legal representative (that is, his executors or administrators).

Act 1883, sect. 34.

"(2) Every such application must be made within six months of the decease of such person, and must contain a declaration by the legal representative that he believes such person to be the true and first inventor of the invention."

Inventor dying before grant of patent.

The Patent Rules, 1890, provide that—

"An application for a patent by the legal representative of a person who has died possessed of an invention shall be accompanied by an official copy of, or an extract from, his will or the letters of administration granted of his estate and effects, in proof of the applicant's title as such legal representative."

Rule 20.

---

* Marsden v. Saville Street Foundry and Engineering Co., 1878, L.R., 3 Ex. D. 203.

This general power of applying for letters patent is, however, limited by the rule that the grant must, unless he be no longer alive, be to the true and first inventor, so that it appears finally that the application must be made by the true and first inventor, or the personal representatives of a deceased true and first inventor, either alone or in conjuntion with other persons or corporations.

The advantage of allowing a joint application to be made by the inventor and others is that each of the applicants has the right of using the invention for which the letters patent are granted without license from their co-applicants, and that by simple agreement between the inventor and a co-applicant who is financing his invention, the latter can obtain control of the patent without the expense of any deed of assignment or license. *Advantages of joint applications.*

The words true and first inventor soon came under judicial consideration, and were held to include an importer into this realm of a new manufacture, that is of a manufacture new so far as this realm is concerned. Thus in 1691 it was declared that— *Inventor includes importer.*

"A grant of a monopoly may be to the first inventor by 21 Jac. I; and if the invention be new in England a patent may be granted, though the thing was practised beyond the sea before: for the statute speaks of new manufactures within this realm; so that if they be new here, it is within the statute, for the Act intended to encourage new devices useful to the kingdom, and whether learned by travel or study, it is the same thing." *

---

* Edgeberry v. Stephens, 1691, 2 Salk. 447 ; 1 W.P.C. 35 ; see also Elmslie v. Boursier, 1869, L.R., 9 Eq. 217.

Importer may be abroad. — It is not necessary that the importer should be in England, the importation may be only by the application for letters patent; for it has been held that a patent can be granted to an alien resident abroad for an invention communicated to him abroad by another alien.*

Importer may be receiver only. — Again, "the first and true inventor" may merely be a receiver of the invention from abroad, and in this case we must distinguish two classes.

Importer an agent. — First, there is the ordinary case in which a foreign inventor communicates his invention to an agent in this country, who applies for a patent for it as on a communication from abroad, and who, when the patent is granted, holds it in trust for his foreign correspondent; and this is *Agent may improve on invention.* the case even when the agent improves upon the invention which has been communicated to him.†

Importer not an agent. — The second case is where an invention is communicated to a person in this country without any intention of his applying for a patent on behalf of his correspondent. In this case he is entitled to apply for a patent in his own name and on his own account, for it was held that—

May apply for patent on his own account. — "Any person not being in a confidential position towards the first inventor, receiving from a person abroad an invention, is entitled, perhaps not in a strictly moral view, but at all events according to law, to take out a patent on his own account for the invention so communicated." ‡

Communication must be from abroad. — It is, however, absolutely necessary that the

---

* *Re* Wirth's patent, 1879, 12 Ch. D. 303.
† Moser *v.* Marsden, C.A., 1893, 10 R.P.C. 350.
‡ Steedman *v.* Marsh, 1856, 2 Jur. N.S. 391.

communication (except in the case of an application by the personal representatives of a deceased inventor) should be received from some person not in the United Kingdom. It has been held that—

"The communication made in England by one British subject to another does not make the latter a first and true inventor to whom a valid patent can be granted."*

Except in the case of an importer the first and true inventor must be the actual inventor,—that is, he must himself have exercised inventive genius in discovering the invention; as Chief Justice Tindal said: *Applicant must be real inventor.*

"A man may publish to the world that which is perfectly new in all its uses, and has not before been enjoyed, and yet he may not be the first and true inventor; he may have borrowed it from some other person, he may have taken it from a book, he may have learned it from a specification, and then the Legislature never intended that a person who had taken all his knowledge from the act of another, from the labours and assiduity and ingenuity of another, should be the man who was to receive the benefit of another's skill."†

In the same case, however, he also stated:

"It would not be sufficient to destroy this patent to show that learned persons in their studies had foreseen or had found out this discovery that is afterwards made public, or that a man in his private warehouse had by various experiments endeavoured to discover it and failed, and had given it up."

This inventive genius may, however, be exercised in developing the suggestions of others. It *Invention may be suggested by another.*

* Marsden v. Saville Street Foundry and Engineering Co., 1878, L.R., 3 Ex. D. 203.
† Gibson and Campbell v. Brand, 1841, 1 W.P.C. 628.

was held in the Court of Appeal, in the well-known bustle case, that—

> "If a mere suggestion is made upon which the mind of the inventor has to work, and out of which the mind of the inventor produces something that is different from, an improvement upon, and a distinct variation from the suggestion, I apprehend the fact that it has been suggested by the reading of a specification, or by looking at the drawings of a specification, will not prevent his having a right to patent his invention." *

<small>Invention may be application of others' work.</small>

The invention itself may consist entirely in the application of knowledge gained from the works of others; as Lord Justice James has said:

> "Even if it could be shown that a patentee had made his discovery of a consecutive process by studying, collating, and applying a number of facts discriminated in the pages of such works, his diligent study of such works would as much entitle him to the character of an inventor as the diligent study of the works of nature would." †

<small>Inventor may have assistants.</small>

In the process of invention the inventor may receive assistance and even important suggestions from others, and yet he may be entitled to describe himself as the true and first inventor; he may employ servants to carry out experiments for him, and even to work on their own account on comparatively slight suggestions from him, and yet he may be entitled to a patent for the result of their labours. In an old case the law on this subject was stated by Justice Erle with great clearness as follows:

> "I take the law to be that if a person has discovered an improved principle, and employs engineers, agents, or other

---

* American Braided Wire Co. v. Thompson and Co., C.A., 1888, 5 R.P.C. 120.

† Von Heyden v. Neustadt, 1880, 50 L.J. Ch. 128.

persons to assist him in carrying out that principle, and they, in the course of the experiments arising from that employment, make valuable discoveries accessory to the main principle, and tending to carry that out in a better manner, such improvements are the property of the inventor of the original improved principle, and may be embodied in his patent." *

The employer, however, must have some claim to be described as the inventor; he must have exercised some inventive genius, even though it may not have been much: if the servant alone by his own ingenuity makes the invention, the fact that in working it out he was using his master's property and time is not enough to deprive him of the right to a patent, or to entitle his master to obtain a patent for the invention of his servant.† *[margin: Applicant must exercise some invention.]*

There is, lastly, the very important case of rival inventors. If two persons, wholly unconnected with one another, at different times, make the same invention, which of them is entitled to call himself the true and first inventor? *[margin: Rival inventors.]*

The law on this subject is quite clear: the person entitled to a patent for an invention is the person who first goes to the Crown and applies for a patent. This law was declared by Chief Justice Tindal in the following terms: *[margin: First to apply is entitled to patent.]*

"There may be many discoverers starting at the same time, many rivals that may be running on the same road at the same time, and the first who comes to the Crown and takes out a patent, it not being generally known to the public, is the man who has a right to clothe himself with the authority of the patent, and to enjoy its benefits." ‡

* Allen v. Rawson, 1845, 1 C.B. 566.
† Heald's application, 1891, 8 R.P.C. 429.
‡ Cornish v. Keene, 1835, 1 W.P.C. 508.

Since patents are dated as of the date and in the order of application, this now may be taken as equivalent to stating that the man whose application for a patent first reaches the Patent Office is the true and first inventor, and is entitled to the patent.

Re-discovery may be invention. Provided an earlier inventor has not published his invention, the fact that the applicant for a patent has only re-discovered what had been first discovered by another does not in any way affect his right to a patent. This question arose in a very early case which was afterwards referred to in the House of Lords in the following terms:

"Dollond was patentee of a new method of making object-glasses, but it was objected that one Dr. Hall had made the same discovery before him.

"Dr. Hall, however, had confined it to his closet, and the public were not acquainted with it. Dollond was held to be the true and first inventor."*

---

* Dollond's case, 1758, 2 H. Bl. 470.

CHAPTER IV.

HOW TO OBTAIN A PATENT.

THE next matter for consideration is, what must a duly qualified party in possession of a patentable invention do in order to obtain a patent?

The grant of a patent in this country is almost entirely a formal matter; it is true that every application is referred to an examiner whose duty it is to report to the Comptroller, but this examination is confined to seeing whether the application is in proper form, and the invention fairly described by the applicant. *Grant a formal matter.*

The Comptroller also has power to refuse to grant a patent for an invention of which the use would, in his opinion, be contrary to law or morality; and this power has been exercised in the case of an application for a patent for a lottery machine.* *Act 1883, sect. 86. Immoral patent may be refused.*

In some cases the grant may be opposed by persons whose rights would be affected by the grant of the patent as applied for; and if their opposition be upheld the grant may be refused, or certain conditions may be imposed on the applicant. *Grant may be opposed.*

In any case before exercising any discretionary power adversely to the applicant the Comptroller must, if required so to do, hear the applicant, *Comptroller must hear applicant.*

* Griff. 20.

and his decision is subject to appeal to the law officer.

Usual course.

With these exceptions the rule is that an application made in due form is accepted, and when a complete specification has been filed a patent is sealed in due course. No examination as to whether the invention is novel, or as to whether it is proper subject-matter for a patent, is made by the Patent Office, the whole responsibility of this being thrown on the applicant.

No examination as to validity.

Who makes the application.

An application for a patent may be made by the applicant or applicants to the Patent Office direct, or through an agent; in the latter case the agent is entitled to sign all the necessary papers with the exception of the application form, which must in every case be signed by the applicant or applicants.

Forms of application.

Three forms are provided, on one of which an application for a patent must be made.

See p. 243.

Patent Form A is for an application by the true and first inventor or inventors, or their personal representatives, either alone or in conjunction with others.

See p. 245.

Patent Form A 1 is for an application made in respect of an invention communicated from abroad by an agent on behalf of his foreign correspondent.

See p. 247.

Patent Form A 2 is to be used in making an application under the foreign and colonial arrangements.

[For obtaining these forms see page 272.]

How to fill up application form.

Whichever form is used, it must bear an impressed stamp for £1, must be filled in with the names and addresses of the applicants and the title of the invention, and must be signed by the applicant, or if there be more than one, by each of the applicants; if the application be on behalf of a firm, every member of the firm must sign, and if on behalf of a corporation or company, the secretary, or some officer of the company should sign the form, adding the words " for the company."*

Under the " Patents Rules, 1890 "—

"An application for a patent must be signed by the applicant; but all other communications between the applicant and the Comptroller, and all attendances by the applicant upon the Comptroller, may be made by or through an agent duly authorised to the satisfaction of the Comptroller, and, if he so require, resident in the United Kingdom." Patent Rule 8.

"The application shall be accompanied by a statement of an address to which all notices, requisitions, and communications of every kind may be made by the Comptroller, or by the Board of Trade, and such statement shall thereafter be binding upon the applicant, unless and until a substituted statement of address shall be furnished by him to the Comptroller. He may in any particular case require that the address mentioned in this rule be in the United Kingdom." Patent Rule 9.

On the backs of Forms A and A 1 will be found two forms of statement as to the address to which notices are to be forwarded: the first is for use when application is made through an agent, and contains an authority to the agent to act in the matter; the second is for use when the application is made direct. In every case one of these forms must be filled in and signed by the applicant or each of the applicants as the case may be. Address to which notices may be sent.

Any change of the address to which notices are Change of address.

* Patent Office Circular.

LAW OF PATENTS.

<small>P. 267.</small>

to be sent must be notified to the Comptroller on Patent Form R, which must bear a stamp for 5s.

<small>How the form of application is to be dealt with.</small>

The form of application when duly filled up may be left by hand at the Patent Office or sent by post addressed to the Comptroller, Patent Office, Southampton Buildings, Chancery Lane, London, W.C.

<small>For full details see Chap. V, p. 60. (4).</small>

It must be accompanied by two copies of either a provisional specification or a complete specification; in the latter case one copy must bear an impressed stamp for £3.

<small>Act 1883, sect. 5. (3).</small>

"A provisional specification must describe the nature of the invention, and be accompanied by drawings if required."

"A complete specification, whether left on application or subsequently, must particularly describe and ascertain the nature of the invention, and in what manner it is to be performed, and must be accompanied by drawings if required."

<small>(5).</small>

"A specification, whether provisional or complete, must commence with the title, and in the case of a complete specification must end with a distinct statement of the invention claimed."

<small>Drawings with provisional specification. Act 1886, sect. 2.

Patent Rule 33.</small>

It is not usual for drawings to accompany a provisional specification, but if any are sent, others like them need not be sent a second time with the complete specification, and in it they may be referred to as the drawings left with the provisional specification.

Preparing Specifications for Filing.

<small>P. 249.

P. 250.</small>

A provisional specification must be commenced on Patent Form B, and a complete specification must be commenced on Patent Form C; the rest of the specification in each case must be on strong wide-ruled paper of size 13 inches by 8 inches, with a margin of 2 inches on the left-hand side. All specifications must be in English, and must be written or printed in large and legible characters. Patent Forms B and C are issued in duplicate with Application Forms A, A 1, and A 2.

Form B does not require any stamp, but one copy of Form C must bear an impressed stamp for £3.

Paper properly ruled for the continuation of specifications may be obtained from any law stationer under the name of "patent paper." *Paper for specifications.*

Each copy of the specification must be signed by the agent through whom the application is made, or if made without an agent by the applicant or applicants. *Each copy must be signed.*

Sizes and Methods of preparing Drawings accompanying Provisional or Complete Specifications.
(Patent Rules, 1890, 30 to 33.)

"30. The provisional or complete specification need not be accompanied by drawings if the specification sufficiently describes the invention without them; but if drawings are furnished they should accompany the provisional or complete specification to which they refer, except in the case provided for by Rule 33. No drawing or sketch, such as requires a special engraving for letterpress, should appear in the specification itself. *Drawings for specifications.*

"31. Drawings (if any) must be delivered at the Patent Office either in a flat state or on rollers, so as to be free from folds, breaks, or creases.

"They must be made on pure white, hot-pressed, rolled, or calendered drawing-paper of smooth surface and good quality, and, where possible, without colour or Indian ink washes. *Requirements as to paper and*

"They must be on sheets of one of the two following sizes *size of drawings.*

(the smaller being preferable): 13 inches at the sides by 8 inches at the top and bottom, or 13 inches at the sides by 16 inches at the top and bottom, including margin, which must be ½ an inch wide.

"If there are more figures than can be shown on one of the smaller sized sheets, two or more of these sheets should be used in preference to employing the larger size. When an exceptionally large drawing is required, it should be *continued* on subsequent sheets. There is no limit to the number of sheets that may be sent in.

<small>Quality of ink.</small>
"To ensure their satisfactory reproduction, the drawings must be executed with *absolutely black Indian ink; the same strength and colour of fine and shade lines to be maintained throughout.* Section lines and lines for effect, or shading lines, must not be closely drawn. A specimen drawing is inserted in illustration of this requirement.

<small>Reference figures and letters.</small>
"Reference figures and letters must be bold, distinct, not less than one eighth of an inch in height; and the same letters should be used in different views of the same parts. In cases of complicated drawings the reference letters must be shown outside the figure, and connected with the part referred to by a fine line.

<small>Scale of drawings.</small>
"The scale adopted should be large enough to show clearly wherein the invention consists, and only so much of the apparatus, machine, &c., need be shown as effects this purpose. When the scale is shown on the drawing it should be denoted, *not* by words, but by a drawn scale, as illustrated in the specimen.

<small>Drawings to bear the name of applicant, &c.</small>
"Drawings must bear the name of the applicant (and in the case of drawings left with a complete specification after a provisional specification, the number and year of the application) in the *left-hand top corner;* the number of sheets of drawings sent and the number of each sheet in the *right-hand top corner;* and the signature of the applicant or his agent in the *right-hand bottom corner.*

"No written description of the invention should appear on the drawings.

<small>Restrictions as to wood engravings.</small>
"Wood engravings, or representations of the invention, other than the drawings prepared as above described, will not be

Specimen drawing for Specifications.

Border line ½ an inch from edge of paper.

A.D. 18   No.   (Sheets)
Smith's Specification.   Sheet

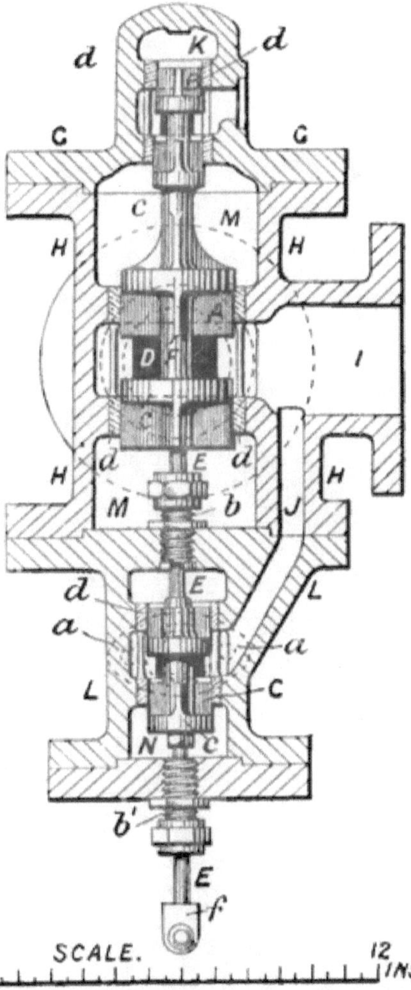

FIG. I.

Jas. Smith (Applicant)
or Jones & Co.
Agents for Applicant

SCALE. 0 — 12 INS.

Border line ½ an inch from edge of paper.

Size of paper for Specification drawing { 13 inches by 8 inches. or 23 .... " 16 inches

received unless of such a character as to be suitable for reproduction by the process of photo-lithography.

"32. A *fac-simile* of the original drawings, but *without* colour or Indian-ink washes, and prepared strictly in accordance with the regulations prescribed in Rule 31, must accompany the originals, and be marked 'true copy.'" *Copies of drawings.*

"33. If an applicant desires to adopt the drawings lodged with his provisional specification as the drawings for his complete specification, he should refer to them as those 'left with the provisional specification.'" *Provisional drawings used for complete specification.*

Procedure after Application is sent.

"Applications for patents sent by prepaid letter through the post shall, as far as may be practicable, be opened and numbered in the order in which the letters containing the same have been respectively delivered in the ordinary course of post. *Patent Rule 18. Applications, how numbered.*

"Applications left at the Patent Office otherwise than through the post shall be in like manner numbered in the order of their receipt at the Patent Office."

It is, however, provided that a letter sent through the post shall be deemed to have been left at the Patent Office at the time when it would be delivered in the ordinary course of post; so that if for any reason the delivery were delayed beyond the time when it should have taken place in the ordinary course of post, it is submitted that the applicant might claim to have his application dated and treated as having been received at the time at which, but for the delay in transmission, it would have reached the Patent Office. *Act 1883, sect. 97. Postal applications, when deemed received.*

Even if the application never reached the Patent Office at all, and the loss was afterwards made good by leaving fresh copies of the appli- *Application lost in post.*

4

cation and specifications, it is submitted that the applicant would be entitled not to suffer by the default of the post office.

There is no discrimination made between inland and foreign post.

It is provided that—

<small>Application to be referred to an examiner. Act 1883, sect. 6.</small>
"The Comptroller shall refer every application to an examiner, who shall ascertain and report to the Comptroller whether the nature of the invention has been fairly described, and the application, specification, and drawings (if any) have been prepared in the prescribed manner, and the title sufficiently indicates the subject-matter of the invention.

<small>When report of examiner is unsatisfactory. Sect. 7.</small>
"(1) If the examiner reports that the nature of the invention is not fairly described, or that the application, specification, or drawings has not or have not been prepared in the prescribed manner, or that the title does not sufficiently indicate the subject-matter of the invention, the Comptroller may refuse to accept the application, or may require that the application or specification or drawings be amended before he proceeds with the application; and in the latter case the application shall, if the Comptroller so directs, bear date as from the time when the requirement is complied with."

<small>No fee for amendment before acceptance.</small>
When the Comptroller exercises this power to require an amendment before acceptance, no fee can be charged for making the amendment.* The provisional specification and application may be amended in this way; and it is doubtful whether the title can be amended in any other way.

<small>Sect. 13. Patent to be for one invention only.</small>
The Act of 1883 provides that a patent shall be granted for one invention only, though it may contain more than one claim; but that if a patent

---

* Re Dart, Gr. P.C. 307.

HOW TO OBTAIN A PATENT. 51

has been granted which comprises more than one invention, that fact shall not affect its validity.

The fact that an application comprises more than one invention is a ground on which the Comptroller might refuse to accept the application; and it is provided that in such a case— *Where application comprises more than one invention.*

"Where a person making application for a patent includes therein by mistake, inadvertence, or otherwise, more than one invention, he may, after the refusal of the Comptroller to accept such application, amend the same so as to apply to one invention only, and may make application for separate patents for each such invention accordingly. *Patent Rule 19.*

Separate patents may be granted for them.

"Every such application shall, if the applicant notify his desire to that effect to the Comptroller, bear the date of the first application, and shall, together therewith, be proceeded with in the manner prescribed by the said Act and by these rules as if every such application had been originally made on that date."

"Before exercising any discretionary power given to the Comptroller by the said Acts adversely to the applicant for a patent, the Comptroller shall give ten days' notice, or such longer notice as he may think fit, to the applicant of the time when he may be heard personally or by his agent before the Comptroller." *Exercise of discretionary power by Comptroller. Patent Rule 11.*

"Within five days from the date when such notice would be delivered in the ordinary course of post, or such longer time as the Comptroller may appoint in such notice, the applicant shall notify to the Comptroller whether or not he intends to be heard upon the matter." *Notice of hearing. Patent Rule 12.*

This notification to the Comptroller need not be in any particular form.

"Whether the applicant desires to be heard or not, the Comptroller may at any time require him to submit a statement in writing within a time to be notified by the Comptroller, or to *Patent Rule 13. Explanations by applicant.*

attend before him and make oral explanations with respect to such matters as the Comptroller may require.

Patent Rule 14. Decision to be notified.

"The decision or determination of the Comptroller in the exercise of any such discretionary power as aforesaid shall be notified by him to the applicant, and any other person affected thereby."

Act 1888, sect. 2 (2). Appeal to law officer.

"Where the Comptroller refuses to accept an application or requires an amendment, the applicant may appeal from his decision to the law officer."

Act 1888, sect. 2 (3).

"The law officer shall, if required, hear the applicant and the Comptroller, and may make an order determining whether and subject to what conditions, if any, the application shall be accepted."

Costs of appeal. Sect. 2 (4); Patent Rule 21. Acceptance, how advertised.

"The Comptroller neither gives nor receives costs of an appeal to the law officer."*

"The Comptroller shall, when an application has been accepted, give notice thereof to the applicant, *and shall advertise such acceptance in the official journal of the Patent Office.*"

More than one application for the same invention.

It may happen that more than one application is made in respect of the same invention, and for some reason a patent on a later application may be sealed before the first application is complete, so that when a patent would naturally be sealed on the first application the invention is already patented on a later one. To meet such a case it is provided—

Act 1883, sect. 13.

"that in case of more than one application for a patent for the same invention, the sealing of a patent on one of those applications shall not prevent the sealing of a patent on an earlier application."

But in order to allow the later applicant to avoid the expense of litigation with the earlier applicant, it is also provided that—

* *Re* Lake, 1887, Gr. A.P.C. 16.

"If after an application has been made, but before a patent has been sealed, another application for a patent is made, accompanied by a specification bearing the same or a similar title, the Comptroller, if he thinks fit, on the request of the second applicant, or of his legal representative, may, within two months of the grant of a patent on the first application, either decline to proceed with the second application or allow the surrender of the patent, if any, granted thereon." Later applicant may withdraw. Act 1883, sect. 7 (5), as amended. Act 1888, sect. 2 (5).

This last provision enables the second applicant to avoid the expense either of opposition, when his patent has not been sealed, or of a Petition of Revocation when his patent has been sealed.

Provisional Protection.

"Where an application for a patent in respect of an invention has been accepted, the invention may, during the period between the date of the application and the date of sealing such patent be used and published without prejudice to the patent to be granted for the same; and such protection from the consequences of use and publication is in this Act referred to as provisional protection." Act 1883, sect. 14.

The effect of such provisional protection varies somewhat according as a provisional or complete specification has accompanied the application. It is only where a provisional specification is filed that the protection is what is generally spoken of as provisional protection; this enables the applicant (or his legal representatives), at any time within nine months (or on payment of a fine of £2 within ten months) of the date on which his application was received at the Patent Office, to leave a complete specification and obtain a patent Effect of provisional protection. Protection by acceptance of provisional specification.

for his invention, and the patent so granted will bear the date of his first application.

Complete specification may embody improvements made in interval.

In this complete specification he can embody any improvement of his original invention which can be brought within the terms of the provisional specification, and during all the nine months he can use his invention in public, and make any experiments and trials which may be deemed advisable, without thereby affecting his patent.

Invention may be used in public.

Article may not be called patent.

At the same time he cannot describe his invention as patented, and cannot prevent others from using it, until a complete specification has been accepted, so that if the patent is for an article which is in immediate demand, he is not in such an advantageous position as if he had filed his complete specification at first, and obtained full protection for his invention.

Protection by acceptance of complete specification.

When an application accompanied by a complete specification is accepted the protection is precisely similar to that which is afforded by the acceptance of a complete specification filed after a provisional, and is practically equal to the protection of an actual patent for every purpose except the taking of legal proceedings; it is as though both the specifications had been accepted on the same day, and does not require any separate consideration.

Completion of Application by Complete Specification.

Act 1883, sect. 8. A complete specification

After the application accompanied by a provisional specification has been accepted, the applicant can complete his application by handing in at the Patent Office, or by sending by post to the Comptroller, at any time within nine calendar months of the date of his application (or on payment of a fine of £2, for which Patent Form U must be used, within ten months of his application) two copies of a complete specification. *may be left after the application.* *See p. 270.*

These must be handed in, or posted in due time to be received in the ordinary course of post, at the Patent Office before midnight on the same day of the ninth or tenth month, as the case may be, from the date of application. If this day should fall on Christmas Day or Good Friday, or on a Saturday or Sunday, or any day observed as a holiday at the Bank of England, or any day observed as a day of public fast or thanksgiving, which are called excluded days, the complete specification need not reach the Patent Office until the day next following such excluded day, or days if two or more of them occur consecutively. *How and where complete specification must be left. Sect. 98.*

If the office is closed, the policeman in charge will take documents up till midnight.

The complete specification must be prepared in the manner above described for preparing specifications, using Form C for the first sheet, and must be sent to the Patent Office in duplicate, one copy bearing an impressed stamp for £3; each copy must be dated and signed by the applicant or applicants, or, where application is made through an agent, by the agent. *Preparation of complete specification for filing, see p. 46.*

A patent is not, however, invalid because the complete specification is signed only by some of *Patent not invalid if all applicants do not sign the complete specification.* the applicants; but the patent in that case will apparently be granted only to those who sign, and the others will be taken to have retired from the application.*

Act 1883, sect. 9. Specifications, &c., referred to an examiner.
"(1) Where a complete specification is left after a provisional specification, the Comptroller shall refer both specifications to an examiner for the purpose of ascertaining whether the complete specification has been prepared in the prescribed manner, and whether the invention particularly described in the complete specification is substantially the same as that which is described in the provisional specification."

[N.B.—The fact of an examiner not having found any difference in the inventions described in the two specifications is no evidence that no such difference exists.]

"(2) If the examiner reports that the conditions hereinbefore contained have not been complied with, the Comptroller may refuse to accept the complete specification unless and until the same shall have been amended to his satisfaction; but any such refusal shall be subject to appeal to the law officer.

Appeal to law officer.

"(3) The law officer shall, if required, hear the applicant and the Comptroller, and may make an order determining whether and subject to what conditions (if any) the complete specification shall be accepted.

Time for acceptance is limited.
"(4) Unless a complete specification is accepted within twelve months from the date of application, then (save in the case of an appeal having been lodged against the refusal to accept) the application shall (subject to an extension of time being obtained) at the expiration of those twelve months become void."

Act 1885, sect. 3.
Enlargement of time for acceptance.
See p. 271.

The applicant may get the time for acceptance enlarged for three months by making application to the Comptroller on Patent Form V, properly stamped. The stamp required is £2, £4, or £6

* *Re* Grenfell and McEvoy's patent, 1890, 7 R.P.C. 151.

respectively, according as the extension sought does not exceed one, two, or three months.

"Reports of examiners shall not in any case be published or be open to public inspection, and shall not be liable to production or inspection in any legal proceeding other than an appeal to the law officer under this Act, unless the Court or officer having power to order discovery in such legal proceeding shall certify that such production or inspection is desirable in the interests of justice, and ought to be allowed." Act 1883, sect. 9 (5). Reports of examiners not published.

On the acceptance of the complete specification the Comptroller advertises the acceptance in the official journal; and upon the publication of such acceptance, the application and specification or specifications with the drawings (if any) may be inspected at the Patent Office upon payment of a fee of one shilling. Advertisement of acceptance of complete specification. Sect. 10. Patent Rule 22. Specification may be inspected after acceptance.

The specifications and drawings are printed three weeks after the complete specification has been accepted,* and may be purchased at the sale branch of the Patent Office at the uniform price of 8d. This includes the cost of inland postage, and, in case of an application by post, the cost of the postage stamp required on the application. Printing and sale of specifications.

A postal application for a specification should be made on Patent Form C¹, which may be obtained at any money order office, but is kept in stock only at certain principal offices. How to obtain a specification by post. See p. 251.

Within two months from the date of the advertisement of the acceptance of a complete specification the grant of the patent may be opposed upon certain grounds (full particulars of opposition are given in Chap. VII). Grant of patent may be opposed within two months of acceptance.

* Patent Office Circular.

How patent is sealed. Act 1883, sect. 12.

"(1) If there is no opposition, or, in case of opposition, if the determination is in favour of the grant of a patent, the Comptroller shall cause a patent to be sealed with the seal of the Patent Office.

"(2) A patent so sealed shall have the same effect as if it were sealed with the Great Seal of the United Kingdom.

Sealing must be within fixed time from application.

"(3) A patent shall be sealed as soon as may be, and not after the expiration of fifteen months from the date of application, except in the cases hereinafter mentioned, that is to say:

"(a) Where the sealing is delayed by an appeal to the law officer, or by opposition to the grant of the patent, the patent may be sealed at such time as the law officer may direct."

Act 1885, sect. 3.

Extension of time for sealing.

If the time for leaving the complete specification or for the acceptance of the complete specification has been extended, a further extension of four months after the expiration of the fifteen months is allowed for the sealing of the patent.

If there is no opposition the patent is usually sealed about ten weeks after the date of the acceptance of the complete specification.*

Date of patent. Act 1883, sect. 13.

"Every patent shall be dated and sealed as of the day of application, provided that no proceedings shall be taken in respect of an infringement committed before the publication of the complete specification."

No legal proceedings can be commenced before sealing. Act 1883, sect. 15.

Proceedings for infringement can be commenced only after the patent is sealed, but may refer back to the date of publication of the complete specification.

Lost patent may be replaced. Act 1883, sect. 37.

"If a patent is lost or destroyed, or its non-production is accounted for to the satisfaction of the Comptroller, the Comptroller may at any time cause a duplicate thereof to be sealed."

Application for a duplicate to be sealed must

* Patent Office Circular.

be made on Patent Form N, and the application must bear an impressed stamp for £2. *See p. 263.*

"If the person making the application die before the expiration of the fifteen months aforesaid, the patent may be granted to his legal representative, and sealed at any time within twelve months after the death of the applicant." *Where applicant dies before sealing. Act 1883, sect. 12 (3, b).*

In the case of the applicant dying before the complete specification has been left at the Patent Office, the legal representatives should produce the Probate or Letters of Administration to the Comptroller, who will allow the subsequent stages of the application to be carried out in their names.

They are then entitled to send the complete specification in due course, but there is no special provision as to the time within which this must be done. It will be seen that if the death takes place early in the fifteen months, the time within which the patent must be sealed may be materially shortened; if, therefore, an applicant dies before his complete specification has been left, the legal representatives if they wish to continue the application should not delay too long, and so risk having their application defeated by lapse of time.

Where the application has been made through an agent, a further authorisation is needed before he can proceed with the application.

If the complete specification has been filed and nothing is done, the patent will be sealed in the name of the deceased applicant; but if the legal representatives produce the Probate or Letters of Administration to the Comptroller, the patent will be granted to them instead.

CHAPTER V.

SPECIFICATIONS.

Two kinds of specification,

provisional

and complete.

In the preceding chapter we have considered only the form in which specifications must be prepared for accompanying or following an application for a patent to the Patent Office, and it was noticed that there are two kinds of specification, either of which may accompany the application. It was also seen that if only a provisional specification accompanies the application it is necessary, in order to obtain a patent, to supplement it by sending to the Patent Office within nine months, or at most within ten months after the date of the application, a complete specification of the invention for which the protection of a patent is sought.

In the present chapter we have to deal with the substance of the specifications, and only in very small degree with their form; we are dealing with the draft, and not with the finished copies that are sent to the Patent Office.

The Title of a Specification.

Specification must commence with the title. Sect. 5 (5).

The Act of 1883 provides that a specification, whether provisional or complete, must commence with the title; so that the first thing to be decided upon in drafting a specification is the title.

It will be seen that in the form of grant it is recited that the inventor has represented that he is in possession of an invention for (here follows the title of the invention). Now if this title is not one which ought to be applied to the invention for which protection is sought, the applicant has made a misrepresentation, or, as it is sometimes called, "a false suggestion;" and the effect of this will be that the patent, when granted, will be of no effect. Therefore it is very important that the specification should commence with a suitable title.

<small>See p. 7.</small>

<small>Title must be suitably chosen,</small>

<small>or patent will be void.</small>

There have been cases in which the title has been considered to be more general than the invention warranted, and it has been made clear that if the title embraces more than the actual invention, so as to make the invention seem greater than it really is, then the patent will be invalid.

<small>Title may be too general.</small>

Thus, in one case where the title conveyed the intelligence that by the invention an instrument gave "new notes" which had never before been produced, while as a matter of fact the instrument only produced "one new note," the patent was held bad for a false suggestion in the title.*

In another case, the accuracy of the judgment in which was afterwards questioned by a higher court, a patent for "an improved mode of lighting cities, towns, and villages," which contained only

---

* Bainbridge v. Wigley, 1810, Parl. Rep. 197; cf. also Bloxam v. Elsee, 1827, 6 B. & C. 178; 3 L. J. (O.S.), Q.B. 93.

a description of an improved street lamp, was held to be invalid on the same ground.*

What may be called a machine.

It is sometimes rather difficult to know what ought to be made the title of an invention; for instance, in the case of a machine it is dangerous to call it a "machine," since that may make the invention appear wider than it really is. Chief Justice Gibbs gave the following instruction to the jury as to the effect of describing an invention as "a machine for the manufacture of bobbin lace or twist lace:"

"If you think that he has invented an engine which consists of a perfectly new conformation of parts, though all the parts were used before, yet he will be entitled to support his patent for a new machine. If a combination of a certain number of parts up to a given point existed before, and Mr. Brown's invention sprung from that point, and added other combinations to it, then I think his specification stating the whole machine as his invention is bad."†

"Machine" generally too broad.

We thus see that the title "machine" by itself is only applicable to what is an entirely new machine, and that in most cases it should be described in rather narrower terms; for instance, as "an improved machine," or "improvements in machines."

New or improved method or machine is a safe description.

The judgment of Justice Cresswell, in a case where an invention had been described as "a new or improved method," seems to apply as well to a machine as to a method, and gives us a very

---

* Cochrane v. Smethurst, 1816, 1 Stark 205; questioned in Cook v. Pearce, 1843, 8 Q.B. 1063.

† Bovill v. Moore, 1815, Dav. P.C. 361.

SPECIFICATIONS.

safe title for use where any doubt exists as to how an invention ought to be described.

He said:

"If a part of the method be new, so as to produce a result that, as a whole, is new, surely it may be called a new or improved method. If the method be altogether new, surely it may be called an improved method. They seem to be convertible terms."*

This gives us good reason to use the words "new or improved" when in doubt as to which an invention really is, and should always be borne in mind in deciding upon the title for a patent.

Provisional Specification.

"A provisional specification must describe the nature of the invention, and be accompanied by drawings if required." Act 1883, sect. 5 (3).

It is, as has been already pointed out, unusual for drawings to accompany a provisional specification. Drawings are unusual.

In speaking of the office of a provisional specification in 1866, Lord Chancellor Chelmsford said: The office of a provisional specification.

"It seems clear that the office of the provisional specification is to describe the nature of the invention, not with minute particularity, but with sufficient precision and accuracy to inform the law officer what is to be the subject-matter of the patent. It is not at all necessary that the provisional specification should describe the mode or modes in which the invention is to be worked or carried out. That is left to the complete specification."†

It is not, however, any objection to a patent if the provisional specification does describe a Provisional may describe a mode of carrying out

---

* Beard v. Egerton, 1846, 3 C.B. 123.

† Penn v. Bibby, 1866, L.R. 2 Ch. 132.

mode of carrying out the invention, even though the mode shown in the complete specification should be a different and a better one. This point was decided by the Court of Appeal in 1887 in the following words:

<small>the invention.</small>

<small>Complete may describe different method from that in provisional.</small>
"A patentee putting in a provisional specification showing the nature of his invention is not bound to describe a way in which that can be carried into effect and operation; but if he does describe a way of doing it, and, before he files his complete specification, he either finds out improvements in that way, or a different way of carrying into effect that which is described as his invention in the provisional specification, he is bound to give the public the benefit of what he has discovered as regards the mode of carrying the invention, the nature of which must be described in the provisional specification, into effect, even although there may be improvement and even invention, which was not known to him at the time."*

<small>Details should be avoided in provisional,</small>

<small>and general language used instead.</small>
Thus the inventor may please himself about giving details in his provisional specification; as, however, details are not required, it would seem better not to give them, but in the provisional specification to use general terms sufficiently wide to cover any improvements which are likely to occur during the time of provisional protection, and just sufficiently definite to enable the inventor to point out what part of the provisional specification describes the invention detailed in the complete specification. If this rule be followed there will not be much fear of the patent being upset upon the ground of disconformity, and this is all that really needs to be guarded against in framing a provisional specification.

* Woodward v. Sansum, 1887, C.A., 4 R.P.C. 175.

The Complete Specification.

Although it is very important to have the provisional specification well drawn, it is of supreme importance to have the complete specification as perfect as possible, since it is to the complete specification that reference must be made to see what the invention really consists in, and what the patentee claims as his monopoly. *[Should be as perfect as possible.]*

" A complete specification, whether left on application or subsequently, must particularly describe and ascertain the nature of the invention, and in what manner it is to be performed, and must be accompanied by drawings if required." *[Act 1883, sect. 5 (i).]*

If a provisional specification has been left with the application, it is necessary that the complete specification should describe the same invention as is described in the provisional specification.* *[Must describe same invention as provisional.]*

The patent is granted on the application, and is for the invention which is described in the provisional specification, although the patent is not sealed until the complete specification, giving a more perfect description of the invention, has been filed; and if anything is not within the provisional specification the patent cannot protect it. This was clearly laid down by Lord Blackburn in the House of Lords; he said: *[Nothing outside provisional specification can be protected.]*

" Look at the nature of the invention described in the provisional specification, and say whether this which you have been doing, and which you say was a part of the patent, is fairly within the nature of the invention you have described.

---

* Vickers *v.* Siddell, 1890, H.L., 7 R.P.C. 303; Nuttall *v.* Hargreaves, 1891, C.A., 8 R.P.C. 450.

In that case you are protected; but if it is a new and separate invention and a different one, then you are not protected."*

Mode of carrying out invention may differ in specifications.
"The provisional and complete specifications may describe different modes of carrying out an invention; but if both are really within the same invention described not minutely, but in general terms in the provisional specification, this will not render the patent bad, even though the complete may contain an improvement on what is described in the provisional." †

Improvements in complete specification.
But although the complete specification may contain an improvement on what is described in the provisional specification, the improvement must not be anything in the nature of an independent invention.‡

The law on this point was very clearly stated by Lord Blackburn in the House of Lords. He said:

"I cannot but think that . . . . . . when the nature of an invention has been described in the provisional specification in the way which has been mentioned, if something were found out during the six months to make the invention work better, or with respect to the mode in which the operation is to be performed—a thing which is very likely to happen,—still the nature of the invention remains the same, and it is no objection that in the complete specification which comes afterwards the invention or application is described more particularly and in more detail, or even if it be shown that there has been more discovery made, and so as to make the invention which is described in the provisional specification really workable.

"If nothing more is done than that, I think it is good; but as soon as it comes to be more than that, and the patentee says in the provisional specification I describe my invention

---

* Bailey v. Roberton, 1878, 3 App. Cas. 1075.
† Woodward v. Sansum and Co., 1887, C.A., 4 R.P.C. 166.
‡ Watling v. Stevens, 1886, C.A., 3 R.P.C. 147.

as A, and in the complete specification he says, I describe A and also B, then, as far as regards B, it is void because the letters patent were granted for the invention that was described in the provisional specification, and do not cover the invention that is described in the other."*

If, however, the complete specification describes something not in the provisional simply for the sake of publishing it, and does not attempt to claim it as part of the invention protected by the patent, it is no objection to the patent; indeed, it is sometimes advisable to take this course in order to prevent others from taking out a patent for some minor detail which the original applicant does not wish to make the subject of a separate application. *Complete specification may describe what it could not claim so as to publish it. This is often advisable.*

Since the complete specification must contain details of the invention described in the provisional specification, it acts as a definer of what the provisional specification had stated to be the subject-matter of the application; and it is no objection to a complete specification that the invention described in it is smaller than what appeared from the provisional specification to be in prospect, provided the invention be not so narrowed as to make the title too general, and so render the patent void for a false suggestion in the title. *Complete defines provisional, and may narrow its scope.*

Thus far the complete specification has been dealt with so far as necessary with reference to the provisional specification, and of course the above applies only to cases in which a provisional specification has accompanied the application; what follows applies to any complete speci-

Bailey v. Roberton, 1878, 3 App. Cas. 1075.

fication, whether it accompanies the application or follows it.

<small>Act 1883, sect. 5. Requirements of complete specification.</small>

A complete specification—

(*a*) Must commence with the title;

(*b*) Must particularly describe and ascertain the nature of the invention, and in what manner the same is to be performed;

(*c*) Must be accompanied by drawings (or must refer to drawings already sent with the provisional specification) if required; and—

(*d*) Must end with a distinct statement of the invention claimed.

Nothing further need be said about (*a*), since what has been already said applies equally to all specifications, whether provisional or complete.

<small>Drawings supplement letterpress</small>

(*b*) and (*c*) may be considered together; the drawings and the letterpress together form the specification, any deficiency in the one being supplemented by the other; and their relative importance varies according to the class of invention which it is sought to protect. In some cases drawings may be not only unnecessary, but quite out of the question, and in such cases the wording of the specification is all-important; while in others the drawings by themselves would be sufficient to show what the invention is, and the letterpress is merely a brief description of the drawings.

No rule can be given as to how far the applicant should rely on the letterpress, and how far on drawings; but, as a rule, where drawings are of any use, the more they are used the better.

<small>Only what is described is protected.</small>

The letters patent contain a recital that "the

inventor hath by his complete specification particularly described the nature of his invention," and the letters patent are granted only for the invention so described.

This is a recital of very great importance, since it is a recital of what the applicant has done in order to entitle himself to the grant of a patent; it is a recital of the consideration for the grant, and if it be not true, the consideration has failed, and the patent is of no effect. *Consideration for grant.*

The applicant must give the public the full benefit of his invention; he must not attempt to keep back anything which he knows to be of value in working the invention, in the hope of combining the advantages of a patent with those of a trade secret. It was stated by Justice Buller, in 1785, that— *Applicant must not keep back any useful information for working the invention.*

"It is clearly settled as law, that a man, to entitle himself to the benefit of a patent for a monopoly, must disclose his secret, and specify his invention in such a way that others may be taught by it to do the thing for which the patent is granted; for the end and meaning of the specification is to teach the public, after the term for which the patent is granted, what the art is, and it must put the public in possession of the secret in as ample and beneficial a way as the patentee uses it." * *To whom a specification is addressed.*

It is thus very important to know how much it is necessary for the applicant to go into details of his invention, and to ascertain this it is well to see to what class of persons a specification is supposed to be addressed. The following statement of the law on this subject was given by Jessel, late Master of the Rolls, in 1875.

* Rex v. Arkwright, 1785, 1 W.P.C. 66.

"It is plain that the specification of a patent is not addressed to people who are ignorant of the subject-matter. If it is a mechanical invention you have, first of all, scientific mechanicians of the first class, eminent engineers; then you have scientific mechanicians of the second class, managers of great manufactories, great employers of labour, persons who have studied mechanics; ... and in this class I should include foremen, being men of superior intelligence, who, like their masters, would be capable of invention, and like the scientific engineers would be able to find out what was meant even from slight hints and still more imperfect descriptions, and would be able to supplement so as to succeed even from a defective description, and even more than that, would be able to correct an erroneous description. That is what I would say of the first two classes, which I will call the scientific classes. The other class consists of the ordinary workman, using that amount of skill and intelligence which is fairly to be expected of him—not a careless man, but a careful man, though not possessing that great scientific knowledge or power of invention which would enable him by himself, unaided, to supplement a defective description, or correct an erroneous description. . . .

"It will be a bad specification if the first two classes only understand it, and if the third class do not."*

This statement of the law is practically identical with that laid down in 1836 by Baron Alderson. He said:

"The specification ought to be framed so as not to call upon a person to have recourse to more than those ordinary means of knowledge (not invention) which a workman of competent skill in his art and trade may be presumed to have. You may call upon him to exercise all the existing knowledge common to the trade, but you cannot call upon him to exercise anything more. You have no right to call upon him to tax his ingenuity or invention.

"The specification of a patent must not merely suggest something that will set the mind of an ingenious man at work, but

---

* Plimpton v. Malcolmson, 1876, 3 Ch. D. 568.

SPECIFICATIONS.

it must actually and plainly set forth what the invention is, and how it is to be carried into effect, so as to save a party the trouble of making experiments and trials."*

The specification must not be misleading or ambiguous; it must not lead a person attempting to put the invention in practice into a course of experiments. *(Must not be ambiguous or misleading.)*

This was stated as law as far back as 1787 in the following language:

"It is incumbent on the patentee to give a specification of the invention in the clearest and most unequivocal terms of which the subject is capable. And if it appear that there is any unnecessary ambiguity affectedly introduced into the specification, or anything which tends to mislead the public, in that case the patent is void.... If the process as directed by the specification does not produce that which the patent professes to do, the patent itself is void. It is certainly of consequence that the terms of a specification should express the invention in the clearest and most specific manner, so that a man of science may be able to produce the thing intended without the necessity of trying experiments."† *(Process described must produce right result.)*

The rule that *no experiments* may be required does not, however, apply to every case; the Court of Appeal in 1889 laid down the rule that—

"The specification must be sufficiently clear to enable a person conversant in the subject without invention to carry out the invention; but not necessarily to enable him to do the work without any trial or experiment, which, when it is new or especially delicate, may frequently be necessary, however clear the description may be."‡ *(In some cases trial may be needed to carry out specification,)*

But, although experiment may be still needed *(but it must not be equivocal.)*

---

* Morgan *v.* Seaward, 1836, 1 W.P.C. 174.
† Turner *v.* Winter, 1787, 1 W.P.C. 80, 81.
‡ Edison and Swan Electric Light Co. *v.* Holland, 1889, C.A., 6 R.P.C. 243; see also Beard *v.* Egerton, 1849, 8 C.B. 206.

in order to put the invention in practice, there must be nothing to put the public on a wrong track.

"If the specification upon a fair interpretation be equivocal it is insufficient."*

Specification need show only one method,

The applicant is not bound to describe every way known to him of carrying out his invention; it is sufficient if he shows one useful way, even though it may turn out not to be the most beneficial way.

but may give more provided they will all work.

He may give several ways, but must be careful only to give ways that will give the required result; for—

"If you describe in a specification two ways of doing a thing, and by one way it cannot be done, the specification is bad." †

Generic term not always sufficient.

"It is not sufficient to describe a material by a generic term comprising many species, the majority of which would be unsuitable;" ‡

but if a patent be for a process which may be applied to a large class of substances, it is no objection to prove that it is only some of these substances which will give a useful result.§

Nature of chemical product need not be given.

In a chemical patent it is not necessary to state what is the exact chemical nature of the product produced by a process; it is the commercial, not the chemical value of the product that is the subject of the patent.‖

* Hastings v. Brown, 1853, 1 E. & B., p. 454.
† Beard v. Egerton, 1846, 19 L.J. 39.
‡ Wegmann v. Corcoran, 1879, 13 Ch. D. 65.
§ Badische Anilin v. Levinstein, 1887, H.L., 4 R.P.C. 419.
‖ Leonhardt v. Kalle, 1895, 12 R.P.C. 103.

The applicant should be careful to avoid mistakes in his directions or drawings; but a mistake will not necessarily render the patent bad unless it is likely to mislead the public, or amounts to a false suggestion. Lord Chancellor Westbury in 1866 laid down the following rule on this question: *Mistakes should be avoided. What mistakes will render patent bad.*

> "The statement that an error in a specification which any workman of ordinary skill and experience would perceive and correct will not vitiate a patent is true only of such errors as appear on the face of the specification or the drawings it refers to, or which would be at once discovered and corrected in following out the instructions given for any process or manufacture. The reason is because such errors cannot possibly mislead; but it is not true of errors which are discoverable only by experiment and further inquiry, nor of an erroneous statement amounting to a false suggestion, even though the error would be at once observed by a workman possessed of ordinary knowledge of the subject." *

Claims.

A complete specification must end with a distinct statement of the invention claimed. *Act 1883, sect. 5.*

After the invention has been described at length in the specification, and by means of references to the drawings accompanying it, the applicant must state shortly what it is that he claims to have invented. This is done by means of a claiming clause containing one or more claims which must define clearly what it is that the patent is meant to protect. These claims are means for warning the public what they must *Claiming clause. Warning the public.*

---

* Simpson *v.* Holliday, 1866, 15 N.R. 340; L.R. 1 H.L. 315.

avoid doing if they do not wish to incur the risk of an action for infringement.*

A usual form of preface to the claims is—

Form of clause.

"Having now particularly described the nature of my invention, and in what manner the same is to be performed, I declare that what I claim is . . . ."

Although the Act of 1883 requires a complete specification to end with a distinct statement of the invention claimed, and it would be the duty of the Comptroller to refuse to accept, or at any rate to require the amendment of a specification that did not comply with this requirement, it has **Absence of claims does not make patent bad.** happened that a complete specification without any distinct claiming clause has been accepted; and a patent having been granted, it was held that the omission of a claiming clause did not of itself render the patent invalid.†

New and old distinguished in claims. In a patent for an improvement on an existing machine or process the specification must distinguish what is new from what is old.‡

The claims themselves are usually sufficient for this purpose, but where this is not the case it may often be conveniently done by means of **Disclaiming clauses.** what is called a disclaiming clause, which either precedes the claiming clause or is made to form a part of it.

A disclaiming clause usually commences by

---

* Campion *v.* Benyon, 1821, 3 B. & B. 10; Gibson *v.* Brand and Scott, 1821, N.R. 890.

† Vickers *v.* Siddell, 1890, H.L., 7 R.P.C. 306.

‡ Foxwell *v.* Bostock, 1861, 4 De G.J. & S. 313; Holmes *v.* L. & N.W.R. Co., 1852, 12 C.B. 831.

stating that the applicant knows that certain things have been either done, or proposed to be done, and that he does not claim them, and then he proceeds to state what he does claim.

If the applicant knows of any machine or process which might be put forward as an anticipation, or if his invention differs but slightly from what is described in some earlier specification or book, he should always insert a disclaimer in his specification; he will thus avoid, or at least considerably lessen, any chance of opposition, and also the danger of getting his patent upset on the ground of its being anticipated. It is only necessary to distinguish what is new from what is old when the invention consists in an improvement on an old machine or process; where the invention consists of a combination, and where the claim is clearly only for a combination, it is not necessary to distinguish what part of the combination (if any) is new from what is old;* so that where the claim is for a combination, even though every part be old, there will be no need for a disclaimer. *[margin: Often advisable to avoid an anticipation.]* *[margin: New and old must be distinguished in an improvement, but not in a new combination.]*

It may, as a rule, be said that what is aimed at in framing the claims is to make the patent cover as much as possible consistently with safety, and in framing a disclaimer to make it include everything that would but for it anticipate the patent, and no more. *[margin: Object to be aimed at in framing claim and disclaimer.]*

The proper wording of both is of the greatest importance, and should receive the most careful attention; and it is this part of a specification *[margin: Claims often sent to counsel.]*

* Harrison v. The Anderston Foundry Co., 1876, 1 App. Cas. 574; see also Proctor v. Bennis, 1887, 36 Ch. D. 740.

which is most frequently left to be settled by counsel.

Act 1883, sect. 33. More than one claim allowed,

Although a patent can only be granted for one invention, it may contain more than one claim.

Now it is one feature of an English patent that if any part of it is bad, the whole patent fails; it therefore follows that if one out of a large number of claims can be shown to be bad, all the other claims are of no effect.

but everything claimed must be new.

Claims for subordinate integers in combination.

Since a patent for a new combination may also be made to cover any new parts or subordinate integers which form part of the whole combination claimed, a single patent may be made to cover several distinct improvements in a machine, each of these improvements being made the subject of a separate claim; but the inventor should be very careful to claim only those parts which are really novel, for if it should turn out that one or more of these supposed improvements were not new, the whole patent would be invalidated,* and before the patentee could do anything to prevent infringements of what were really his inventions he would be put to the expense and delay of amending his specification by striking out claims which ought never to have been made.

* Brunton v. Hawkes, 1821, 4 B. & A. 550; Gillett v. Wilby, 1839, 1 W.P.C. 270.

CHAPTER VI.

OPPOSITION TO THE GRANT OF A PATENT.

"(1) Any person may, at any time within two months from the date of the advertisement of the acceptance of a complete specification, give notice at the Patent Office of opposition to the grant of the patent on the ground of the applicant having obtained the invention from him, or from a person of whom he is the legal representative; or on the ground that the invention has been patented in this country on an application of prior date; or on the ground that the complete specification describes or claims an invention other than that described in the provisional specification, and that such other invention forms the subject of an application made by the opponent in the interval between the leaving of the provisional specification and the leaving of the complete specification; but on no other ground.   *Act 1883, sect. 11. Notice of grounds for opposition. Act 1888, sect. 4.*

"(2) Where such notice is given the Comptroller shall give notice of the opposition to the applicant, and shall, on the expiration of those two months, after hearing the applicant and the person so giving notice, if desirous of being heard, decide on the case, but subject to appeal to the law officer. *Act 1883, sect. 11. Notice to applicant.*

"(3) The law officer shall, if required, hear the applicant, and any person so giving notice and being, in the opinion of the law officer, entitled to be heard in opposition to the grant, and shall determine whether the grant ought or ought not to be made. *Appeal to law officer.*

"(4) The law officer may, if he thinks fit, obtain the assistance of an expert, who shall be paid such remuneration as the law officer, with the consent of the Treasury, shall appoint." *Law officer may employ expert.*

"A notice of opposition to the grant of a patent shall be on Form D, and shall state the ground or grounds on which the person giving such notice (hereinafter in Rules 37, 38, 41, and 43 called the opponent) intends to oppose the grant, and must be signed by him. Such notice shall state his address *Patent Rule 34. P. 82.*

for service in the United Kingdom, and shall be accompanied by an unstamped copy.

Patent Rule 35.
"On receipt of such notice a copy thereof shall be transmitted by the Comptroller to the applicant."

First ground of opposition.
The first ground of opposition is that the applicant is not the true and first inventor, but obtained the invention from the opponent, and for this to succeed the obtaining must have been within the United Kingdom. There need not be any fraud in the obtaining of the invention from the opponent, but of course in some cases there may have been fraud, and in such cases evidence of the fraud should be given before the Comptroller, since, if no evidence of fraud is given before the Comptroller, it will not be be possible to introduce the subject before the law officer.*

Who may oppose.
The opponent on this ground must be the actual person from whom the applicant obtained the invention or his legal representative.† This latter term appears to apply only to the legal personal representative of a deceased person, who, as we have seen, has much the same rights, so far as the inventions of such person are concerned, as the inventor himself would have had if he had lived.

Thus this ground is practically confined to persons who could themselves have properly applied for the patent which they are opposing.

Patent Rule 13. Evidence as to the obtaining must be given.
"Where the ground of opposition is that the applicant has obtained the invention from the opponent, or from a person of whom such opponent is the legal representative, unless evidence in support of such allegation be left at the Patent Office

* *Re* Bairstow, 1888, 5 R.P.C. 286.
† *Re* Edmunds, 1888, Griff. 281.

within the time prescribed by these rules the opposition shall be deemed to be abandoned, and a patent shall be sealed forthwith." <small>See p. 82.</small>

Where the opponent proves that the applicant obtained a substantial part of his invention from him, but the applicant has also made improvements of merit, the patent may be sealed subject to an agreement being filed at the Patent Office for securing to the opponent the full rights of a joint patentee;* or the patent may be sealed to the applicant and opponent as joint inventors.†

The second ground of opposition is "that the invention has been patented in this country on an application of prior date." <small>Second ground of opposition.</small>

"Where the ground or one of the grounds of opposition is that the invention has been patented in this country on an application of prior date, the number and date of such prior application shall be specified in the notice." <small>Patent Rule 36. Number and date of prior patent required.</small>

The prior patent need not have been actually sealed, but the complete specification must have been accepted; and it does not matter whether the prior patent is an existing or an expired patent. <small>Prior patent need not be actually sealed.</small>

The words of the Act that any person may oppose on this ground appear to be of the most general nature possible, and no doubt many would suppose that it was intended to allow any person who could point out that the invention claimed was clearly old, because it had been already the subject of a patent, to oppose the grant of what would thus clearly be an illegal monopoly. <small>Who may oppose on second ground.</small>

According to the Act it seems clear that any

---

* *Re* Luke, 1886, Griff. 294.

† *Re* Eadie, Griff. 279.

person may give notice of opposition, and also that the Comptroller must hear such person if he is desirous of being heard; but on appeal the law officer is required to hear such person only if he is, in the opinion of the law officer, entitled to be heard in opposition to the grant. Law officers have used this power of refusing to hear an opponent to greatly restrict the class of persons who are able practically to oppose the grant, and from the decision of the law officer there is no appeal. In a leading case on this question Sir Edward Clarke, Solicitor-General, said:

Opponent must be interested in prior patent. "The only class of persons who are entitled to be heard in opposition before the law officer are persons who are interested with a legitimate and real interest in the prior patent upon which an application is opposed, or persons who, while they have not patented the invention, have yet been the originators of it, from whom the person seeking the patent has obtained it."*

Prior patent may have expired. It has been clearly held that the fact that the prior patent has expired does not affect the validity of the opposition,† and it is certainly rather difficult to see how anyone can be interested with a legitimate and real interest in an expired patent except as one of the public who are in free possession of the invention disclosed in that patent, especially as the same law officer has held that the fact of manufacturing under the prior patent was not sufficient interest to entitle a person to be heard.‡ In the above case § he did not

---

* *Re* Heath and Frost, 1886, Griff. 290.
† *Re* Lancaster, 1884, Griff. 293.
‡ *Re* Macevoy, 1880, 5 R.P.C. 285.
§ *Re* Heath and Frost, 1886, Griff. 285.

disapprove of the decision in the leading case of *re* Glossop, where Lord Herschell, then Solicitor-General, said :

"I shall hesitate very much before I say that any member of the public can come in and oppose a patent and raise an inquiry and cause an appeal of this sort who has no interest in it, and who simply says, 'Do not ask me what my interest is, because I have none, except that I am going to show you that this patent is the same as that,' because that system might be used so as to cause a vast amount of annoyance and expense of a most objectionable character to patentees. I know that it was intended to prevent that. In the present case the opponent purchased a prior patent, which he says has anticipated the present invention, and he has been working under it, and he is a manufacturer who has been making machines in accordance with that patent. Although that patent has now become public property, I do not think that I ought to hold that he is not a person entitled to be heard."

It thus appears that it is useless for any person to oppose under the second ground unless he is interested in the prior patent either as patentee or as licensee,* or as an applicant whose complete specification has been accepted.

Although the law officers are not absolutely bound by previous decisions, these decisions as to the *locus standi* of an opponent having been followed, there is but little chance of their being now departed from, and there being no appeal from the law officer's decision, the correctness of this rule cannot be reviewed by any higher authority. Effect of decisions of law officers.

The last ground of opposition was introduced in 1888 to meet the danger of an earlier applicant stealing his invention from a later applicant, who Third ground of opposition.

* *Re* Hill, 1888, 5 R.P.C. 599.

had either filed a complete specification or otherwise published his invention during the term of the earlier applicant's provisional protection.

Except under the first ground of opposition it is not necessary to produce any evidence before the Comptroller. In that case, as we have seen, evidence is required, and in other cases evidence may be used.

<small>Evidence before Comptroller.</small>
<small>Patent Rule 11. 17 A.</small>

The Comptroller cannot take evidence *vivâ voce*, and all evidence used before him must be given by way of statutory declarations, which must be in the same form as is used in the High Court of Justice. They must be headed in the matter or matters to which they relate, and they must be divided into paragraphs, consecutively numbered, each paragraph so far as possible being confined to one subject.

<small>Patent Rule 17. Statutory Declarations, how to be made.</small>

"The statutory declarations required by the Acts and Rules or used in any proceedings thereunder shall be made and subscribed as follows :

"(a) In the United Kingdom, before any justice of the peace, or any commissioner or other officer authorised by law in any part of the United Kingdom to administer an oath for the purpose of any legal proceeding ; and

"(b) In any other part of Her Majesty's dominions, before any court, judge, justice of the peace, or any officer authorised by law to administer an oath there for the purpose of a legal proceeding ; and

"(c) If made out of Her Majesty's dominions, before a British minister, or person exercising the functions of a British minister, or a Consul, Vice-Consul, or other person exercising the functions of a British Consul, or a notary public, or before a judge or magistrate."

<small>Patent Rule 37.</small>

"Within fourteen days after the expiration of two months from the date of the advertisement of the acceptance of a complete specification, the opponent may leave at the Patent Office statutory declarations in support of his opposition, and on so leaving shall deliver to the applicant a list thereof." Opponent's evidence.

"Within fourteen days from the delivery of such list the applicant may leave at the Patent Office statutory declarations in answer, and on so leaving shall deliver to the opponent a list thereof, and within fourteen days from such delivery the opponent may leave at the Patent Office his statutory declarations in reply, and on so leaving shall deliver to the applicant a list thereof. Such last-mentioned declarations shall be confined to matters strictly in reply. Patent Rule 38. Evidence in answer and reply.

"Copies of the declarations mentioned in this and the last preceding rule may be obtained either from the Patent Office or from the opposite party." Copies of declarations.

"No further evidence shall be left on either side except by leave of the Comptroller upon the written consent of the parties duly notified to him, or by special leave of the Comptroller on application in writing made to him for that purpose." Patent Rule 39.

"Either party making such application shall give notice thereof to the opposite party, who shall be entitled to oppose the application." Patent Rule 40.

"On the completion of the evidence, or at such other time as he may see fit, the Comptroller shall appoint a time for the hearing of the case, and shall give to the parties ten days' notice at the least of such appointment. Patent Rule 41. Notice of hearing.

"If the applicant or opponent desires to be heard he must forthwith send the Comptroller an application on Form E (bearing an impressed stamp for £1). The Comptroller may refuse to hear either party who has not sent such application for hearing. If neither party applies to be heard the Comptroller shall decide the case, and notify his decision to the parties."

"On the hearing of the case no opposition shall be allowed in respect of any ground not stated in the notice of opposition, and where the ground or one of the grounds is that the invention has been patented in this country on an application of prior date, the opposition shall not be allowed upon such ground unless the number and date of such prior application shall have been duly specified in the notice of opposition." Patent Rule 42. Opposition on hearing restricted to grounds stated in notice.

Patent Rule 44. Decision to be notified.

"The decision of the Comptroller, after hearing any party who applies under Rule 41, shall be notified by him to the parties."

Appeals to law officer.

From the decision of the Comptroller an appeal lies to the law officer; the procedure on appeal in an opposition either to a grant or to an amendment is the same, and is dealt with in a separate chapter (see p. 115 in Chapter XI).

The hearing before the law officer is by way of rehearing, and *vivâ voce* evidence may be given, so that the witnesses may be cross-examined. In a complex case where *vivâ voce* evidence is practically indispensable, the evidence laid before the Comptroller may be of only a formal nature raising the issues, and the real contest may be deferred until the hearing by the law officer. Where either party wishes to adopt this procedure they should, if practicable, come to an agreement with the other party as to the evidence that shall be given.

When opposition is likely to succeed.

In order to actually prevent a patent being sealed, it is necessary for the opponent to have an extraordinarily strong case; if the grant is refused, the applicant is left entirely without remedy; while if the patent is sealed, it is always open to impeachment in the Courts, and if proved to have been wrongly sealed can always be revoked; it is, therefore, comparatively seldom that the grant is wholly refused.

In a case of opposition Sir Edward Clarke, Sol.-Gen., laid down the following strict rule:

"The law officer should only stop the issue of a patent if,

having examined the evidence, he is so clearly of opinion that the opponent has made out his case that he would, if a jury were to find in favour of the applicant, refuse to accept it, and overrule the decision on the ground that it was perverse and contrary to the obvious weight and effect of the evidence."*

And of course this rule applies equally to a decision of the Comptroller.

The same eminent law officer was of opinion that—

" Where there is a strongly controverted question of scientific anticipation the patent should not be stopped."†

But this was before he stated the above rule, which may be taken as a perfect test of whether the sealing will be refused.

As a general rule an opposition is entered not so much for the purpose of stopping the patent as for forcing the applicant to make an amendment by way of disclaimer of something which the opponent is interested in. *Disclaimer may be ordered.*

Disclaimers are of two kinds, special and general.

In a special disclaimer the applicant mentions some prior patent, and states that he does not claim anything described therein, or something to that effect.

A special disclaimer will be required only in very special cases where the prior patent is a master patent, or the later invention is simply a modification of the earlier one. If the applicant can prove that there was any public knowledge

---

* *Re* Stuart's Application, 1892, 9 R.P.C. 452.
† *Re* Lake, 1889, 6 R.P.C. 550.

on the subject of the application at the date of the prior application, he will only be compelled to insert a general disclaimer, not mentioning the prior patent, but only disclaiming what had been before claimed.

CHAPTER VII.

KEEPING UP A PATENT.

WHEN a patent has been sealed the applicant becomes the patentee, and in all matters connected with the patent the patentee is the person concerned.

The Act of 1883 defines the "patentee" as the person for the time being entitled to the benefit of the patent. Thus if a patentee assigns his patent to any person or persons (including Corporations) he ceases at once to be patentee, and the assignee or assignees become patentee or patentees in their turn. Now, as any act or thing which may be required to be done in connection with a patent is always left to the patentee, it must be remembered that in all that follows relating to patents the patentee for the time being, and not the original patentee, is referred to under the term "patentee." *Patentee defined. Sect. 46.*

"(1) The term limited in every patent for the duration thereof shall be fourteen years from its date.

"(2) But every patent shall, notwithstanding anything therein or in this Act, cease if the patentee fails to make the prescribed payments within the prescribed times." *Term of patent. Act 1883, sect. 17.*

The fees of £1 and £3, paid with the application and complete specification, keep the patent in force. *Fees must be paid to keep patent in force.*

force until the expiration of the fourth year from the date of application. In order to keep the patent in force beyond the fourth year the patentee must, before the expiration of the fourth and of each succeeding year during the term of the patent, pay the prescribed fee.

<small>Patent Rules, 1892 (2nd set), 4.</small>

The fees payable in respect of a patent, and the manner of payment of such fees, are regulated by the Board of Trade, and they have been altered from time to time by that authority. The present scale of fees, with the times of payment, will be found at page 239.

<small>Fees, how fixed. Act 1883, sect. 24.</small>

The latest day for payment of a renewal fee in any year is the date for which the patent was sealed,—that is, in ordinary cases the date on which the application for the patent was made.

<small>Date for payment of renewal fees.</small>

Payment must be made by way of Patent Form J, duly stamped, which must be sent to the Patent Office for entry of the payment in the register.

<small>Fees, how paid. P. 259. Patent Rules, 1892 (2nd set), 4.</small>

This must be sent to the Patent Office so as to be received before midnight of the day on which the payment falls due, unless that day should fall on Christmas Day, Good Friday, or on a Saturday or Sunday, or any day observed as a holiday at the Bank of England, or any day observed as a day of public fast or thanksgiving. These are called excluded days, and a payment due on an excluded day may be made up to midnight on the day next following such excluded day, or days if two or more of them occur consecutively.

<small>Act 1883, sect. 98.</small>

Payment may be made by prepaid letter through the post, and if so made will be deemed to have been made at the time when the letter containing

<small>Payment by post. Act 1883, sect. 97.</small>

the same would be delivered in the ordinary course of post. It is sufficient to prove that the letter was properly addressed and put into the post.

The patentee may pay in advance the whole or any portion of the aggregate of the prescribed annual fees. *Fees may be paid in advance.*

"On due compliance with these rules, and as soon as may be after such respective periods as aforesaid, or any enlargement thereof respectively duly granted, the Comptroller shall issue a certificate that the prescribed payment has been duly made." *Certificate of payment. Patent Rules, No. 48.*

If payment be not made in time, the time may be extended for not more than three months on payment of a fine. The Act of 1883 provides that— *Enlargement of time for payment.*

"If, nevertheless, in any case, by accident, mistake, or inadvertence, a patentee fails to make any prescribed payment within the prescribed time, he may apply to the Comptroller for an enlargement of the time for making that payment. *Sect. 17 (3).*

"Thereupon the Comptroller shall, if satisfied that the failure has arisen from any of the above-mentioned causes, on receipt of the prescribed fee for enlargement, not exceeding ten pounds, enlarge the time accordingly, subject to the following conditions : *Sub-sect. (4).*

"(*a*) The time for making any payment shall not in any case be enlarged for more than three months.

"(*b*) If any proceeding shall be taken in respect of an infringement of the patent committed after a failure to make any payment within the prescribed time, and before the enlargement thereof, the Court before which the proceeding is proposed to be taken may, if it shall think fit, refuse to award or give any damages in respect of such infringement." *No damage for infringements during enlargement of time.*

"An application for an enlargement of the time for making a prescribed payment shall state in detail the circumstances in which the patentee by accident, mistake, or inadvertence has failed to make such payment, and the Comptroller may require *Patentee must show why fee was not paid in time.*

Patent Rules, No. 49. the patentee to substantiate by such proof as he may think necessary the allegations contained in the application for enlargement."

P. 260. Application for enlargement of the time for payment of a renewal fee must be made on Patent Form K duly stamped. The fees are £3, £7, and £10 for enlargements of one, two, or three months respectively.

CHAPTER VIII.

RIGHTS OF PATENTEE.

SUBJECT to the due payment of the fees as they become due, the patent gives protection for fourteen years from the date of application, and we must now consider briefly what are the rights which the possession of letters patent for an invention confers upon the patentee for the time being.

"Every patent when sealed shall have effect throughout the United Kingdom and the Isle of Man." Range of patent.
Act 1883, sect. 16.

It does not extend to the Channel Islands, nor to any colony or foreign possession; for these separate patents must be obtained as for foreign countries.

The Act of 1883 provides that—

"A patentee may assign his patent for any place in or part of the United Kingdom or Isle of Man as effectually as if the patent were originally granted to extend to that place or part only." Assignment of patent. Sect. 36.

This of course implies that the patentee may assign his patent for the whole of the United Kingdom and Isle of Man.

Although a patent is personal property an assignment must be by deed; in order to be effectual it must be duly stamped, and registered at the Patent Office; and from the date of such Assignment must be by deed.

registration the assignee, whether of part or of the whole of the patent, takes, so far as what is assigned to him is concerned, the place of the assignor. If the patent is assigned for any part of the kingdom the assignee becomes the patentee for that part, with all the rights of an ordinary patentee, so far as his district is concerned.

<small>Assignee becomes patentee.</small>

When a person sells a patent, he of course implies that he has a good title to sell it; but he sells it for what it is, and does not by so selling it in any way warrant its validity.* Of course the sale may be subject to a covenant on the part of the vendor to hold himself responsible if the patent should be declared bad, but this is exceptional, and usually *caveat emptor* is the rule.

<small>Assignor does not warrant validity.</small>

On referring to the form of grant it will be seen that the Crown doth by the letters patent—

<small>What is granted to the patentee.</small>

"give and grant unto the said patentee our especial license, full power, sole privilege, and authority that the said patentee by himself, his agents or licensees, and no others, may at all times hereafter during the terms of years herein mentioned make, use, exercise, and vend the said invention within our United Kingdom of Great Britain and Ireland, and Isle of Man, in such manner as to him or them may seem meet, and that the said patentee *shall have and enjoy* the whole profit and advantage from time to time accruing by reason of the said invention."

<small>Act 1883, Sched. 1.</small>

This gives to the patentee a monopoly of the invention for the term of the patent,—that is, he may during that time make and sell the patented article at his own price without any risk of competition, and he may also sell or supply the

<small>Patentee has a monopoly.</small>

<small>May sell subject to conditions as to user,</small>

* Monforts v. Marsden, 1895, 12 R.P.C. 266.

article subject to any conditions as to the manner or the locality in which it may be used.

If the patentee wishes to restrict the manner in which the patented article may be used, clear notice of the restriction must be given to the purchaser before the article is sold ;* for when an article is sold without any restriction on the buyer the sale gives an absolute right as against the seller to use the article in any way the buyer may think fit. This will include using or selling the article in any country where the vendor owns a patent for the article at the time of sale.† *but must give notice of restrictions before sale.*

We have seen that a patent may be granted to several persons jointly ; and even if originally granted to a single person the grantee may assign it to more than one person, and thus several persons may become joint owners, or, as they may then be called, joint patentees. *Joint owners of a patent.*

When there are several joint owners of a patent, each of them is at liberty, unless he is bound by some agreement to the contrary, to work the patent on his own account; he can manufacture and sell articles made under it without the consent of his co-owners, and he need not account to them for any profits which he may so make.‡ *A joint owner can work invention alone.*

Whether he can grant licenses and receive royalties without accounting for the sums so received does not appear to have ever been *Whether joint owner can grant licenses on his own account. Joint owner may sell part of his share.*

* Incandescent Gas Light Co., Ltd., v. Cantelo, 1895, 12 R.P.C. 262.

† Société anonyme de Glaces v. Tiljhman's Sand Blast Co., 1883, 25 Ch. D. 1.

‡ Steers v. Rogers, 1893, H.L., 10 R.P.C. 245.

decided;* but he can of course sell a part of his share, and the purchaser will then be entitled to work the patent on his own account; and as the price of such a share might be paid as an annuity, and would practically amount to a royalty, there really seems no reason why he should not also have power to grant a license.

Persons not owners entitled to benefit.

Besides joint owners, there may be persons who, though they are not owners, are entitled to share in the profits of the patent; thus an owner may assign a share of the profits while remaining sole proprietor. In such a case the assignee of profits can claim an account from a licensee; but the account must be taken in the presence of the assignor and of all persons interested so as to bind them.†

Accounts of licensees where joint owners.

Licensees.

The use of the word "licensees" implies that not only may the patentee by himself and his agents work his invention, but that he may license others to do so, and this is often the most valuable right attaching to the possession of a patent. The subject of licenses is treated fully in Chapter IX.

P. 9.

The grant continues:

Infringement forbidden.

"And to the end that the said patentee may have and enjoy the sole use and exercise and the full benefit of the said invention, we do by these presents, for us, our heirs and successors, strictly command all our subjects whatsoever within our United Kingdom of Great Britain and Ireland, and the Isle of Man, that they do not at any time during the continuance of the said term of fourteen years either directly or indirectly make use of or put in practice the said invention, or

---

* Mathers v. Green, 1865, L.R., 1 Ch. 29.
† Bergmann v. Macmillan, 1881, 17 Ch.D. 423.

any part of the same, nor in any wise imitate the same, nor make or cause to be made any addition thereto or subtraction therefrom, whereby to pretend themselves the inventors thereof without the consent, license, or agreement of the said patentee in writing under his hand and seal, on pain of incurring such penalties as may be justly inflicted on such offenders for their contempt of this our royal command, and of being answerable to the patentee according to law for his damages thereby occasioned."

If any person breaks this royal command he is said to have infringed the patentee's monopoly, and the patentee is entitled to bring against such person an action for infringement to restrain future breaches, and to recover damages in respect of past offences. The subject of actions for infringement is fully dealt with later. If any person threatens to infringe the patentee's monopoly without actually doing so, the patentee may bring an action against such person to prevent him from carrying his threat into execution.* For a full consideration of what amounts to infringement see Chapter XIII, p. 125. *Liability of infringers.* *P. 142.* *Threatened infringements.*

Besides bringing actions against infringers a patentee may endeavour to prevent infringements taking place by frightening intending infringers with threats of actions, and this right of threatening is often extremely effective, as the costs of a patent action are almost invariably very great for both parties, whichever side may ultimately be successful. *Threats.*

This question is dealt with in a separate chapter (see p. 160).

The Act of 1883 provides that—

* Frearson v. Loe, 1878, 9 Ch.D. 65.

Patent binds the Crown. Act 1883, sect. 27 (1).

"A patent shall have to all intents the like effect as against Her Majesty the Queen, her heirs and successors, as it has against a subject."

But in cases where the Crown is concerned the patentee has not the same freedom as to the terms on which his invention shall be used as he has generally. It will be seen that by the terms of the grant,—

Patentee must supply articles for public service.

"If the said patentee shall not supply or cause to be supplied for our service all such articles of the said invention as may be required by the officers or commissioners administering any department of our service in such manner, at such times, and at and upon such reasonable prices and terms as shall be settled in manner for the time being by law provided, then, and in any of the said cases, these our letters patent, and all privileges and advantages whatever hereby granted, shall determine and become void, notwithstanding anything hereinbefore contained."

And the Act of 1883 provides that—

Sect. 27 (2).

Terms on which Crown may use invention.

"The officers or authorities administering any department of the service of the Crown may, by themselves, their agents, contractors, or others, at any time after the application, use the invention for the services of the Crown on terms to be before or after the use thereof agreed on, with the approval of the Treasury, between those officers or authorities and the patentee; or, in default of such agreement, on such terms as may be settled by the Treasury after hearing all parties interested."

Crown need not admit validity.

By the grant of letters patent for an invention the Crown is not in any way bound to admit their validity. If any department make use of the invention, such use will very probably be without any agreement with the patentee, and the patentee must take some action to obtain any compensation to which he may consider himself entitled.

If he believes that any department is using or

intends to use his invention, he should write to that department pointing out what his patent is for, and inquiring whether they wish to use his invention. He should also ask, in the event of their admitting user of his invention, that they should come to an agreement with him as to the terms upon which they are to use it. *Procedure if Crown infringes.*

If they admit the fact of user, and do not dispute the validity of his patent, but fail to come to terms with him, he should apply to the Treasury to settle the terms.

If they deny user or deny the validity of his patent, he should apply to the Treasury to nominate some person against whom he may bring any action he may be advised to bring, and who shall defend on behalf of the Crown.* *Where Crown disputes validity.*

This course has been adopted more than once, and has proved very satisfactory, as it enables all matters in dispute to be determined in an ordinary action for infringement; if it were not adopted, the patentee would have to proceed by way of a petition of right.

The patentee will be allowed full inspection of what the department is actually doing, so as to be able to establish the fact of infringement if such really exist. *Patentee has full inspection.*

When the validity of the patent and the fact of infringement have been established in any action that may be taken by the patentee against the nominee of the Treasury, he should again apply to the department to agree upon the terms on which the invention shall be used, and in default *Procedure when validity is established.*

* Nobel's Explosive Co. v. Anderson, 1894, 11 R.P.C. 115.

of their coming to an agreement with him he should again apply to the Treasury to fix the terms.

The Act of 1883 provides that—

<small>Use of invention on foreign vessels. Sect. 43.</small>

"A patent shall not prevent the use of an invention for the purposes of the navigation of a foreign vessel within the jurisdiction of any of Her Majesty's Courts in the United Kingdom or Isle of Man, or the use of an invention in a foreign vessel within that jurisdiction, provided it is not used therein for or in connection with the manufacture or preparation of anything intended to be sold in or exported from the United Kingdom or Isle of Man.

<small>Provision must be mutual.</small>

"But this section shall not extend to vessels of any foreign state of which the laws authorise subjects of such foreign state, having patents or like privileges for the exclusive use or exercise of inventions within its territories, to prevent or interfere with the use of such inventions in British vessels while in the ports of such foreign state, or in the waters within the jurisdiction of its courts, where such inventions are not so used for the manufacture or preparation of anything intended to be sold in or exported from the territories of such foreign state."

CHAPTER IX.

LICENSES.

The grant is that the patentee by himself, his agents or licensees, and no others may, &c. And the grant goes on to forbid any person using the invention without the consent, license, or agreement of the patentee in writing under his hand and seal. Later on it is provided that nothing in the grant shall prevent the granting of licenses in such manner and for such considerations as they may by law be granted. ^{See p 7.}

This shows that the patentee may grant licenses to use his invention; but from the earlier part it would appear that a license to be effective must be in writing under the hand and seal of the patentee; on the other hand, the last proviso makes the power of granting licenses very considerably wider. When the patentee sells a patented article to anyone unconditionally, he thereby impliedly licenses the use of that machine, so that it seems clear that in some circumstances even a parol license can be good. If a license be granted not under seal, the Courts will enforce it against the licensee, as Baron Alderson said— *Patentee may grant licenses. A license should be by deed, but one not under seal will be enforceable.*

"To grant a license not under seal may be a contempt of the Crown, but does not exempt the man to whom it is granted, and who derives a benefit from it, from paying the price of it."*

---

* Chanter v. Dewhurst and another, 1844, 12 M. & W. 823.

We are here only concerned with what may be called real licenses,—that is, definite licenses to make, sell, or use the patented invention.

Licenses usually under seal.
A license not under seal has the advantage of not requiring any stamp; but it is more usual to grant licenses by deed, and this course undoubtedly has advantages for all parties concerned.

Agreement for a license.
An agreement to grant a license would be enforceable in the courts, and would for many purposes be. as good as a license,* so that where the cost of stamps is a consideration it may be as well to use such an agreement, for which the stamp costs only sixpence.

Joint owners and licenses.
Joint owners of a patent may each use the invention without the consent of the rest; but if a joint owner made and sold one of the patented articles, he would have impliedly granted a license to use that article; and there seems to be little doubt that a joint patentee has power to grant licenses of his own motion. It has been suggested that if a joint owner granted a license he would have to account to his co-owners for any royalties received by him,† but the point has never been determined.

A license may be granted even before the complete specification is filed.‡

License usually reserves royalty.
A license may be granted wholly or partly in consideration of a lump sum, but it is more usual to reserve a royalty, either fixed or varying.

---

* Post-card Automatic Supply Co. v. Samuel, 1889, 6 R.P.C. 562.

† Mathers v. Green, 1865, L.R., 1 Ch. 29.

‡ Otto v. Singer, 1890, 7 R.P.C. 7.

When royalties are reserved, it is generally stipulated that if at any time the patent shall be declared invalid the payment of royalties shall cease. If this were not stipulated for by the licensee a declaration of invalidity would not affect the payment of royalty, at least until the patent was revoked ; and any sums paid as royalty under a patent which, though invalid, has not been revoked cannot be recovered from the patentee.* Effect of declaration of invalidity on royalty.

A license is very usually granted for the remainder of the term of the patent and any extension thereof ; and in such a case if it be under seal it cannot be revoked by the licensor.† It may, however, be for a shorter definite period, or it may be for an indefinite time ; in the last case, unless the license required some definite notice to be given, it would be revocable at any time by the licensor upon his giving notice to that effect to the licensee. Term of license. License by deed, when irrevocable. License for indefinite term is revocable.

The grant of a license does not impliedly warrant that the patent is valid, nor that in working under such license the licensee does not infringe an earlier patent.‡ License does not warrant validity

A licensee by deed under a patent is estopped from disputing the validity of the patent,§ and, while he is paying royalties, is not at liberty to deny the title of his licensors ;|| but he may, if Licensee may not dispute validity. Licensee may show that licensor's right has ceased.

* Taylor v. Hare, 1805, 1 W.P.C. 292.
† Guyot v. Thomson, 1894, 11 R.P.C. 541.
‡ Monforts v. Marsden, 1895, 12 R.P.C. 266.
§ Hills v. Laming, 1853, 9 Ex.R. 256.
|| Crossley v. Dixon, 1863, 10 H.L.C. 304.

sued for royalties, show that the licensor's right has expired. Thus, though the licensee could not say that the patent had been declared invalid, he could show that it had been revoked or had lapsed through non-payment of fees.* There is not, however, any implied covenant on the part of a licensor to pay any fees, and where an exclusive licensee covenants to pay a fixed annual royalty during the time for which the patent was granted, the patentee not covenanting to pay the fees for keeping up the patent, the royalty was held to be payable even though the patent had lapsed by reason of non-payment of fees.†

<small>No implied promise to pay renewal fees.</small>

Although a license by deed is irrevocable on the part of the licensor, the licensee can repudiate it, and from the date of such repudiation the license terminates;‡ the repudiation dates from the time when the licensee gives notice to the licensor.

<small>Licensee may repudiate license.</small>

To prevent the licensee repudiating his license, and thereby becoming able to dispute the validity of the patent, it is usual for the license to contain a covenant on the part of the licensee not at any time either directly or indirectly to dispute the validity of the patent.

<small>Licensee usually covenants not to dispute validity.</small>

A license is not assignable unless it is made so in distinct terms, and it is usual to make a license to work under a patent assignable only with the business of the licensee, and to bind the

<small>License is not necessarily assignable.</small>

* Muirhead v. The Commercial Cable Company, 1895, C.A., 12 R.P.C. 39.

† Mills v. Carson, 1892, 9 R.P.C. 338 ; C.A., 10 R.P.C. 9.

‡ Redges v. Mulliner, 1893, 10 R.P.C. 21 ; Crossley v. Dixon, 1863, 10 H.L.C. 293.

licensee not to part with his business without compelling the purchaser to accept a transfer of the license.

A license is often made to extend to more than one patent, and in such a case the royalties are usually made payable until the expiration of the term of the latest patent; in such a case the royalty must be paid without deduction during the whole period, even though the principal patents have expired.* License to use several patents.

In an old case, however, where there was a license granted to use six patents on payment of an annuity of £400 it was held that the consideration was entire, and if it failed partially by reason of one of the patents being invalid, it failed entirely, and no action could be maintained for the money;† so that it is well to be careful in framing a license to use more than one patent to avoid the risk of this occurring. Where one patent held bad.

If a patentee granted an exclusive license for the remainder of the term of the patent without reserving any royalty, he would have parted with his entire interest, and the licensee could probably claim to be registered as owner and to sue in his own name; but where an exclusive license for a limited area and a limited time was granted the licensee was not allowed to sue without joining the licensor.‡ License may be equal to assignment.
Licensee cannot sue alone.

In granting an exclusive license it is usual to give the licensee the right to bring actions Exclusive licensee may have power to sue in name of patentee.

* Siemens *v.* Taylor, 1892, 9 R.P.C. 393.
† Chanter *v.* Leese, 1839, 5 M. & W. 701.
‡ Heap *v.* Hartley, 1889, C.A., 6 R.P.C. 495.

in the patentee's name upon indemnifying him against the costs.

Compulsory Licenses.

Act 1883, sect. 22.

"If, on the petition of any person interested, it is proved to the Board of Trade that by reason of the default of a patentee to grant licenses on reasonable terms—

"(a) The patent is not being worked in the United Kingdom; or

"(b) The reasonable requirements of the public with respect to the invention cannot be supplied; or

"(c) Any person is prevented from working or using to the best advantage an invention of which he is possessed, the Board may order the patentee to grant licenses on such terms as to the amount of royalties, security for payment, or otherwise, as the Board, having regard to the nature of the invention and the circumstances of the case, may deem just, and any such order may be enforced by mandamus."

Patent Rule 60. Petition for compulsory grant of license.

"A petition to the Board of Trade for an order upon a patentee to grant a license shall show clearly the nature of the petitioner's interest, and the ground or grounds upon which he claims to be entitled to relief, and shall state in detail the circumstances of the case, the terms upon which he asks that an order may be made, and the purport of such order."

P. 256.

The petition must be on Patent Form H, and must be accompanied by Patent Form H in duplicate, one copy bearing a stamp for £5.

Patent Rule 61. To be left with evidence at Patent Office.

"The petition and an examined copy thereof shall be left at the Patent Office, accompanied by the affidavits or statutory declarations, and other documentary evidence (if any) tendered by the petitioner in proof of the alleged default of the patentee."

Patent Rule 62. Directions as to further proceedings unless petition refused.

"Upon perusing the petition and evidence, unless the Board of Trade shall be of opinion that the order should be at once refused, they may require the petitioner to attend before the Comptroller, or other person or persons appointed by them, to receive his or their directions as to further proceedings upon the petition."

"If and when a *primâ facie* case for relief has been made out to the satisfaction of the Board of Trade, the petitioner shall upon their requisition, and on or before a day to be named by them, deliver to the patentee copies of the petition and of the affidavits or statutory declarations and other documentary evidence (if any) tendered in support thereof." *Patent Rule 63. Procedure. Petitioner's evidence.*

If the patentee desires to oppose the grant of the license, he must give to the Comptroller notice of his opposition on Patent Form I, bearing a stamp for £5; and— *Patentee may oppose license. p. 258.*

"Within fourteen days after the day of such delivery the patentee shall leave at the Patent Office his affidavits or statutory declarations in opposition to the petition, and deliver copies thereof to the petitioner." *Patent Rule 64. Patentee's evidence.*

"The petitioner within fourteen days from such delivery shall leave at the Patent Office his affidavits or statutory declarations in reply, and deliver copies thereof to the patentee; such last-mentioned affidavits or declarations shall be confined to matters strictly in reply." *Patent Rule 65. Evidence in reply.*

"Subject to any further directions which the Board of Trade may give, the parties shall then be heard at such time, before such person or persons, in such manner, and in accordance with such procedure as the Board of Trade may, in the circumstances of the case, direct, but so that full opportunity shall be given to the patentee to show cause against the petition." *Patent Rule 66. Further proceedings.*

Nothing can be said as to what procedure the Board of Trade would adopt, as no one yet appears to have taken advantage of the provisions for compelling a patentee to grant a license.

CHAPTER X.

AMENDMENT OF SPECIFICATIONS.

Correction of clerical errors.

It may happen that after filing his complete specification the applicant may discover that some clerical error has been made which it would be advisable to correct.

P. 265.

In such a case he should apply to the Comptroller upon Patent Form P (bearing a stamp of £1 or 5s. according to whether the patent is or is not sealed).

The application must be accompanied by a certified copy of the specification with the correction made in red ink.

Invalidity of patent may be cured by amendment.

It may be, however, that after the complete specification is filed the applicant or, if the patent has been sealed, the patentee may discover that there is something in the specification which renders the patent invalid, or at any rate which it would be safer to alter. For instance, he may find that his claims cover something which, without his knowledge, existed before the date of his patent, and it may be possible to alter the specification and so narrow the claim as to exclude that which would, unless the specification were amended, be an anticipation of the inven-

When claim covers something old.

tion. Although the applicant for a patent is expected to examine into what has gone before, so as not to claim anything that is old, there is provision made for enabling him, or the patentee, at any time to so amend the specification as to make the patent, if possible, a valid one.

The original specification may be capable of two constructions, and in such a case the patentee may limit it by amendment to one of these.* Ambiguity may be cleared up.

"An applicant or a patentee may from time to time, by request in writing left at the Patent Office, seek leave to amend his specification, including drawings forming part thereof, by way of disclaimer, correction, or explanation, stating the nature of such amendment and his reasons for the same." Act 1883, sect. 18 (1).

"No amendment shall be allowed that would make the specification, as amended, claim an invention substantially larger than or substantially different from the invention claimed by the specification as it stood before amendment." Amendment must not enlarge claim. Act 1883, sect. 18 (8).

An amendment will, however, be allowed when there is any question of doubt as to its effect.† Allowed when effect doubtful.

The amendment must not make the patent extend to anything which was not discovered at the date of the original specification.‡ Nor must the patentee strike out the original complete claim, and insert a new claim for a subordinate part only.§

* *Re* Rylands, 1888, 5 R.P.C. 665.
† *Re* Lake, 1887, Gr.A.P.C. 16.
‡ *Re* Beck and Justice, 1886, Gr.A.P.C. 10.
§ *Re* Serrell, 1889, 6 R.P.C. 101.

Amendment during Patent Action.

Act 1888, sect. 5.

"The above, however, does not apply when and so long as any action for infringement or proceeding for revocation of a patent is pending."

What is a pending action.

The action or petition must be actually pending,—that is, it must have been commenced and not been tried. A pending appeal to the House of Lords is not a pending action,* and there seems no reason why the same rule should not apply equally to any appeal.

A pending action for threats does not interfere with the amendment of a specification.†

Act 1883, sect. 19. Court may allow amendment and impose terms.

"In an action for infringement of a patent, and in a proceeding for revocation of a patent, the Court or a judge may at any time order that the patentee shall, subject to such terms as to costs and otherwise as the Court or a judge may impose, be at liberty to apply at the Patent Office for leave to amend his specification by way of disclaimer, and may direct that in the meantime the trial or hearing of the action shall be postponed."

Only by disclaimer.

It will be seen that the amendment, when an action or petition is pending, must be limited to disclaimer; it must not be by way of correction or of explanation as in the general case of an amendment.

If leave to apply to amend be given in an action for infringement, it may be made a condition that the amended specification be not used in evidence at the trial,‡ but this would generally necessitate the discontinuance of the action.

---

* Cropper v. Smith, 1884, 28 Ch.D. 151.
† Re Hall, 1888, 21 Q.B.D. 137.
‡ Bray v. Gardner, 1887, C.A., 4 R.P.C. 40.

AMENDMENT OF SPECIFICATIONS.

As a rule the applicants will, in any event, have to pay the costs of the other side up to and including those of the application for leave to apply to amend and consequent upon the amendment (not including, however, costs incurred in opposing the amendment, or of an unsuccessful appeal against the granting of the application).* Costs where amendment is allowed.

Procedure.

"A request for leave to amend a specification must be signed by the applicant or patentee, and accompanied by a duly certified printed copy of the original specification and drawings, showing in red ink the proposed amendment, and shall be advertised by publication of the request and the nature of the proposed amendment in the official journal of the Patent Office, and in such other manner (if any) as the Comptroller may in each case direct." Request to amend, how made. Patent Rule 52.

The application for leave to amend must be made on Patent Form F, which must bear a stamp for £1 10s. or £3, according as the application be made before or after the sealing of the patent. p. 254.

"Where a request for leave to amend is made by or in pursuance of an order of the Court or a judge, an official or verified copy of the order shall be left with the request at the Patent Office." Patent Rule 58. Request during action.

It has been held by a law officer that an application for leave to amend a complete specification before acceptance must be made in this way;† but he failed to explain how a duly

---

* Fusee Vesta v. Bryant and May, 1887, 4 R.P.C. 71.
† Re Jones, Gr. P.C. 313.

certified printed copy should in such a case be provided.

<small>Opposition to amendment. Act 1883, sect. 18 (2). Notice to patentee.</small>
"At any time within one month from its first advertisement any person may give notice at the Patent Office of opposition to the amendment. Where such notice is given, the Comptroller shall give notice of the opposition to the person making the request, and shall hear and decide the case subject to an appeal to the law officer."

<small>Patent Rule 53. Grounds of opposition must be stated.</small>
"A notice of opposition to the amendment shall state the ground or grounds on which the person giving such notice (hereinafter called the opponent) intends to oppose the amendment, and shall be signed by him. Such notice shall state his address for service in the United Kingdom, and shall be accompanied by an unstamped copy."

<small>P. 255.</small>
Notice of opposition to an amendment must be made on Patent Form G in duplicate, one copy bearing an impressed stamp for 10s.

If the notice of opposition be not signed by the opponent, the Comptroller may allow him to sign it subsequently.*

<small>Patent Rule 54.</small>
"On receipt of such notice the copy thereof shall be transmitted by the Comptroller to the applicant (or patentee)."

<small>Evidence in support of opposition. Rule 55.</small>
"Within fourteen days after the expiration of one month from the first advertisement of the application for leave to amend, the opponent may leave at the Patent Office statutory declarations in support of his opposition, and on so leaving shall deliver to the applicant a list thereof."

<small>Form of declarations, Patent Rules 11 & 17A.</small>
Such declarations must be in the same form as is used in the High Court of Justice, and must be headed in the matter or matters to which they relate. They must be divided into paragraphs consecutively numbered, each paragraph being so far as possible confined to one subject.

* *Re* Codd, 1884, Gr.P.C. 305.

AMENDMENT OF SPECIFICATIONS.

The filing of declarations is optional, and the opponent may be able to rely on the reasons which he has given in his notice of opposition.

The rules for signing such declarations are the same as are given on page 82.

"Within fourteen days from the delivery of such list the applicant may leave at the Patent Office statutory declarations in answer, and on so leaving shall deliver to the opponent a list thereof, and within fourteen days from such delivery the opponent may leave at the Patent Office his statutory declarations in reply, and on so leaving shall deliver to the applicant a list thereof. Such last-mentioned declarations shall be confined to matters strictly in reply. Patent Rule 38. Evidence in support of application to amend.
Evidence in reply.

"Copies of the declarations mentioned in this and the last preceding rule may be obtained either from the Patent Office or from the opposite party." Copies of declarations.

"No further evidence shall be left on either side except by leave of the Comptroller upon the written consent of the parties duly notified to him, or by special leave of the Comptroller on application in writing made to him for that purpose." Patent Rule 39. Closing of evidence.

"Either party making such application shall give notice thereof to the opposite party, who shall be entitled to oppose the application." Patent Rule 40.

"On completion of the evidence, or at such other time as he may see fit, the Comptroller shall appoint a time for the hearing of the case, and shall give the parties ten days' notice at the least of such appointment. If the applicant or opponent desires to be heard, he must forthwith send the Comptroller an application on Form E (bearing an impressed stamp for £1). The Comptroller may refuse to hear either party who has not sent such application for hearing. If neither party applies to be heard, the Comptroller shall decide the case and notify his decision to the parties." Patent Rule 41. Notice of hearing by Comptroller.
P. 253.

"The decision of the Comptroller after hearing any party who applies under Rule 41 shall be notified by him to the parties." Patent Rule 42. Decision to be notified to parties. Act 1883, sect. 18 (3).

The decision of the Comptroller is subject to an appeal to the law officer, which must be made according to the law officers' rules (see next chapter).

It is provided that—

Act 1883, sect. 18 (4). Law officer to hear parties.

"The law officer shall, if required, hear the person making the request and the person so giving notice, and being in the opinion of the law officer entitled to be heard in opposition to the request, and shall determine whether and subject to what conditions (if any) the amendment ought to be allowed."

Law officer's decision final.

There do not appear to have been any cases in which the law officer refused to hear the opponent. The decision of the law officer is final on any question coming before him in proceedings for amendment of a specification.

Act 1883, sect. 18 (5). When opponent does not appear.

"Where no notice of opposition is given, or the person so giving notice does not appear, the Comptroller shall determine whether and subject to what conditions (if any) the amendment ought to be allowed."

Act 1883, sect. 94. Patent Rule 11. Exercise of discretionary power by Comptroller.

"Before exercising any discretionary power given to the Comptroller adversely to the applicant for amendment of a specification, the Comptroller shall give ten days' notice, or such longer notice as he may think fit, to the applicant of the time when he may be heard personally or by his agent before the Comptroller."

Patent Rule 12. Notice by applicant.

"Within five days from the date when such notice would be delivered in the ordinary course of post, or such longer time as the Comptroller may appoint in such notice, the applicant shall notify in writing to the Comptroller whether or not he intends to be heard upon the matter."

Patent Rule 13. Comptroller may require statements, &c.

"Whether the applicant desires to be heard or not, the Comptroller may at any time require him to submit a statement in writing within a time to be notified by the Comptroller, or to attend before him and make oral explanations with respect to such matters as the Comptroller may require."

Patent Rule 14. Decision to be notified to parties.

"The decision or determination of the Comptroller in the exercise of any such discretionary power as aforesaid shall be

AMENDMENT OF SPECIFICATIONS.

notified by him to the applicant, and any other person affected thereby."

"When leave to amend is refused by the Comptroller, the person making the request may appeal from his decision to the law officer." Act 1883, sect. 18 (6). Refusal of leave to amend.

"The law officer shall, if required, hear the person making the request and the Comptroller, and may make an order determining whether, and subject to what conditions (if any), the amendment ought to be allowed." Sect. 18 (7).

In case of an appeal against the Comptroller, the Comptroller neither gives nor receives costs, whatever the result, except in very special circumstances.*

If an application to amend refused by the Comptroller be not appealed against, no appeal will be allowed from a similar refusal made on a second application for substantially the same amendment.†

"Where leave to amend is given the applicant shall, if the Comptroller so require, and within a time to be limited by him, leave at the Patent Office a new specification and drawings as amended, to be prepared in accordance with rules 10, 30, and 31" (see p. 47). Patent Rule 57. Requirements when leave is given to amend.

"Every amendment of a specification shall be forthwith advertised by the Comptroller in the official journal of the Patent Office, and in such other manner (if any) as the Comptroller may direct." Patent Rule 59. Advertisement of amendment.

"Leave to amend shall be conclusive as to the right of the party to make the amendment allowed, except in case of fraud; and the amendment shall in all courts and for all purposes be deemed to form part of the specification." Act 1883, sect. 18 (9). Leave to amend conclusive of right to amend.

This does not prevent anyone subsequently showing that the amendment made the specifica- Amendment may be shown to have invalidated patent.

* *Re* Lake, 1887, Gr. A.P.C. 16.
† *Re* Arnold, 1887, Gr. A.P.C. 5.

tion claim an invention substantially larger than or substantially different from the invention claimed by the original specification; and in such a case the patent would be rendered invalid by the amendment.

So far as the bringing of actions is concerned, amendment is complete as soon as conditional leave to amend has been obtained, and the condition has been assented to by the patentee.*

If no conditions are imposed, it would appear that the amendment is complete for this purpose as soon as leave to amend is given.

Act 1883, sect. 20. Effect of amendment on damages. "Where an amendment by way of disclaimer, correction, or explanation has been allowed under this Act, no damages shall be given in any action in respect of the use of the invention before the disclaimer, correction, or explanation, unless the patentee establishes to the satisfaction of the Court that his original claim was framed in good faith and with reasonable skill and knowledge."

* Andrew and Co., Ltd., v. Crossley Brothers, Ltd., 1891, C.A., 9 R.P.C. 165.

CHAPTER XI.

PROCEEDINGS BEFORE LAW OFFICERS.

It has been seen that the decision of the Comptroller is always subject to an appeal to the law officer, that is to Attorney or Solicitor General.

The decision of the law officer, whether he be Attorney-General or Solicitor-General, is final on every matter before him; and he is not a court to which a prohibition can go, so that there is never any way of testing the correctness of his decision.* Decision of law officer is final.

"When any person intends to appeal to the law officer from a decision of the Comptroller in any case in which such appeal is given by the Act, he shall within fourteen days from the date of the decision appealed against file in the Patent Office a notice of such his intention." L.O.R. 1. Notice of appeal.

The notice of intention to appeal must be on Patent Form T, which must bear a stamp for £3, and must be sent to the Comptroller at the Patent Office. P. 269.

The notice of appeal need not be signed by the appellant himself; signature by his authorised agent is sufficient.†

* *Re* Van Gelder, 1889, 6 R.P.C. 28.
† *Re* Anderson and McKinnell, 1887, Gr.A.P.C. 23.

The fourteen days run, in case of leave being given to amend, from the day of forwarding to the opponent a copy of the amendment as approved by the Comptroller.*

L.O.R. 5. "No appeal shall be entertained of which notice is not given within fourteen days from the date of the decision appealed against, or such further time as the Comptroller may allow, except by special leave upon application to the law officer."

When notice has been given just before the fourteen days expire, and the party receiving it desires to give a counter notice the time for giving it will be extended.†

Form of notice, L.O.R. 2. "Such notice shall state the nature of the decision appealed against, and whether the appeal is from the whole or part only, and if so, what part of such decision."

Law officer will only hear arguments on points mentioned in notice. When notice of appeal is given as to part only of the Comptroller's decision, and the party receiving such notice desires to question other parts, he must give a counter notice.‡

L.O.R. 3. Notice of Appeal, to whom sent. "A copy of such notice of intention to appeal shall be sent by the party so intending to appeal to the law officer's clerk at room 549, Royal Courts of Justice, London; and when there has been an opposition before the Comptroller, to the opponent or opponents; and when the Comptroller has refused to seal a patent on the ground that a previous application for a patent for the same invention is pending, to the prior applicant."

When the appeal is by an opponent he need not give notice to the applicant,§ but the law officer provides for giving such notice.‖

---

* *Re* Chandler, 1886, Gr. 270.
† *Re* Bairstow, 1888, 5 R.P.C. 289.
‡ Ibid.
§ *Re* Anderson and McKinnell, 1887, Gr.A.P.C. 23.
‖ *Re* Hill, 1888, 5 R.P.C. 601.

"Upon notice of appeal being filed, the Comptroller shall forthwith transmit to the law officer's clerk all the papers relating to the matter of the application in respect of which such appeal is made." L.O.R. 4.

"Seven days' notice, at least, of the time and place appointed for the hearing of any appeal shall be given by the law officer's clerk, unless special leave be given by the law officer that any shorter notice be given." Notice of hearing, L.O.R. 6.

"Such notice shall in all cases be given to the Comptroller and the appellant; and when there has been an opposition before the Comptroller to the opponent or opponents, and when the Comptroller has refused to seal a patent on the ground that an application for a patent for the same invention is pending, to the prior applicant." L.O.R. 7.

In case of opposition to either the grant of a patent or the amendment of a specification the law officer is only required to hear the opponent if he is in the opinion of the law officer a person entitled to be heard in opposition; but he must in any case hear the applicant, and when the Comptroller is respondent he also is entitled to be heard. Whom law officer must hear. Act 1883, sects. 11 (3) and 18 (4). Sects. 9 (3) and 18 (7).

If the appellant does not appear at the hearing the appeal will be dismissed with costs.* Appellant not appearing

If the appeal be withdrawn without sufficient reason being assigned for the withdrawal the appellant will have to pay the costs.† or withdrawing.

If the respondent does not appear, but explains his non-appearance to the satisfaction of the law officer, another day will be appointed for hearing the appeal, and the respondent will be ordered to pay the costs of the day.‡ Respondent not appearing.

* *Re* Dietz, 1889, 6 R.P.C. 297.
† *Re* Knight, 1887, Gr. A.P.C. 35.
‡ *Re* Ainsworth, 1885, Gr. 269.

In case of opposition to the grant of a patent—

Law officer may employ expert. Act 1883, sect. 11 (4).
"the law officer may, if he thinks fit, obtain the assistance of an expert, who shall be paid such remuneration as the law officer, with the consent of the Treasury, shall appoint."

L.O.R. 8. Evidence on appeal.
"The evidence used on appeal to the law officer shall be the same as that used at the hearing before the Comptroller; and no further evidence shall be given, save as to matters which have occurred or come to the knowledge of either party, after the date of the decision appealed against, except with the leave of the law officer upon application for that purpose."

Evidence before Comptroller is documentary.
We have seen that the evidence before the Comptroller is entirely documentary; he cannot take *vivâ voce* evidence under any circumstances, and therefore in a very complicated case the proceedings before him are often of a formal character, just sufficient evidence being given to raise the questions at issue; an appeal to the law officer is then made, and that alone is seriously contested.

Law officers may take virâ voce evidence. Act 1883, sect. 38.
The law officers may examine witnesses on oath, and administer oaths for that purpose; so that the objection as to documentary evidence being required does not apply to an appeal.

Attendance of witnesses may be ordered. L.O.R. 9.
"The law officer shall, at the request of either party, order the attendance at the hearing on appeal, for the purpose of being cross-examined, of any person who has made a declaration, in the matter to which the appeal relates, unless in the opinion of the law officer there is good ground for not making such order."

L.O.R. 10.
"Any person requiring the attendance of a witness for cross-examination shall tender to the witness whose attendance is required a reasonable sum for conduct money."

No costs before Comptroller.
The Comptroller has no power to award any costs to either party directly or indirectly; but

the law officer may order costs to be paid by either party, and any such order may be made a rule of the Court (*i. e.* of the High Court of Justice). <small>Law officer may give costs. Act 1883, sect. 38.</small>

"Where the law officer orders that costs shall be paid by any party to another, he may fix the amount of such costs; and if he shall not think fit to fix the amount thereof, he shall direct by whom and in what manner the amount of such costs shall be ascertained." <small>Law officer may fix amount of costs. L.O.R. 11.</small>

As a rule the law officer fixes the costs; the amount awarded is quite an arbitrary one, often five guineas, but sometimes double that sum may be awarded when the evidence is of an expensive kind.

"If any costs so ordered to be paid be not paid within fourteen days after the amount thereof has been so fixed or ascertained, or such shorter period as shall be directed by the law officer, the party to whom such costs are to be paid may apply to the law officer for an order for payment under the provisions of section 38 of the Act (*i. e.* to make the order a rule of the Court). <small>Recovery of costs. L.O.R. 12. Act 1883, sect. 38.</small>

"All documentary evidence required or allowed by the law officer to be filed shall be subject to the same regulations, in all respects, as apply to the procedure before the Comptroller, and shall be filed in the Patent Office, unless the law officer shall order to the contrary." <small>Form of documentary evidence. L.O.R. 13.</small>

"No further evidence shall be left on either side except by leave of the Comptroller upon the written consent of the parties duly notified to him, or by special leave of the Comptroller on application in writing made to him for that purpose. <small>Patent Rule 39. Fresh evidence.</small>

"Either party making such application shall give notice thereof to the opposite party, who shall be entitled to oppose the application." <small>Notice to leave fresh evidence. Patent Rule 40.</small>

Notices to law officer's clerk.

"14. Any notice or other document required to be given to the law officer's clerk, under these rules, may be sent by a pre-paid letter through the post."

The Act of 1883 provides that—

Sect. 38.

"The law officers may from time to time make, alter, and rescind rules regulating references and appeals to the law officers and the practice and procedure before them under this part of this Act."

CHAPTER XII.

PROFESSIONAL ASSISTANCE IN PATENT MATTERS.

To aid intending applicants for patents, and to enable them to make their applications in proper form, the Patent Office publishes a circular of information which will be found very useful. This circular is supplied gratis at the Patent Office. *Patent Office Circular.*

A careful examination of this and of a few specifications will be sufficient to enable an intelligent person to make an application for a patent without professional aid, without much risk of making any serious mistakes so far as formal matters are concerned.

The choice of a suitable title and the drafting of a provisional specification do not generally present any great difficulty, and provided the title is applicable to the invention, and not too wide, and the provisional specification gives a fair outline of the invention sufficiently general to cover all probable improvements, there is no fear of going far wrong. When, however, it becomes a question of the complete specification and its claims, the greatest care and skill are required, and as a rule it is advisable for the applicant to obtain professional assistance. *Title must be applicable to invention.* *Complete specification requires great care.*

Before settling the claims it is very important to know what has been done before in the same connection, so as to be able to make the claims *Knowledge of what has gone before is essential.*

cover all that is really new and nothing that is old. For this purpose it is often advisable to supplement the applicant's knowledge by making a search through the specifications of previous patents. Such a search involves considerable expenditure of time, and the applicant may not feel prepared to spend several days at the Patent Office or elsewhere on work of this description. Of course he need not necessarily employ a regular patent agent for making a search, but one who is accustomed to the work is more likely to carry it out effectively than one who has had little or no experience in such matters.

<small>Searches.</small>

Such work is usually entrusted to a patent agent, of whom there are many in London and other places; their business consists in conducting all kinds of work, other than legal proceedings, in connection with patents. Formerly any person, however ignorant of patent business, could style himself a patent agent; but the Act of 1888 provided that—

<small>Patent agents.</small>

<small>Who may call themselves patent agents. Sect. 1 (1).</small>

"A person shall not be entitled to describe himself as a patent agent, whether by advertisement, by description on his place of business, by any document issued by him, or otherwise, unless he is registered as a patent agent."

"If any person describes himself as a patent agent in contravention of this section he shall be liable on summary conviction to a fine not exceeding twenty pounds."

<small>Penalty for using the name patent agent improperly. Sub-sect. 4.</small>

<small>Anyone may act as agent in patent matters.</small>

Providing he does not describe himself as a patent agent, any person can act as agent for another in patent business; and the signing of a specification as agent for the applicant is not sufficient to render him liable to the fine.* This

* Graham v. Fanta, 1892. Div. Ct., 9 R.P.C. 164.

would probably apply to any other patent business, but it would be certainly unwise in ordinary circumstances for an applicant to employ as his agent any person whose name is not on the Register. *but employment of patent agent is advisable.*

A patent agent cannot undertake the conduct of an action for infringement, or to restrain threats, or of a petition for revocation or prolongation, which must be conducted by the party in person or through a solicitor like any other legal proceedings; but in all proceedings before the Comptroller and the law officers it is unusual to employ a solicitor, and his place is generally taken by a patent agent, though, as has been said, the Acts and Rules do not require that the person who acts as agent for an applicant, patentee, or opponent need be a patent agent. *Patent agent cannot do solicitor's work.*

At a hearing before the Comptroller or a law officer it is very usual for the parties to be represented by counsel. Such proceedings form an exception to the general rule that in contentious business counsel must receive their instructions from a solicitor, for in them the employment of a member of the other branch of the legal profession is unnecessary and unusual, and counsel take their briefs from the agent. *Counsel may be employed.*

Besides the contentious proceedings in which professional assistance is generally absolutely necessary, there are many matters in which it is advisable for a patentee not to trust to his own unaided powers. For settling the complete specification, amendments, or licenses professional aid is generally very advisable; many a patent, which might have been of great value, has been *Non-contentious business.*

irretrievably ruined by having the claims badly drawn in the first instance. Settling an amendment or disclaimer is usually a matter of some nicety, where experience is of great advantage.

<small>Specifications and licenses often settled by counsel.</small>

The drafting of specifications is generally carried out by a patent agent, but it is very usual to lay the draft specification before some counsel who makes a speciality of patent matters, and let him settle the claims.

The settling of an amendment or disclaimer is also very usually left to counsel.

<small>Proceedings on sale of a patent.</small>

When a patent is sold, the vendor does not usually in any way warrant its validity,* and the intending purchaser usually requires some search to be made to see if the patent has been anticipated, and generally requires the specifications and the results of any searches to be laid before counsel, and an opinion favorable to the validity of the patent to be obtained before the purchase is completed.

<small>Counsel's opinion usually required by purchaser.</small>

In all these non-contentious matters the instructions for counsel are usually prepared and submitted by a solicitor or patent agent; but as in other non-contentious matters—such, for instance, as the well-known case of giving instructions for drawing up a will—they may, if preferred, be drawn up and submitted to counsel by the parties themselves, who may thus avoid the double expense involved in the more usual procedure.

* Monforts v. Marsden, 1895, C.A., 12 R.P.C. 270.

CHAPTER XIII.

INFRINGEMENT.

Letters patent confer upon the patentee, his agents and licensees, the sole right to make, use, exercise, and vend the invention in the United Kingdom and the Isle of Man in such manner as to him or them may seem meet.

If any person without the license of the patentee makes, uses, exercises, or vends the invention, such person is said to have infringed the letters patent; and the patentee is entitled to bring an action for infringement against him. In such an action, unless the patent is held bad, if he prove that the infringement has taken place, the patentee will be entitled to judgment against the infringer for an injunction to restrain any future infringements, for an account of the profits which the infringer has made by his wrongful acts, or in the alternative for an inquiry into the damages which the patentee has suffered by the infringements, and lastly for an order requiring the delivery up upon oath to the patentee or the destruction of all the infringing articles which may be at the time in the possession of the infringer.

Patentee may bring action for infringement.

Penalties of infringers.

The patentee is not even obliged to wait until

Patentee may sue before infringement.

his patent has been actually infringed; if any person threatens to do what the patentee considers will be an infringement of his patent, he can bring an action to restrain the threatened infringement;* of course in such a case there is no question of damages, and the only relief possible is an injunction. In order to succeed the patentee must show that his patent is valid, and that the defendant has threatened and continues to threaten to do something which would actually infringe the patent.

Generally better to wait for infringement to take place.

Except when it is very clear that what is threatened will be an infringement, it is safer to wait until the infringement takes place, and in the meantime to threaten to proceed against infringers (see Threats, p. 160).

What constitutes infringement.

The question of what constitutes an infringement is one of great importance both to the patentee and to the public; since the latter are entitled to know what they may do without infringing and becoming liable to the severe penalties inflicted on infringers.

The first question that may arise in respect of an alleged infringement is "does the article or process alleged to be an infringement come within the scope of the invention described and claimed in the complete specification? since this alone is protected by the patent. This, of course, depends partly on the construction of the specification, which is a matter of law for the consideration of the Court; but when the meaning of the specification is clear, the question of infringement is one

Construction of specification.

* Frearson v. Loe, 1878, 9 Ch. D. 65.

of fact, and if the case be tried by a jury, must be left to them to answer.

A second question which may arise is whether, granted that the article or process would otherwise be an infringement, the facts of the case are such that what the defendant did was done under an implied license from the patentee, and therefore did not amount to an infringement. In such a case there may, of course, be questions of what actually happened, but when these are answered the question of infringement becomes a matter of law for the Court to decide. *Is the user complained of an infringement?*

The question as to whether the alleged infringement does or does not come within the scope of the invention protected by a patent is sometimes one of considerable difficulty, even after the meaning of the complete specification is made clear. Of course, where the infringer has simply taken the invention as described no difficulty arises; but this is not by any means the most usual case. More usually an infringer, starting with the intention of using the invention described in the specification, disguises it by making slight alterations here and there, by using something which is different from what is described in the specification, but which will produce the same effect, or by adding or subtracting something, perhaps in itself of considerable importance, so that at first sight what he does appears to be quite different from what is described in the specification, and it is only after careful examination and with full knowledge of all the particulars that the fact of infringement becomes clear. *Does alleged infringement come within scope of patent?* *Effect of alterations from invention described in specification.*

Substitution of an equivalent.

Perhaps the simplest alteration that an infringer can make in an invention described by a specification is to substitute for the method described some other method which will produce the same result. This, according as the invention is mechanical or chemical, is called using a mechanical or chemical equivalent. In his specification the applicant need not describe every method of carrying out his invention, and if he describes one method, this will be sufficient to prevent others from using what at the date of his specification *What is an equivalent?* was well known to be an equivalent method. The patent will not, however, protect him against the use of any method which, though really equivalent to that described by him in his specification, was not at the date of the specification known to be an equivalent; in such a case there is invention in the discovery of the equivalent which may be the subject of another patent.

In the leading case on this subject it was said:

Equivalent must be known at date of patent.
" The specification must be read as persons acquainted with the subject would read it at the time it was made; and if it could be construed as containing any chemical equivalents, it must be such as are known to such persons at that time; but those which are not known at the time as equivalents, and afterwards are found to answer the same purpose, are not included in the specification. They are new inventions."*

It is not, however, in every case that the introduction of an equivalent fails to secure immunity *Substitution of equivalent in combination may not be an infringement.* from infringement. In the case of a patent for a combination, all depends on whether the substitution takes place in an important or unimportant

* Heath v. Unwin, H.L. 1855, 2 W.P.C. 314.

part. As a general rule a patent for a combination protects only the actual thing described, and is not infringed by the use of a different combination, even though the same results are produced in similar ways by each.

Thus:

"Where there is a well-known machine, and there is an improvement in a part of that machinery for effecting the old object, though in a better way, you must confine the patentee to the improvement which he claims in effecting that particular object. It does not come to the question whether this is or not a mechanical equivalent; it is, 'Have you really taken in substance that which was the invention of the plaintiff, protected by his patent?'"*

But although in the case of a patent for a combination the question of equivalents may not be of importance, this is not by any means always the case. It was laid down that— [But this is not always true.]

"A patent for a new combination or arrangement is to be entitled to the same protection and on the same principles as every other patent. In fact, every patent, or almost every patent, is a patent for a new combination. The patent is for the entire combination; but there is, or may be, an essence or substance of the invention underlying the mere accident of form, and that invention, like every other invention, may be appropriated by a theft in a disguised or mutilated form; and it will be in every case a question of fact whether the alleged piracy is the same in substance and in fact, or is a substantially new or different combination."†

And in the Court of Appeal in a recent case it was clearly stated that a patent for a combination

---

* Boyd v. Horrocks, 1889, C.A., 6 R.P.C. 159; see also Brown v. Jackson [1895], A.C. 416.

† Clarke v. Adie, 1875, L.R., 10 Ch. 675.

may be infringed by taking the essential part with mechanical equivalents for some of the parts.*

<small>When essential part of combination is taken.</small>

Besides the use of mechanical or chemical equivalents, there may be many ways in which an infringer may endeavour to conceal the fact of infringement. As a general statement of the law on this subject we may take the words of Chief Justice Tindal in a case decided in 1841. He said:

<small>Test of infringement.</small>

"Where a party has obtained a patent for a new invention, or a discovery he has made by his own ingenuity, it is not in the power of any other person, simply by varying in form or in immaterial circumstances the nature or subject-matter of that discovery, either to obtain a patent for it himself, or to use it without the leave of the patentee, because that would be in effect and in substance an invasion of the right; and, therefore, what you have to look at upon the present occasion is not simply whether in form or in circumstances, that may be more or less immaterial, that which has been done by the defendants varies from the specification of the plaintiff's patent, but to see whether in reality, in substance, and in effect, the defendants have availed themselves of the plaintiff's invention in order to make that fabric.

"There can be no doubt whatever, that, although one man has obtained a patent for a given object, there are many modes still open for other men of ingenuity to obtain a patent for the same object. There may be many roads leading to one place, and if a man has by dint of his own genius and discovery, after a patent has been obtained, been able to give to the public without reference to the former one, or borrowing from the former one, a new and superior mode of arriving at the same end, there can be no objection to his taking out a patent for that purpose. But he has no right whatever to take, if I may so say, a leaf out of his neighbour's book, for he must be contented to rest upon his

---

* Peckover v. Rowland, 1893, C.A., 10 R.P.C. 234.

own skill and labour for the discovery, and he must not avail himself of that which had before been granted exclusively to another."*

This statement of the law has often been repeated in different words by the highest authority. Thus Lord Chancellor Cairns said :

"That which is protected by a patent is that which is specified, and that which is held to be an infringement must be an infringement of that which is specified. But I agree that it will not be the less an infringement because it has been coloured or disguised by additions or subtractions, which additions or subtractions may exist, and yet the thing protected may be taken notwithstanding."† *[margin: Infringement must be of what is described, but may be altered so as to conceal fact of infringement.]*

In every case the fact of infringement is one to be decided on the evidence, and does not depend on other cases, and the above only serve as aids in showing what must be the object in view in considering the evidence. This has been stated in the following language : *[margin: Infringement is matter of fact depending on evidence.]*

"You must ask yourself whether the substance and pith of the invention is taken substantially. A mere addition to the original machine will not prevent the new machine from being an infringement; nor will diminishing or subtracting this or that part of the original machine necessarily prevent an infringement of it from taking place. You must recall yourself, after making allowance for the subtraction, to the question whether in substance the invention has been borrowed."‡

And to this nothing can with advantage be added.

In order to be liable as an infringer it is not *[margin: Infringement by selling]*

---

* Walton v. Potter, 1841, 1 W.P.C. 586.

† Dudgeon v. Thompson, 1877, 3 App. Cas. 44.

‡ Franklin Hocking and Co., Ltd., v. Franklin Hocking, 1887, C.A., 4 R.P.C. 442.

always necessary to actually carry out the invention protected by a patent; it may be enough to constitute infringement for a person to make all the parts of a patented machine, and to supply these parts to others in a form in which they can easily put them together, and thus use the patented invention.*

<small>Parts of invention.</small>

It is not necessary for a person either to use or to sell that which infringes a patent in order to be rendered liable for infringement. The mere making and keeping infringing articles in his possession is sufficient. Thus in one case where a patent was about to expire, and defendant had made a large number of the patented articles ready to be thrown on the market as soon as the monopoly had expired, an injunction was granted to restrain the sale of such articles both before and after the time limited by the patent.†

<small>Infringement by making only.</small>

<small>Others may not prepare to flood market on expiration of patent.</small>

Again, the infringement may be only by user of the patented invention without either making or selling. The purchaser of an infringing article infringes the patent every time he uses such an article, and is liable to the like penalties as any other infringer. If this were not so, it would be easy to defeat the patentee's rights by getting some man of straw to make the infringing article for sale to the person who wanted to use it.

<small>Infringement by user only.</small>

<small>Purchaser may infringe.</small>

But, as we have seen, when the patentee himself supplies the article, he may supply it on any terms he thinks fit, and may license it to be

<small>Restricted user.</small>

---

* United Telephone Co. v. Dale, 1884, 25 Ch. D. 778.
† Crossley v. Beverley, 1829, 1 Russ. & M. 166 n.

used or dealt with in a restricted manner only. For instance, a patentee who had a patent only in this country would be prepared to supply the patented article for export at a lower rate than for home use, since abroad anyone could lawfully supply such articles, and he would have all foreign manufacturers to compete with for the market. In such a case it would be an infringement to use in this country an article sold for export; in fact, the offence would be practically the same as that of importing into this country an article made in infringement of the patent, and this is in itself an infringement.* <small>*Articles for export only may not be used here. Infringement by importation.*</small>

But, unless there is some clear indication to the contrary, notified to the purchaser before sale, where a patentee manufactures in England and abroad, the sale of the article in one country implies a license to use it in the other. This, however, only applies where the patentee has not parted with any of his patent rights, since, if he has assigned the foreign patent in either country, he cannot sell the article so as to defeat the rights of the assignee.† <small>*Sale implies license to use.*</small>

Not only may the patentee supply an article for export, but he may supply an article and limit the manner or the locality in which it may be used in this country; and in that case, provided the purchaser is before purchasing made aware of <small>*Locality for user may be limited.*</small>

---

* Von Heyden v. Neustadt, 1880, 14 Ch. D. 230; Walton v. Lavater, 1860, 8 C.B.N.S. 162; Wright v. Hitchcock, 1870, L.R. 5, Ex. 37.

† Betts v. Willmott, 1871, 6 Ch. 239; cf. Société Anonyme de Glaces v. Tilghman's Sand Blast Co., 1883, C.A., 25 Ch. D. 1.

the limitation, any use beyond the limits specified will constitute an infringement.*

Patentee must not cause infringement. The patentee must not in any way be instrumental in causing the infringement to be committed; thus the making of an infringing article under the instructions of the patentee's agent is not an infringement; for the patentee must not lay a trap for anyone so as to entangle an innocent party in litigation.†

* Incandescent Gas Light Co., Ltd., v. Cantelo, 1895, 12 R.P.C. 262.

† Kelly v. Batchelar, 1893, 10 R.P.C. 289.

CHAPTER XIV.

ACTIONS FOR INFRINGEMENT.

IF a patentee believes that any person has made use of his invention without license from him—that is, that any person has infringed his monopoly—he may bring against such person an action for infringement of his patent.

An action for infringement in England must be brought in the High Court of Justice or in the County Palatine Court of Lancaster. In the High Court the action may be commenced in either the Chancery or Queen's Bench Division, and the choice of plaintiffs is divided nearly equally between the two. *Court in which action must be brought. Act 1888, sect. 26.*

An action for infringement of a patent, however small the amount of damage may be, cannot be tried in a county court.* *Cannot be tried in county court.*

The Act of 1883 provides that—

"The provisions of this Act conferring a special jurisdiction on the court as defined by this Act shall not, except so far as the jurisdiction extends, affect the jurisdiction of any court in Scotland or Ireland in any proceedings relating to patents, or to designs, or to trade marks; and with reference to any such proceedings in Scotland the term 'the court' shall mean any Lord Ordinary of the Court of Session, and the term 'court of appeal' shall mean either division of the said court; and with reference to any such proceedings in Ireland, the terms 'the *Actions in Scotland and Ireland. Sect. 111 (1).*

---

* Reg. v. Judge of C. Ct. of Halifax, 1891, C.A., 8 R.P.C. 338.

court' and 'the court of appeal' respectively mean the High Court of Justice in Ireland and Her Majesty's Court of Appeal in Ireland."

<small>No action till patent is sealed, relates back to acceptance. Act 1883, sect. 13.</small>

An action for infringement cannot be commenced until the patent is actually sealed; but it may relate back to all infringements committed after the date of publication of the complete specification.

Parties.

<small>Registered owner can sue.</small>

The registered owner of the patent is usually a plaintiff, even though he may only be in the position of a trustee; but it appears that a *cestui que trust* may sue in his own name.* This would enable an equitable assignee to sue; but,

<small>Registration not necessary, but advisable.</small>

except when his assignor is the defendant, the assignment ought to be by deed, and it is better to have the assignment registered before commencing the action.

If the plaintiff is a registered owner, he is under no necessity for proving any assignment to him, but can describe himself as a registered proprietor.

<small>A joint owner may sue alone.</small>

When there are joint owners of a patent, any one of them can sue for infringement without the rest: if the defendant wishes to avoid the possibility of having several actions against him in respect of the same infringement, he should at once apply to join the other owners as parties.†

<small>Formerly registration necessary before action.</small>

Formerly an assignee of a patent could not sue for infringement until the assignment had been

---

* Speckhart *v.* Campbell, C.A., 'Times,' March 13th, 1884.
† Sheehan *v.* G. E. Rail. Co., 1880, 16 Ch. D. 59.

registered;* but when the assignment was registered the registration had relation back, and gave a right to sue as from the date of the assignment.†

A mortgagor in possession of a patent can sue for infringement without joining the mortgagee; but if it appear to the judge desirable that the mortgagee should be a party he ought to join him.‡ *Mortgagor may sue alone.*

A licensee, even when his license is an exclusive one, cannot sue in his own name without joining the patentee.§ *Licensee cannot sue alone.*

The writ usually claims— *Form of writ.*

(1) An injunction to restrain the defendant, his servants and agents, from infringing the plaintiff's letters patent (usually adding the title, date, and number of the patent).

(2) Damages, or, at the option of the plaintiff, an account of profits.

(3) Delivery up to the plaintiff or destruction of all articles in the defendant's possession made in infringement of the said letters patent.

(4) Costs (adding, when a certificate of validity has been obtained in a previous trial) between solicitor and client.

An action for an injunction may be commenced before the defendant has actually infringed if he has threatened to do so,‖ but in this case only (1) and (4) will be required.

* Chollet v. Hoffman, 1857, 7 E. & B. 686.
† Hassall v. Wright and others, 1870, L.R., 10 Eq. 509.
‡ Van Gelder v. Sowerby Bridge Flour Co., 1890, C.A., 7 R.P.C. 41.
§ Heap v. Hartley, 1890, C.A., 42 Ch. D. 461, 6 R.P.C. 495.
‖ Frearson v. Loe, 1878, 9 Ch. D. 65.

But although an injunction may be granted to restrain infringement where there is an intention to infringe, but no actual infringement; no injunction will be granted where there is no intention to infringe, even though there may have been a past infringement.*

Who may be defendants.

Any party who is alleged to have infringed directly or indirectly may be made a defendant. Thus it has been held right to commence an action against carriers who have in their possession infringing articles, and on discovery to add the owners as defendants; † but custom-house agents for foreign importers are not liable to be thus attacked.‡

Directors of a company may be joined.

Directors of a company may be liable for infringements by the company, and if made defendants with the company are personally liable to pay the costs of the plaintiffs.§

When defendant is out of the jurisdiction.

If the defendant is an importer resident out of the jurisdiction the plaintiff must not delay the commencement of his action until the term of his patent has nearly expired, as he will then have no ground for claiming an injunction, and will be unable to obtain leave to serve the defendant out of the jurisdiction; or if he obtains leave to serve, the service will be liable to be set aside. In such a case his only remedy is to sue the persons who in this country have purchased infringing

---

* Proctor v. Bailey, 1889, C.A., 6 R.P.C. 538.
† The Washburn and Moen Manufacturing Co. v. Q., 1889, 6 R.P.C. 398.
‡ Nobels Explosive Co. v. Jones, 1882, 8 App. Cas. 1.
§ Betts v. De Vitre, 11 Jur., p. 9.

articles, since he has no right of action abroad against an infringer in this country only.

The manufacturer and purchaser of an infringing machine may be sued together,* but the manufacturer cannot claim to be added as a defendant in an action against the purchaser;† if, however, he has given the purchaser an indemnity he may be allowed to defend as a third party, and in such a case if unsuccessful he will be liable for the plaintiff's costs.‡

The Act of 1883 provides that—

"In an action for infringement of a patent, the Court or a judge may, on the application of either party, make such order for an injunction, inspection, or account, and impose such terms and give such directions respecting the same and the proceedings thereon as the Court or a judge may see fit." Orders during action. Sect. 30.

Interim Injunctions.

If the plaintiff intends to apply for an interim injunction, he should do so as soon as possible after the defendant has entered an appearance; he may with special leave in an urgent case do so before appearance. When to be applied for.

The application is made by motion or summons according to the division in which the action is commenced, and asks for an injunction to restrain the defendant, his servants and agents from making, using, exercising, or vending the invention for which the letters patent were granted. Application, how made.

---

* Proctor *v.* Bennis, 1887, 36 Ch. D. 740.
† Moser *v.* Marsden, 1892, C.A., 9 R.P.C. 214.
‡ Edison and Swan Electric Light Co. *v.* Holland, 1889, C.A., 6 R.P.C. 287.

<small>Evidence on application for interim injunction.</small>
Upon the hearing the plaintiff must be prepared with evidence of the infringement, or of the intention to infringe, of the validity of his patent, and also of his title.

<small>Defendant not appearing.</small>
If the defendant does not appear on a motion for an interim injunction, an injunction will be granted upon the plaintiff filing an affidavit stating that the patent is good and valid, and has not been anticipated.*

<small>Validity not disputed.</small>
If the defendant appears and does not dispute the validity of the patent, and there is good evidence of intention to infringe on his part, an injunction will be granted.†

<small>When injunction is resisted.</small>
<small>Plaintiff must have *primâ facie* evidence of validity.</small>
<small>Plaintiff must show account insufficient.</small>
If, however, the defendant appears and resists the injunction the plaintiff will not obtain an injunction unless he can show that for many years the validity of the patent has been unquestioned, and his monopoly has been complete and free from infringement, or that the validity of the patent has been upheld in a previous trial; and also that he will not be sufficiently protected if the defendants keep an account of all the profits they make by the alleged infringements.

<small>When infringement doubtful no injunction granted.</small>
<small>Account may be ordered to be kept.</small>
If there is any reasonable doubt as to whether what the defendant is doing amounts to infringement, or if the defendant seriously disputes the validity of the patent, no injunction will be granted, but as a rule the defendant will be ordered to keep an account of his profits, and the motion or summons will be ordered to stand

---

* Clarke v. Nichols, 1895, 12 R.P.C. 310.
† Howes v. Webber, 1894, 11 R.P.C. 586.

over until the trial of the action or further order.

If the defendant undertakes not to infringe until the trial of the action or further order, the motion will stand over with liberty to apply.* <small>*Defendant undertaking not to infringe.*</small>

Where there is good evidence of infringement, the strongest ground for an injunction is that the validity of the patent has been established in a previous trial; but where the defendants offered to pay a reasonable sum into court and to keep an account an interim injunction was refused, though the patent had been so upheld.† When an interim injunction is granted the plaintiff must give the defendant an undertaking in damages in case he should not succeed in the action. <small>*Previous action on validity is useful. Defendant giving security and keeping an account. Plaintiff must give undertaking in damages.*</small>

Statement of Claim.

The Act of 1883 provides that—

"In an action for infringement of a patent the plaintiff must deliver with his statement of claim, or by order of the Court or the judge, at any subsequent time, particulars of the breaches complained of." <small>Sect. 29 (1).</small>

The statement of claim is usually a formal document which states the title of the plaintiffs to the letters patent, alleges that the said letters patent are good and valid, and that the defendant has infringed in the manner shown in the particulars of breaches delivered with it. <small>*Form of statement of claim.*</small>

The particulars of breaches must be the best <small>*Particulars of breaches.*</small>

---

* Lyon *v.* Mayor, &c., Newcastle-upon-Tyne, 1894, 11 R.P.C. 218.

† The North British Rubber Co., Ltd., *v.* The Gormully and Jeffry Manufacturing Co., 1895, 12 R.P.C. 17.

that the plaintiff is able to give, but it is obvious that without full discovery the plaintiff cannot give very full particulars. He should give any instances of which he is aware, and may add a general statement as to other infringements. Where the patent has more than one claim the plaintiff should state which claims are alleged to have been infringed.*

Should state kind of infringement complained of.
The particulars should say in what way the defendant has infringed or threatened to infringe, i. e. by manufacture, sale, or user, and the plaintiff is bound by these particulars, so that if he has not alleged infringement by manufacture in the particulars, he cannot complain of manufacture at the trial.† In cases where the plaintiff is unable to give particulars as to what part of his patent has been infringed, he may apply for an order for liberty to inspect the defendant's alleged infringement before delivery of the statement of claim.‡

Inspection before statement of claim.

Complicated machine.
Where the alleged infringement is at all complicated, the particulars should specify what part of the article complained of is alleged to infringe.

Particulars must show what plaintiff complains of.
No general rule can be given as to how explicit the particulars need be, except that they must be such as to leave no reasonable doubt in the mind of the defendant as to what is the case he has to meet.

Particulars need not interpret claim.
It is not, however, necessary for the plaintiff, when alleging that a certain claim has been in-

* Haslam v. Hall, 1887, 4 R.P.C. 203.
† Hener v. Hardie, 1894, 11 R.P.C. 421.
‡ Drake v. Muntz's Metal Co., 1886, 3 R.P.C. 43.

fringed, to tell the defendant what he considers to be the meaning of that claim.*

Since part of the relief sought is an injunction to restrain infringements, evidence of infringements committed after the issue of the writ may be of service to the plaintiff; but such evidence can only be given if proper notice be given to the defendant that such infringements will be relied upon. *Infringement after writ.*

The particulars of breaches, however, usually state that the plaintiff will claim full compensation in respect of all infringements committed by the defendant up till the date of the judgment. *Compensation claimed for all infringements.*

The particulars of breaches form part of the pleadings in the action, and are usually settled and signed by counsel. *Particulars signed by counsel.*

If the defendant admits some infringements, but denies all others, the plaintiff can move for judgment on the pleadings; but the inquiry into damages must be confined to the admitted cases of infringement.† *Defendant admitting infringement.*

Defence.

Three courses are open to the defendant in an action for infringement, success in any one of which will entitle him to judgment in the action. He may show—

(1) That the plaintiff is not entitled to sue under the patent; *Forms of defence.*

---

* Wenham Co. v. Champion Co., 1891, 8 R.P.C. 22.
† United Telephone Co. v. Donohoe, 1886, 31 Ch. D. 399.

(2) That he has not infringed the patent; and
(3) That the patent is bad.

Licensee may not dispute validity,

The first course is open to him except when he is a licensee under the plaintiff, and continues to pay royalties to him; for as long as he is paying royalties he may not dispute his licensor's title;*

but may show that plaintiff has no title.

but, provided he does not continue to pay royalties, it is open to a licensee to show that his licensor's title has expired.†

No infringement is a complete defence.

It is of course a complete answer to the plaintiff's claim if the defendant can show that he has done nothing which infringes the patent.

Licensee need not admit interpretation of patentee.

The fact that a man has taken a license under the patent does not involve any assumption that the interpretation put on the specification by the patentee is to be accepted by him as the true one; thus Lord Chancellor Cairns said:

"A licensee is entitled to have it ascertained what is the ambit, what is the field which is covered by the specification as properly construed; and he is entitled to say, 'Inside of that field I have not come; so far as I have worked I have worked outside the limit which is covered by it as properly construed, and therefore I am not bound to make any of those payments which are stipulated in my license as payments to be made for working the patent.'"‡

Licensee may have ambiguous specification construed by Court.

Thus a licensee, although he may not dispute the validity of the patent, is entitled to have the specification construed by the Court; and if it is ambiguous, or requires explanation, he may give evidence of the state of public knowledge at the

---

* Crossley v. Dixon, 1863, 10 H.L.C. 304.
† Muirhead v. The Commercial Cable Co., 1895, 12 R.P.C. 39.
‡ Clark v. Adie (No. 2), 1877, 2 App. Cas. 426.

date of the patent to show that the patentee could not be taken to have intended to include what he is doing.*

There are several cases in which the defendant is not allowed to dispute the validity of the plaintiff's patent. <small>Defendant may not always dispute validity.</small>

If the question of validity has been determined in a previous action to which he was a party, or if in such an action he has submitted to an injunction, he may not again dispute the validity of the patent.† <small>Estoppel by record.</small>

If the defendant has formerly been an owner of the patent, and has assigned his share to the plaintiff or his predecessor in title, he cannot dispute the validity of the patent, for that would be to derogate from his own grant.‡ <small>By being an assignor.</small>

The assignment must, however, be by him in order to thus bind him; for if the assignment was only by the trustee in the bankruptcy of the defendant, he is at liberty to dispute the validity of the patent on the ground of want of novelty, or insufficiency of the specification,§ or presumably on any other ground. <small>Actual party only is estopped by assignment.</small>

His assignment only binds him, it does not bind his partner;‖ and a like rule applies where the defendant has been the defendant in a previous action.¶ <small>or by record.</small>

---

* Crosthwaite v. Steel, 1889, 6 R.P.C. 190.

† Moore v. Thomson, 1890, H.L., 7 R.P.C. 325.

‡ Chambers v. Crichley, 1864, 33 Beav. 374; Walton v. Lavater, 1860, 8 C.B.N.S. 162.

§ Smith v. Cropper, 1885, 10 App. Cas. 249.

‖ Heugh v. Chamberlain, 1877, 25 W.R. 742.

¶ Goucher v. Clayton, 1864, 5, 11 Jur. N.S. 107.

Licensee by deed is estopped from disputing validity, but may repudiate license.

If the defendant is a licensee by deed under the patent he cannot dispute its validity;* he can, however, at any time repudiate the license, and from the time of such repudiation the license terminates;† so that a licensee even by deed may give notice to the plaintiff that he repudiates the license, and then, unless he is under covenant not to dispute the validity of the patent, he may raise the question in his defence. It is not, however, sufficient for him simply to plead in his defence that the license has been abandoned,‡ since this is not notice that such is the case, and until the notice is given he may not dispute the validity of the patent.

Repudiation must precede defence.

Equitable licensee may be estopped.

The rule that a licensee may not dispute validity may in some cases apply also to persons not licensed by deed, but who are only equitable licensees; thus it has been held that the defendant in an infringement action cannot both claim to be an equitable licensee and also question the validity; he must choose one or the other alternative.§

Licensee only is estopped.

It is only the actual licensee who is unable to dispute the validity; the fact of a person having been a licensee does not prevent his partner raising the question.‖

Usual defence.

Subject to these limitations, the defendant

* Hills v. Laming, 1853, 9 Ex. R. 256.
† Redges v. Mulliner, 1893, 10 R.P.C. 21; Crossley v. Dixon, 1863, 10 H.L.C. 293.
‡ Cheetham v. Nuthall, 1893, 10 R.P.C. 321.
§ Post-card Automatic Supply Co. v. Samuel, 1889, 6 R.P.C. 560; and see Crossley v. Dixon, 1863, 10 H.L.C. 293.
‖ Goucher v. Clayton. 1864, 11 Jur. N.S. 107.

ACTIONS FOR INFRINGEMENT. 147

usually raises all these issues in his defence. He does not admit the plaintiff's title, he denies that he has infringed, and he alleges that the patent is invalid.

The Act of 1883 provides that—

> "The defendant must deliver with his statement of defence, or, by order of the Court or a judge, at any subsequent time, particulars of any objections on which he relies in support thereof.
>
> "If the defendant disputes the validity of the patent, the particulars delivered by him must state on what grounds he disputes it, and if one of those grounds is want of novelty, must state the time and place of the previous publication or user alleged by him."

Particulars of objections to validity must be given. Sect. 29, (2), (3).

The defence is usually a formal document, and all objections to the validity of the patent are left to be dealt with in the particulars, which are usually settled and signed by counsel. *Form of defence.*

The particulars of objections in an action for infringement are similar to those in a petition for revocation, and to those required in an action for threats where the validity of the patent is put in issue; and the subject is dealt with in a separate chapter. *Form of particulars of objection.*

In an action for infringement where there is more than one defendant, one of them may have no defence because he cannot deny infringement, and yet the plaintiff may not be entitled to judgment, since another defendant disputes the validity of his patent; and if this defence should succeed, it would enable the other defendant to escape judgment.* *When one defendant cannot dispute validity plaintiff cannot get judgment.*

---

* Cropper *v.* Smith, 1885, H.L., 2 R.P.C. 17.

Particulars may be amended. Act 1883, sect. 29 (5).

"Particulars delivered may be from time to time amended by leave of the Court or a judge."

Particulars of objections are important.

It is not necessary for the plaintiff to deliver very minute particulars of breaches; it is sufficient if he proves a single breach, but it is most important for the defendant to make his particulars of objections as perfect as possible; and if after the delivery of his defence he finds out any really strong objection to the patent which is not included in his particulars, he should apply

Conditions for amendment.

for leave to deliver further particulars. This will probably be given subject to the defendant paying any costs incurred between the delivery of the original and further particulars, if the plaintiff should discontinue within a given time after the delivery of the further particulars.* In the case of either plaintiff or defendant, care must be taken to give particulars of all that they

No evidence of matter not in particulars.

intend to put in evidence at the trial, for the Act of 1883 provides that—

Sect. 29 (4).

"At the hearing no evidence shall, except by leave of the Court or a judge, be admitted in proof of any alleged infringement or objection of which particulars are not so delivered."

Inspection.

Plaintiff can obtain inspection.

If the plaintiff is able to make out a *primâ facie* case of infringement he can in general obtain an order entitling him to inspect the defendant's works if such inspection would assist him in proving his case.

* Ehrlich v. Ihlee, 1887, 4 R.P.C. 115.

The defendant may answer his application for inspection by alleging that it would disclose trade secrets, and in such a case the Court will appoint an independent expert to make a secret report to it on the question. An expert appointed for this purpose may not be called as a witness by either side, or at least if called must only be asked such questions as are approved by the judge.*　*Defendant may allege trade secret.*

The defendant may also, if he can show good reason for it, obtain an order for the inspection of what the plaintiff is doing under his patent. When the utility of the invention is in issue, the defendant might wish to show that the plaintiff did not use his own invention because it would not work, and in such a case he would require to know exactly what the plaintiff was doing.　*Defendant may inspect plaintiff's works.*

In making an order for inspection the judge may in his discretion give directions as to the costs incurred in the inspection.　*Cost of inspection in discretion of judge.*

Interrogatories and Discovery.

Each party may apply for discovery, and leave to serve interrogatories in an action for infringement as in an ordinary action. The plaintiff may not interrogate the defendant as to what he is doing in a general way, but the plaintiff can interrogate the defendant as to whether he uses each successive step or part of the patented process or machine; and where the interrogatories are directed to the steps of a process, it is no answer for the　*No general interrogatory on infringement.*　*Interrogatories as to steps in process.*

* The Plating Co. *v.* Farquharson, 1879-83, Griff. 187.

defendant to say that some of them are immaterial and constitute a trade secret.*

<small>Names of customers cannot be asked.</small>

A defendant who denies infringement may be asked if he sold certain specified articles to specified persons, but he cannot, until after judgment, be made to disclose the names of customers in a general way.†

If he admits the sale of certain goods, but denies that they are infringements, the question of who purchased them may be irrelevant.

The defendant may interrogate the plaintiff as to whether he has succeeded in using his patented invention without any alteration or addition; but not as to what those alterations or additions are, since this is not necessarily relevant to the matter in dispute.‡

Consolidation of Actions.

Under the rules of the Supreme Court—

"Causes or matters pending in the same division of the High Court may be consolidated by an order of the Court or a judge in the manner formerly in use in the courts of Common Law."§

<small>Consolidation must be on application of defendants.</small>

In these courts actions could be consolidated only at the instance of the defendants; ‖ and, if the defendants applied for and obtained an order for consolidating the actions, the plaintiff had to

---

* Benno Jaffé *v.* John Richardson and Co., Limited, 1893, 10 R.P.C. 136.

† Lister *v.* Norton, 1885, 2 R.P.C. 68.

‡ Rylands *v.* Ashley's Patent Bottle Co., 1890, C.A., 7 R.P.C. 175.

§ R.S.C., O. 49, r. 8.

‖ Amos *v.* Chadwick, 1877, 4 Ch. D. 869; Lush's Practice, 3rd ed., p. 965.

choose which he would proceed with first, and proceedings in the others were stayed until the first had been disposed of.

If in the one tried, the plaintiff was successful, the other defendants were bound by the result; but if the plaintiff was unsuccessful, he could, unless he had consented to be bound by the result of the first, proceed with the others. *Defendants only bound by order.*

The orders made in various cases are so worded as only to bind the defendants; but there might be a great hardship inflicted on the other defendants if the one selected for attack did not appear and defend the action, and provision is usually made for such a case.* *Where first defendant fails to defend.*

When several actions have been consolidated, and the defendant in the representative case refuses to appeal against an adverse judgment, the Court may substitute one of the other defendants, who are bound by the decision, to prosecute an appeal.† *Appeals.*

Although true consolidation applies only when there are several defendants sued by one plaintiff, when several plaintiffs have brought actions against the same defendant the Court may, under its general jurisdiction, extend the time for taking the next step in the rest of the actions until a test action has been tried; and where the first action fails to be a real trial of the issue, a second may be substituted as a test action.‡ *Several actions against one defendant.*

* See Bovill v. Ainscough, 1867, Plimpton v. Spiller, 1876, Johnasson v. Palgrave, Lawson, Pat. Pract., 2nd edit., pp. 495 seqq.

† Briton, &c., Life Assurance v. Jones, 1889, 60 L.T. 637.

‡ Amos v. Chadwick, 1877, 4 Ch. D. 869; Bennett v. Lord Bury, 5 C.P.D. 339.

Defendant in test case not defending. Where an order has been made in one action that another should be treated as a test case, and at the trial the defendant does not appear, this does not affect the binding nature of the test case.*

* The Edison United Phonograph Company & The Edison Bell Phonograph Company, Limited, *v.* T. Lewis Young, 1894, 11 R.P.C. 489.

CHAPTER XV.

REVOCATION OF LETTERS PATENT.

It will be seen that the letters patent are granted subject to the condition—

"that if at any time during the said term it be made to appear to us, our heirs or successors, or our Privy Council, that this our grant is contrary to law, or prejudicial or inconvenient to our subjects in general, or that the said invention is not a new invention as to the public use and exercise thereof within our United Kingdom of Great Britain and Ireland, and Isle of Man, or that the said patentee is not the first and true inventor thereof within this realm as aforesaid, these our letters patent shall forthwith determine, and be void to all intents and purposes." See p. 9.

The Act of 1883 provides that—

"Revocation of a patent may be obtained on petition to the Court." Form of proceedings for revocation. Sect. 26 (1).

But this does not apply to a patent which has been assigned to the Secretary of State for War, and in relation to which he has certified that it is his opinion that in the interest of the public service the particulars of the invention and of the manner in which it is to be performed should be kept secret. Sect. 44 (9). See p. 224.

"Proceedings in Scotland for revocation of a patent shall be in the form of an action of reduction at the instance of the Lord Advocate, or at the instance of a party having interest with his In Scotland. Sect. 109.

concurrence, which concurrence may be given on just cause shown only.

"Service of all writs and summonses in that action shall be made according to the forms and practice existing at the commencement of this Act."

The Act of 1883 provided that—

<small>Grounds for revocation. Sect. 26 (3).</small> "Every ground on which a patent might, at the commencement of this Act, be repealed by *scire facias* shall be available by way of defence to an action of infringement, and shall also be a ground of revocation."

These grounds will be fully discussed in the chapter on Particulars of Objections, and need not be here further mentioned.

In one case it was suggested that a patent for a medicinal preparation which contained poison was bad (presumably as prejudicial or inconvenient to subjects in general), because it was taken out to defeat the provisions of the Pharmacy Acts; but this was declared not to be a ground upon which it could be revoked.*

<small>Who may present petitions for revocation. Sect. 26 (4).</small> "A petition for revocation of a patent may be presented by—
"(a) The Attorney-General in England or Ireland, or the Lord Advocate in Scotland:
"(b) Any person authorised by the Attorney-General in England or Ireland, or the Lord Advocate in Scotland:
"(c) Any person alleging that the patent was obtained in fraud of his rights, or of the rights of any person under or through whom he claims:
"(d) Any person alleging that he, or any person under or through whom he claims, was the true inventor of any invention included in the claim of the patentee:
"(e) Any person alleging that he, or any person under or through whom he claims an interest in any trade, busi-

---

* Vaisey's Patent, 1894, 11 R.P.C. 592.

ness, or manufacture, had publicly manufactured, used, or sold, within this realm, before the date of the patent, anything claimed by the patentee as his invention."

When a person petitions under (c), (d), or (e), he must state in his petition under which head or heads he is petitioning; and until he has proved that he has a *locus standi* under one of the heads mentioned in the petition, the Court will not entertain any evidence as to the invalidity of the patent.* Petitioner must prove his *locus standi*, or petition will not be heard.

Under (c) the person who presents the petition must show that the patent was obtained in fraud of his rights,—that is, that the patentee has been guilty of dishonest and culpable acts in obtaining it; the petition must be in the name of the person so defrauded, it cannot be presented by his attorney in his own name.† It is more advantageous to present a petition under the head (c) than any of the others, since—

"Where a patent has been revoked on the ground of fraud, the Comptroller may, on the application of the true inventor made in accordance with the provisions of this Act, grant to him a patent in lieu of and bearing the same date as the date of revocation of the patent so revoked, but the patent so granted shall cease on the expiration of the term for which the revoked patent was granted." Where there is fraud patent may be granted to person defrauded. Act 1883, sect. 26 (8).

Unless the person petitioning can bring himself under (c), (d), or (e), he must obtain the fiat of the Attorney-General authorising him to present the petition. When Attorney-General's fiat must be obtained.

The person who desires to obtain the Attorney- How to obtain fiat.

---

* Avery's Patent, 1887, C.A., 4 R.P.C. 322, 36 Ch.D. 307.
† Ibid.

General's fiat must send to the law officer's clerk at room 549, Royal Courts of Justice, the following documents:

(1) Memorial to the Attorney-General asking for his authority, and stating all the circumstances. (On judicature paper.)

(2) Statutory declaration verifying the statements in the memorial. (On judicature paper.)

(3) Two copies of the proposed petition, and of the particulars of objections proposed to be delivered.

(4) Certificate by a barrister that the petition is proper to be authorised by the Attorney-General. (On foolscap.)

(5) Certificate by a solicitor that the proposed petitioner is a proper person to be a petitioner, and that he is competent to answer the costs of all proceedings in connection with the petition if unsuccessful.

(6) Declaration by the applicant that the validity of the patent cannot be disputed in any legal proceedings then pending. (On foolscap.)

Fiat may be granted ex parte. Sometimes the Attorney-General grants or refuses his fiat *ex parte*, and sometimes he directs notice to be given to the patentee or persons interested that they may appear before him and oppose the granting of his fiat.

No costs for proceedings to obtain fiat. The Attorney-General has no power to award costs to any person on an application for his fiat,*

* Griff. 320.

unless by consent they be made costs in the cause; and where this has not been done, costs before the Attorney-General will not be allowed to a successful petitioner at the trial of the petition.*

A petition for revocation is a proceeding on behalf of the public, and it is so far not a proceeding *inter partes* that neither party is estopped from raising anew points which have been already decided in a previous action for infringement by the respondent against the petitioner.† Petition is not *inter partes*.

"The plaintiff must deliver with his petition particulars of the objections on which he means to rely, and no evidence shall, except by leave of the Court or a judge, be admitted in proof of any objection of which particulars are not so delivered.

"Particulars delivered may be from time to time amended by leave of the Court or a judge." Particulars of objection must be delivered. Petitioner bound by particulars. Act 1883, sect. 26 (5), (6).

The particulars of objections in a petition for revocation are similar to those in an action for infringement.

No certificate as to the reasonableness of the particulars is required in a petition for revocation in order to obtain the costs thereof.‡

The petitioner may obtain directions from the Court as to what persons are to be served with the petition; all parties beneficially interested in the patent should be made respondents to the petition.§

There is no power to serve a petition of revocation out of the jurisdiction; but if ample notice Respondent out of jurisdiction.

* Rendell's Patent, 1894, Lanc. Ct., 11 R.P.C. 277.
† Deeley's Patent, 1895, C.A., 12 R.P.C. 199.
‡ Gaulard & Gibbs Patent, 1888, 5 R.P.C. 526; C.A., 6 R.P.C. 215.
§ Avery's Patent, 1887, 4 R.P.C. 152, C.A. 322.

be given to the respondent the Court will make an order *nisi* for the petition to be set down for trial in the list of witness actions.*

First hearing of petition. — The petition is usually filed in the Chancery Division, and comes on to be heard on affidavit evidence in the usual way.

When revocation is unopposed. — When the respondent appears and consents to the revocation, an order for revocation will be made with costs without evidence being taken.†

When opposed usually tried as witness action. — As a general rule, when the respondent appears and opposes the revocation, he applies for the petition to be tried on *vivâ voce* evidence, and in that event it is set down in the witness list, and comes on for trial in its turn.‡

No security for costs by respondent. — If a foreign respondent applies to have a petition for revocation tried on *vivâ voce* evidence, he will not have to give security for costs.§

Conduct of petition before trial. — A petition for revocation almost exactly resembles an action in the manner in which it is conducted; interrogatories may be administered, and discovery and inspection ordered, as in an action for infringement.‖

Trial may be at assizes. — The petition may be sent for trial to the assizes, and when fraud is alleged the trial may *Jury.* — be ordered to be by jury.¶ See chapter on Trial, p. 177.

---

* Drummond's Patent, 1889, 43 Ch. D. 80, 6 R.P.C. 576, 59 L.J.Ch. 576. Cf. Görz & Högh's Patent [1895], W.N. 105.
† Sleight's Patent, 1893, 10 R.P.C. 447.
‡ Gaulard and Gibbs' Patent, 34 Ch. D. 386.
§ Miller's Patent, 1894, 11 R.P.C. 55.
‖ Haddan's Patent, Griff. 108, 1885, 54 L.J.Ch. 126.
¶ Edge v. Harrison, 1891, 8 R.P.C. 74.

At the trial—

"the defendant shall be entitled to begin, and give evidence in support of the patent, and if the plaintiff gives evidence impeaching the validity of the patent the defendant shall be entitled to reply." Respondent commences. Act 1883, sect. 26 (7).

If the petitioner succeed at the trial the Court will declare the patent invalid, and order its revocation. This is carried out by registration of the order at the Patent Office.

The costs of a petition of revocation usually follow the event. While the petition is pending, the patentee may apply to the Court for leave to apply to amend his specification by disclaimer, and the petition will be stayed pending the amendment being made; if after amendment the petitioner does not wish to proceed, he will be entitled to his costs up to and including those of the application for leave to apply to amend.* Costs. Amendment pending petition. Act 1883, sect. 19.

In case of an appeal the registration will be stayed pending the appeal. Even after the Court has made an order for revocation, it seems that the specification may still be amended;† and since a pending appeal is not a pending action, there seems no reason why the amendment in such a case should be restricted to disclaimer. Amendment after judgment. P. 108.

* Deeley's Patent, 1894, 11 R.P.C. 72.
† Deeley's Patent, 1895, C.A., 12 R.P.C. 199.

CHAPTER XVI.

THREATS.

To bring actions.

A PATENTEE not only has the right of bringing actions and recovering damages against those who infringe his patent, but he may by threats endeavour to prevent others from infringing. It is open to him to say, " I have a patent for this invention, and I give warning that I may bring an action against anyone whom I find infringing my patent."

Patentee may threaten to bring actions.

Purchaser of infringement is liable.

Now we have seen that the purchaser of an infringing article, if he uses that article, is liable for infringement of the patent; and in most cases the advantage he would obtain by purchasing an infringing article instead of one made by, or under license from, the patentee would be very small compared with the loss he would inevitably suffer were he made the defendant in an action for infringement. It is therefore very probable that if an intending purchaser were aware that an article is the subject of a patent, he would take care not to run the risk of infringing, and would consequently purchase the licensed rather than the infringing article. It seems, then, that threats against the purchasers of infringing articles are very likely to be of use to the patentee, and

Purchaser would probably prefer not to infringe.

if he has any reason to suspect that his patent is being infringed he should take every opportunity of warning the public of the possible consequences of infringement. *Warning to purchasers may stop infringement.*

Of course a patentee is not obliged to bring an action against every person he may find infringing his patent, even though he may have threatened in a general way to bring actions. The expense of even a successful patent action is usually considerable, and a patentee could hardly be expected to take proceedings against any infringer unless he could feel certain of getting whatever damages and costs might be awarded to him if successful. Even if he fully believed that his patent was a valid one, the patentee might consider that by means of threats he could keep the amount of any infringements within such narrow limits, that his loss of profits by them would not be so great as to justify him in incurring the cost of an action. *Patentee not obliged to sue for an infringement.* *Threats might avoid necessity for action.*

In any case the patentee would probably consider prevention better than cure, and deem an advertisement containing a threat at least not inferior to one of a more peaceful nature. *Prevention better than cure.*

As there is always great risk in a patent action, if a patentee could prevent infringement by means of threats it would, in almost all cases, be to his advantage to do so. *An action is always risky.*

If the threats are intended only to prevent possible infringements of a valid patent they can hardly be said to be capable of injuring anybody, since the most they can do is to prevent what would be wrongful competition with the patentee's monopoly. *Injury by threats to others.*

Threats may do serious injury.

It may happen, however, that there are infringements going on, and the effect of the patentee's threats may be very serious for those who have actually commenced competing with him; for threats, if effectively used, will entirely ruin the trade of such rivals.

but no damage if patent be good.

If the patent be valid the ruin of their trade will not be any injustice to the rivals of the patentee, since their competition is an illegal one; but if the patent be invalid, there is no reason why its possessor should be placed in a more favorable position than his rivals in trade.

Patent no guarantee of novelty.

Now we have seen that the grant of a patent is of itself no guarantee whatever of the novelty of the invention, and thus it might happen that the possessor of a patent would ruin his rivals in trade by threatening to bring actions which

Threats might prevent validity being contested.

could not be carried to a successful termination, because the patent itself was invalid; and yet as the patentee might prefer to threaten only, and not to run the risk of an action, the validity of the patent might never come in dispute unless some one took proceedings to get the patent revoked.

Patent might be ambiguous.

Again, the wording of the patent might be such that without judicial interpretation there might well be doubts as to whether what was being done in competition with the patentee was really an infringement at all, and this could not be well determined in proceedings for revocation of the patent.

In order to prevent a patentee continuing to threaten indefinitely without putting his patent into court, the Act of 1883 provided that—

"Where any person claiming to be the patentee of an invention, by circulars, advertisements, or otherwise threatens any other person with any legal proceedings or liability in respect of any alleged manufacture, use, sale, or purchase of the invention, any person or persons aggrieved thereby may bring an action against him, and may obtain an injunction against the continuance of such threats, and may recover such damage (if any) as may have been sustained thereby if the alleged manufacture, use, sale, or purchase to which the threats related was not in fact an infringement of any legal rights of the person making such threats. Provided that this section shall not apply if the person making such threats with due diligence commences and prosecutes an action for infringement of his patent."

Limitation of threats. Act 1883, sect. 32.

Person threatening must bring action.

The first question which arises on this section is what is meant by "threatening any other person." How far can it be taken to apply to a general threat to bring actions against infringers?

What constitutes a threat.

In 1887 it was laid down by the Court of Appeal that—

"Everybody has still a right to issue a general warning to pirates not to pirate, and to infringers not to infringe, and to warn the public that the patent to which the patentee is entitled, and under which he claims, is one which he intends to enforce; but it does not follow that because a threat is so worded as in mere language apparently and grammatically to apply only to the future, that therefore it may not be in any particular case in substance and in fact applicable to what has been done. It might be really directed against the sale and manufacture of some machines which the patentee considered infringements, and would none the less be a threat because it was worded in a general way as a warning to all persons not to infringe."*

General warnings may be threats.

In 1891, however, Mr. Justice Wright said:

"The section of the Act is limited to threats, and I do not think it subjects a patentee to an action for publishing a general

---

* Challender v. Royle, 1887, C.A., 4 R.P.C. 375, 36 Ch. D. 425.

statement that he claims to be the owner of a valid patent, which covers all articles of a particular description."*

This left the question still open to doubt, but in the succeeding year the Court of Appeal again affirmed the doctrine that a general warning may be a threat; and the threat may be directed against a proposed infringement, and render the patentee liable to an action.†

And in the year following the Court of Appeal made the following statements as to the effect of the section :

"The object of the section was to give an action for damages where there was not one before, and to enable an action to be brought against a man who uses threats unless he will or does follow up his threats by commencing an action himself.

Not even general threats are allowed unless the threatener is qualified under the Act.

"You are not to threaten even in a general kind of way, which might not be regarded as a threat to any particular person; you are not to do it even by a circular or advertisement, but if you do threaten, no action is to lie against you if you will prosecute the person who is aimed at by your threats.

"The Legislature desires that threats of patent actions shall not hang over a man's head, that the sword of Damocles, in such a case, should either not be suspended, or should fall at once; and it is with that view that the section seems to be framed.

"You shall not threaten legal proceedings unless the manufacture to which the threat applies infringes the legal right of the threatener, or unless the threatener is about to forthwith bring an action to show the validity of his threats. If he cannot bring himself within these two saving clauses at the end of the section, then the section absolutely forbids a man threatening legal proceedings with regard to a patent at all." ‡

---

* Ungar v. Sugg, 1891, 8 R.P.C. 385.
† Johnson v. Edge, 1892, C.A., 9 R.P.C. 142.
‡ Skinner v. Perry, 1893, C.A., 10 R.P.C. 1.

THREATS.   165

It thus appears that there are only two conditions under which a person can use even the most general kind of threat without being liable for any damage which his threats may cause. It will be well to examine these two conditions carefully, and to see exactly what each amounts to. *(Conditions under which threats may be issued.)*

The first is that he shall be able to show that the manufacture to which the threat applies infringes a legal right belonging to him. In order to do this he must have a legal title to the patent,* and must also be able to show that his patent is a valid one, for if not he has no legal rights; you cannot infringe a bad patent.† He must also prove that his threats were directed only against manufactures which came within the scope of his patent. *(Must prove infringement of legal right.)*

The other alternative is for him to commence an action for infringement, and to prosecute it with due diligence. The action must be brought by the person who threatens,‡ and must be a *bonâ fide* action for infringement, and not a collusive action;§ it need not be brought against the person who is the plaintiff in the action for threats, but it would require a great deal to prove that an action brought against the plaintiff in an action for threats was not *bonâ fide*.‖ *(or must commence an action. Action may be against any infringer. An advantage to sue plaintiff for threats.)*

The action need not be such as to test the *(Action need not test validity.)*

---

* Kensington Electric, &c., v. Lane Fox Electrical, 1891, 8 R.P.C. 277.

† Blakey v. Latham, 1889, C.A., 6 R.P.C. 190.

‡ Kensington Electric v. Lane Fox Electrical, 1891, 8 R.P.C. 277.

§ Challender v. Royle, 1887, C.A., 36 Ch. D. 425, 4 R.P.C. 363.

‖ Colley v. Hart, 1890, 7 R.P.C. 101.

validity of the patent; an action for royalties against a licensee who cannot dispute the validity of the patent is sufficient to bring the patentee within the proviso.*

Action for threats after an infringement action is vexatious.
If the action for infringement be commenced before the commencement of the action for threats, the latter action will be vexatious;† but

Both actions must be on same kind of infringement.
the bringing of an action for infringement does not form a defence to an action for threats when what is done by the plaintiff in the action for threats is not similar to that for which the action for infringement is brought.‡

The action, then, must be for an infringement of the same class as that which is threatened; and it must also be commenced and prosecuted with due diligence.

What is due diligence?
The question as to what constitutes due diligence in commencing an action for infringement depends entirely on the circumstances of the case, and no rule can be laid down.§

When a patentee has had an action for threats commenced against him he is justified in waiting a reasonable time to have a statement of claim delivered, and see whether he can combine the

Action may be by counter-claim.
action for infringement with the action for threats by a counter-claim.§ In an earlier case, however, when the threats had been continued for over a year, and then the patentee, on being sued to

---

* Day *v.* Foster, 1890, 7 R.P.C., p. 54.
† Barrett *v.* Day, 1890, 7 R.P.C., p. 54.
‡ Combined Weighing Machine Co. *v.* Automatic Weighing Machine Co., 1889, 6 R.C.P. 502.
§ Colley *v.* Hart, 1890, 7 R.P.C. 101.

restrain the threats, waited to counter-claim for infringement, and the counter-claim was unsuccessful, it was held that he had not brought an action with due diligence.* *An unsuccessful counter-claim may not be a good defence.*

In a more recent case, however, in which the threats had been continued over a long period, but no action had been taken, and the person aggrieved brought an action to restrain the threats, the defendants, on a motion for an interim injunction to restrain the threats, stated that they could not be sure as to whether the plaintiff did actually infringe, and got an order for inspection of the plaintiff's works. After this they commenced an action for infringement, and the application for an injunction to restrain the threats was refused.† *Patentee not certain of infringement.*

Provided that it is commenced and prosecuted with due diligence, the action for infringement need not be successful in order to protect the patentee from liability for the damage caused by his threats. He may, as long as he is duly prosecuting his action for infringement, continue to threaten, and it is not contempt of court to go so far as to say that "users of infringing articles are liable to damages and injunction in respect of such user."‡ If at any time during the prosecution of his action the patentee finds that it is hopeless to continue the action, he may discontinue it without losing his defence to any action for threats already issued. The action *Action need not be successful. Patentee may threaten while action pending. Action may be discontinued.*

---

* Herrburger *v.* Squire, 1888, 5 R.P.C. 581.
† Edlin *v.* Pneumatic Tyre, &c., 1893, 10 R.P.C. 311.
‡ Fenner *v.* Wilson, 1893, C.A., 10 R.P.C. 283.

need not be successful, and whether it be dismissed at the trial or discontinued when its further prosecution is hopeless makes no difference.* It is right to discontinue and not to go on with a hopeless action, and discontinuance is no evidence of *mala fides* in having commenced the action.†

Summary of law of threats.

As the law stands at present it seems as if the owner of even a hopelessly bad patent may safely use threats, provided he brings an action for infringement against some one within a reasonable time; and if before a reasonable time has expired anyone commences an action to restrain his threats, he may wait until the time comes for delivering a defence, and then raise the question of infringement by way of counter-claim.

Present state of law unsatisfactory.

This is somewhat unsatisfactory, and it is to be hoped that some one will carry a case of this nature to the highest tribunal, that it may be determined whether Colley v. Hart was rightly decided.

Action for Threats.

Particulars.

In an action for threats, the plaintiff is entitled to particulars of the patents under which the threats are issued;‡ and the defendant is entitled to particulars of the threats complained of before putting in a defence, but not to the names of

---

* Colley v. Hart, 1890, 7 R.P.C. 111.

† English and American v. Gare Machine, 1894, 11 R.P.C. 27.

‡ Union Electrical Power Co. v. Electrical Storage, 1888, C.A., 5 R.P.C. 329, 38 Ch. D. 325.

customers whom the plaintiff has, in consequence of the threats, promised to indemnify.*

Where the plaintiff alleges threats by the defendant's agents, particulars of the agents as well as of the threats must be given.†

Plaintiff for threats may allege invalidity;

The plaintiff in his statement of claim usually alleges that the patent is bad for the reasons given in the particulars of objections, and claims a declaration that the patent is invalid.‡

The particulars of objections are similar to those required in other patent actions, and should be delivered with the pleading which denies the validity.

but if not, invalidity may be raised by reply.

Where, however, the statement of claim does not allege invalidity, and the defence alleges validity, the invalidity may be set up in the reply, but in that case leave for a special rejoinder will be given.§

Claims in action for threats.

The plaintiff claims damages for past injuries, and an injunction to restrain threats. If he commences his action without great delay he will as a rule apply for an interim injunction; but where an action for infringement is being prosecuted with due diligence no interim injunction will be granted.‖

Interim injunction.

* Law v. Ashworth, 1890, 7 R.P.C. 86 (Lancaster Court Case).

† Dowson Taylor v. The Drosophore Co., Ltd., 1894, 11 R.P.C. 536 (Lancaster Court Case).

‡ Challender v. Royal, C.A., 1887, 4 R.P.C. 363; Union Electrical Power Co. v. Electrical Power Storage, 1888, C.A., 5 R.P.C. 329, 38 Ch. D. 325.

§ Dowson Taylor and Co., Ltd., v. The Drosophore Co., Ltd., 1895, C.A., 12 R.P.C. 95.

‖ Kurtz v. Spence, 1887, C.A., 4 R.P.C. 427.

Staying of threats action.

If an action for infringement is commenced by the defendant in a threats action against the plaintiff, the latter action will be stayed, and the costs made costs in the infringement action;* but this rule does not apply unless the infringement action involves all the patent upon which the threats are based.†

Damages for threats.

The damage must be really due to the threats, and not to general rumours in the trade, and the natural disinclination of people to run any risk of an action. The question of the amount of damages should be dealt with at the trial, and not referred.‡

Where a contract is stopped by reason of threats, the loss of profits is a proper measure of damages.§

Although the question of the validity of a patent can be tried in an action for threats, it is doubtful whether a valid certificate of validity can be given.‖

When the validity of the patent is in issue the defendant commences, and the procedure is similar to that in an action for infringement.

* Household v. Fairburn, 1884, 1 R.P.C. 109.
† Dowson Taylor v. The Drosophore Co., 1895, 12 R.P.C. 95 (Lancaster Court Case).
‡ Ungar v. Sugg, 1891, 8 R.P.C. 385; C.A., 9 R.P.C. 114.
§ Skinner and Co. v. Perry, 1894, 11 R.P.C. 406.
‖ Crampton v. Patents Investment, 1888, 5 R.P.C. 404.

CHAPTER XVII.

PARTICULARS OF OBJECTIONS.

WHENEVER the validity of a patent is challenged in any proceeding at law, whether in an action for infringement or for threats, or in a petition of revocation, the party who challenges validity must deliver to the party upon whom the task of defending the patent will fall particulars of his objections to the validity of the patent which is challenged.

Particulars of objections required whenever validity is challenged.

At the trial the challenger is confined to the particulars he has delivered, so that it is most important for them to embrace every objection that can be fairly taken to the patent; at the same time judges (especially Mr. Justice Kekewich) have frequently commented severely on the very loose way in which particulars were framed, and on the inclusion in them of objections for sustaining which no evidence was given, and which were really wholly inapplicable.

The particulars should, where necessary, specify the claims against which they are directed, and should in every case be made as precise as possible.

Claims must be specified.

In making out particulars of objections, quality

Feeble objections should be avoided.

is of far greater importance than quantity. A single good objection is sufficient to invalidate a patent; and, although it is of course better to find more than one point against which an attack may be directed, it should always be remembered that one strong objection is better than a dozen weak ones, and that if an objection cannot be sustained it is really a sign of weakness and is far better omitted.

It is not, as a rule, advisable to raise objections on trivial matters in the specification, as a number of trivial objections may incline the Court to favour the patent. In one case, where the only real issue was that of validity, which was decided in favour of the patent, Lord Esher, M.R., said in dismissing an appeal:

> "The defendants have used the exact thing that has been patented; they have used it to a considerable extent, but they say, 'Your patent is a bad one, you cannot sue upon it;' and they have taken, by way of objection, every one of the ordinary objections which are taken under such circumstances,—that is to say, they spell every paragraph and every line in the patent, and try to persuade the Court that some one line or some one sentence in it is so bad that it makes the whole of the patent bad, and prevents the inventor from having the benefit of his invention, however useful or however great it may be. I do not hesitate to say myself that when that is the sort of defence in such a case, the Court ought to look carefully to see whether any one of these objections can be sustained. The Court certainly, under those circumstances, ought not to favour the objection. Those who take such objections as that must prove them strictly. That is my view." *

---

* The Edison Bell Phonograph Co., Ltd., v. Smith, 1894, C.A., 11 R.P.C. 395.

PARTICULARS OF OBJECTIONS. 173

Some of the following objections will usually be found applicable when the validity of the patent is open to attack.

(a) "That the plaintiff (*or the person to whom the patent was granted where there has been an assignment*) was not the true and first inventor of the alleged invention in respect of which the said letters patent were granted." True and first inventor.
Cf. p. 34.

This objection is often used very loosely, but it is really applicable only when it is intended to show that the plaintiff obtained the invention from some other person. It is not a correct way of alleging want of novelty.*

(b) "That the alleged invention is not proper subject-matter for letters patent." Invention not proper subject-matter.

This is applicable only when the alleged invention is *primâ facie* not proper subject-matter; *e. g.* if it is for a principle, or for an illegal or immoral purpose, the ground on which subject-matter is impeached ought to be stated. Cf. p. 16.

(c) "That the alleged invention is not useful." Invention not useful.

This is frequently introduced, though but rarely is it of any avail to the defendant. If, however, it can be sustained, it is a good objection. Cf. p. 17.

(d) "The complete specification does not sufficiently describe and ascertain the nature of the alleged invention comprised therein, and in what manner the same is to be performed. In that, &c. (adding wherein the insufficiency lies)." Specification insufficient.
Cf. p. 65.

This particular must contain particulars of the parts of the invention which are alleged to be in-

---

* Thomson *v.* Macdonald & Co., 1891, 8 R.P.C. 9.

sufficiently described if the defendant is able to point them out.*

Specification ambiguous. Cf. p. 71.

(e) "The specification is ambiguous."

This particular should point out in what way the specification is ambiguous.†

Disconformity. Cf. p. 65.

(f) "That the alleged invention described in the complete specification is different from that described in the provisional specification and title (or one of them) in that . . . ."

This particular must state in what way the inventions described in the specifications differ from one another.‡

Enlargement by amendment. Cf. p. 107.

(g) "That the amendment of the complete specification enlarged the scope of the alleged invention."

Particulars of this objection should be given.

Concealment by patentee. Cf. p. 69.

(h) "That the complete specification did not describe the most beneficial method of carrying out his alleged invention with which the plaintiff was then acquainted."

This should only be used when the defendant is able to point out something which he can show was within the knowledge of the plaintiff at the date of filing the complete specification, which was omitted therefrom; the particular should mention what is complained of.

False suggestion. P. 71.

(i) "That the letters patent were granted on a false suggestion that . . . ."

Particulars of the false suggestion should be given, such as of any words in the complete

---

* Crompton v. Anglo-American Brush Corporation, 1887, C.A., 4 R.P.C. 197; 35 Ch. D. 283.

† Heathfield v. Greenway, 1894, 11 R.P.C. 17.

‡ Anglo-American Brush Corporation v. Crompton, 1887, C.A., 4 R.P.C. 27.

specification which might tend to mislead. This objection in its most general form, and the similar one " that the Crown was deceived," are often used in a very loose manner merely as general forms.

<small>Crown deceived.</small>

(j) "That the alleged invention was anticipated in the following prior publications."

<small>Invention anticipated by prior publication. Cf. p. 27. In specification;</small>

If the prior publications be specifications of English patents the publication need not be proved, but in any other case the time and place of publication must be given in the particulars.

<small>in other publications.</small>

"The parts relied on as anticipations should be specified, not necessarily pages and lines, though this is generally advisable, but where the anticipation is to be found, and what it is."*

<small>Particulars should be very definite.</small>

(k) "That the alleged invention was anticipated by prior public user."

<small>Anticipation by prior public user must be definite. Cf. p. 27.</small>

This particular must give the details of the prior user; it should specify the persons by whom, the places where, the dates at, and the manner in which the prior user took place.†

It is not sufficient to allege prior user over a space of several years many years ago.‡ If general user in a locality is alleged, the plaintiff may interrogate as to the names and addresses of those who so used the invention.§

No order for inspection of anticipating machines will be made unless by consent.‖

---

* Holliday v. Heppenstall, 1889, C.A., 6 R.P.C. 320.
† Penn v. Bibby, 1866, L.R., 1 Eq. 548.
‡ Smith v. Lang, 1890, C.A., 7 R.P.C. 148.
§ Alliance Pure White Lead Syndicate v. MacIvor's Patents, Ltd., 1891, 8 R.P.C. 321.
‖ Garrard v. Edge, 1889, C.A., 6 R.P.C. 372.

(*l*) "Considering the state of public knowledge at the date of the patent, the alleged invention was not proper subject-matter for the grant of letters patent."

<small>Considering public knowledge no subject-matter. Cf. p. 22.</small>

<small>Public knowledge is a matter for evidence.</small>

No particulars of the public knowledge need be given, though it is not unusual to state that the specifications and publications put forward as prior publications will be relied on to prove the state of public knowledge.

<small>A specification is no Proof of public knowledge,</small>

The specification of a prior patent is not evidence of much value as to prior public knowledge;* it must be proved by ordinary evidence, as by that of persons engaged in the trade, but well-known books may also be referred to.†

<small>but books are evidence.</small>

<small>Knowledge of one person not public knowledge.</small>

The knowledge of a particular man is not public knowledge, though it may be an anticipation,‡ since even a single person must not be restrained by a patent from doing that which he was able to do before the date of the grant.

<small>Single specification may not be referred to without notice.</small>

<small>No notice if several publications are referred to.</small>

As evidence of common knowledge a defendant may not without having given notice, in his particulars of objections, of his intention so to do, refer to a single specification, though where several publications are relied on no reference is necessary.§

<small>Hypothetical form of objections.</small>

Sometimes objections (b), (c), (j), (k), and (l) may be put in a hypothetical form, "If the complete specification be construed so as to include the alleged infringement, then," &c.

---

* Peckover *v.* Rowland, 1893, 10 R.P.C. 118.
† Holliday *v.* Heppenstall, 1889, C.A., 6 R.P.C. 320.
‡ Benno Jaffé Fabrik *v.* Richardson, 1894, 11 R.P.C. 102.
§ English and American Machinery Co., Ltd., *v.* Union Boot and Shoe Machine Co., Ltd., 1894, C.A., 11 R.P.C. 367.

CHAPTER XVIII.

TRIAL OF A PATENT ACTION.

IN the term patent action are included the three kinds of action which have been already considered, viz. actions for infringement, actions for threats, and petitions for revocation. What is a patent action?

Although in these three kinds of action the relations of the parties are entirely different, the procedure at trial is practically the same in all, and the three varieties can be conveniently considered together. One procedure in all patent actions.

Any action for infringement may be put down for trial at an assizes, and a petition for revocation may be ordered to be tried at an assizes when that mode of trial appears to the Court to be convenient. Patent action may be tried at assizes,

If set down for trial at an assizes, a patent action will be tried like any other action standing for trial at an assizes, and if in the Chancery Division it must not be sent back to the judge of the Chancery Division because there is no time to try it at the assizes; it must be treated as a remanet, or transferred to a neighbouring assizes.* and must not be sent back to be tried in London for want of time.

* Fairburn v. Household, 1885, C.A., 2 R.P.C. 195.

Issues in a Patent Action.

Revocation. The simplest kind of patent action is a petition for revocation in which only two points can arise, viz. what is the invention claimed in the complete specification? and is the patent for this invention a valid one?

Infringement. In an action for infringement also the same two points arise, and there is the further question, has the defendant infringed?

Threats. In an action for threats there are the further questions, has the defendant threatened? and if so, has he with due diligence commenced and prosecuted an action for infringement?

Construction of the Specification.

The first question for the Court at the trial of any patent action is, what is the invention for which the patent is granted? that is, what does the patentee claim in his complete specification?

Construction is matter of law. The construction of the specification is a matter of law for the Court, but it differs somewhat from that of any other document, since the **Evidence on meaning of specification.** Court will hear the evidence of experts as to what the specification means. Upon this subject Lord Chancellor Westbury in 1861 made the following statement:

"It is undoubtedly true as a proposition of law that the construction of a specification, as the construction of all other written instruments, belongs to the Court; but a specification of an invention contains most generally, if not always, some technical terms, some phrases of art, some processes, and requires generally the aid of the light derived from what are called surrounding circumstances. It is therefore an admitted rule of law that the explanation of the words or technical terms of art, the phrases used in commerce, and the proofs and results of the processes which are described (and in a chemical patent the ascertainment of chemical equivalents)—that all these are matters of fact upon which evidence may be given, contradictory testimony may be deduced, and upon which undoubtedly it is the province, and the right of a jury to decide." *

Notwithstanding that evidence may be required to enable the Court to construe the specification, the construction is so far a matter of law that it forms a precedent, which is binding in any later action brought on the same patent.† Construction forms a precedent.

In ascertaining what is the invention patented the claims must be looked at and construed as forming part of the specification, and must not be dealt with independently of what precedes them.

Upon this subject Lord Esher, M.R., said:

" As to the rule of construction of a patent, when the question is what is the true construction, I cannot doubt myself that the same rules of construction or the same canons of construction are to be applied to the construction of a patent or to any part of it as are used with regard to any other instrument. You must look at the whole of the specification, and then, having looked at the whole, if it is an objection to the claim, see what the claim on the true construction of it is, having regard to the whole of the instrument." ‡

A specification is sometimes capable of bearing more than one construction, and then it becomes Ambiguity.

---

* Hills v. Evans, 1862, 31 L. J.N.S.Ch. 460.

† Edison and Swan v. Holland, C.A., 6 R.P.C. 243.

‡ Edison Bell Phonograph Corporation, Ltd., v. Smith and Young, 1894, C.A., 11 R.P.C. 395.

a question for the Court which construction is to be preferred.

<small>See p. 9. Benevolent construction of specification.</small>

The grant provides that the letters patent shall be construed in the most beneficial sense for the advantage of the patentee, and it has been supposed that this means that the Court is to try and make out a meaning which will make the patent of the greatest benefit to the patentee.

On this subject, which is called the beneficial construction of a patent, Jessel, M.R., in 1882, used the following language:

<small>Rule for construction.</small>

"I have heard judges say, and I have read that other judges have said, that there should be a benevolent interpretation of specifications. What does this mean? I think, as I have explained elsewhere, it means this: when the judges are convinced that there is a genuine, great, and important invention, which, as in some cases, one might almost say, produces a revolution in a given art or manufacture, the judges are not to be astute to find defects in the specification, but on the contrary, if it is possible consistently with the ordinary rules of construction, to put such a construction on the patent as will support it. They are to prefer that construction to another which might possibly commend itself to their minds if the patent was of little worth and of very little importance. That has been carried out over and over again, not only by the Lord Chancellor on appeal, but by the House of Lords. There is, if I may say so, and I think there ought to be, a bias, as between <small>Limit of rule of benevolent construction.</small> two different constructions, in favour of the real improvement and genuine invention, to adopt that construction which supports an invention. Beyond that I think the rule ought not to go."[*]

In a recent case in the Court of Appeal, Lord Justice Kay went somewhat further than this when he laid down the rule that—

---

[*] Otto v. Linford, 1882, C.A., 46 L.T. 39.

"The Court will continue the specification so as to support the patent if it can fairly be done, and will not be astute to find flaws in small matters in a specification with a view to overthrow it. Where any expression is ambiguous the Court will endeavour to give effect to the intentions of the patentee."*

Validity.

When the meaning of the specification has been arrived at, the next question is whether the patent is a valid one. Now we have seen that if a patent be bad in one particular, it is altogether invalid; so that the question of validity resolves itself into the question, has any one of the objections specified in the particulars been sustained? A patent bad in one point is bad altogether.

These objections may involve the construction of the specification, or may be simple questions of fact, as of the sufficiency of the specification, or the utility or novelty of the invention; but since a jury is now rarely employed in the trial of a patent action, these distinctions are not of any great importance.

Probably the question of conformity of the specifications would be a matter of law, which would, when determined form a precedent binding in subsequent trials; but all the other objections seem to be matters of fact, which must be decided *de novo* at each trial.† Most objections are matters of fact.

---

* Edison Bell Phonograph Corporation, Limited, *v.* Smith, 1894, C.A., 11 R.P.C. 400.

† Edison and Swan *v.* Holland, 1889, C.A., 6 R.P.C. 243.

Infringement.

Infringement is a question of fact.

The question of whether the defendant has infringed is one entirely of fact, which would in a trial by jury be left to the jury.

Threats.

Whether a threat has been used.

The question as to whether what was done by the defendant in an action for threats amounted to a threat seems to be one partly of law and partly of fact, and is dealt with in the chapter on Threats.

Due Diligence.

Whether the defendant in an action for threats brought an action with due diligence depends entirely on the circumstances of the case.*

The Hearing of a Patent Action.

The Act of 1883 provides that—

Sect. 28 (1).

Assessor may be applied for by either party.

"In an action or proceeding for infringement or revocation of a patent the Court may, if it think fit, and shall on the request of either of the parties to the proceeding, call in the aid of an assessor specially qualified, and try and hear the case wholly or partially with his assistance. The action shall be tried without a jury unless the Court shall otherwise direct."

How assessor is paid.

Act 1883, sect. 83 (2).

"The remuneration (if any) to be paid to an assessor under this section shall be determined by the Court, and be paid in the same manner as the other expenses of the execution of this Act," that is out of money provided by Parliament.

* Colley v. Hart, 1890, 7 R.P.C. 101.

TRIAL OF A PATENT ACTION.

"In any action for infringement of a patent in Scotland the provisions of this Act, with respect to calling in the aid of an assessor, shall apply, and the action shall be tried without a jury, unless the Court shall otherwise direct; but otherwise nothing shall affect the jurisdiction and forms of process of the courts in Scotland in such an action, or in any action or proceeding respecting a patent hitherto competent to those courts. *Act 1883, sect. 107. Trial in Scotland.*

"For the purposes of this section 'court of appeal' shall mean any court to which such action is appealed."

It would certainly appear that this provision might more often be taken advantage of by suitors, and it would certainly very largely reduce the cost of a patent action; the assessor appointed by the court would not entail any expense for the parties, and if an action were tried in this way there seems no reason why the expense of expert witnesses should not be almost if not entirely avoided. It would be a great boon to a poor plaintiff, to whom the proverbial cost of a patent action must often be a cause of great injustice. *Assessor would reduce cost of action.*

Notwithstanding its apparent beneficence this right to demand an assessor has but seldom been exercised.

Whenever the validity of a patent is in issue the party defending the patent commences, and if any evidence of prior user of the invention be given he will be allowed to call evidence in reply. *Patentee commences.*

Since the person attacking a patent is tied down to his particulars of objections, the patentee really may almost be said to have to open his opponent's case, and to be compelled to prove that what is going to be brought against him is of no effect.

Title usually admitted,

The title of the plaintiff in an action for infringement is usually admitted by consent, as are the specifications and patents; and in one case the defendants, who refused to admit the plaintiff's title, had to pay the costs of proving it, although successful in the action.*

or defendants may have to pay costs of proving it.

Each party must of course carefully consider which points his evidence is to be directed towards, and upon this his choice of witnesses will depend. It is very usual for both sides to call scientific experts, who are really expert advocates of the cause they are called to support rather than witnesses, and it is generally supposed that such experts are not always strictly truthful: an ideal expert witness is a man who is unlikely to be entrapped by the wiles of the opposing counsel into admitting anything which will injure the side on which he is called.

Expert witnesses are usually called.

The scientific witnesses generally have to prepare themselves specially for giving evidence, and come prepared with accounts of experiments which they have made in the course of this preparation. A witness is not compelled to make a general disclosure of all his experiments, though of course, if asked about any particular experiment, he would have to answer as best he can.

Witnesses may make experiments for use as evidence.

When the subject of the patent is mechanical, each party usually produces models and drawings of what they consider that the specification describes, and also of the alleged infringement; models of any articles alleged to anticipate the patent are usually produced, but it is of course

Models and drawings.

Proof of anticipations by models.

* Vorwerk and Son v. Evans and Co., 1890, 7 R.P.C. 174.

advisable where practicable to have the actual articles produced in court, since this will avoid not only the expense of making models and drawings, but also the expense of proving their correctness, and the possibility of conflict of evidence as to what the articles really are. The expert witnesses should be well acquainted with all the models, drawings, and specifications which it is intended to use in evidence. Besides scientific experts it is often necessary or advisable to call trade witnesses to speak to the knowledge possessed by the trade at the date of the patent, and as to the utility of the invention. *[Experts should examine models, drawings, and publications.]* *[Trade witnesses to general knowledge.]*

When the sufficiency of the specification is in issue, workmen may be given the specification, and, without any further assistance, instructed to make what is described; and then they may be called and asked to produce the result of their work. Some small points of evidence have already been dealt with in the chapter on Particulars of Objections. *[Sufficiency proved by workmen.]*

As a general rule all the issues in a patent action are tried together; the question of infringement will be tried separately only if the validity of the patent is admitted,* but where several instances of prior user are alleged, all the evidence on one will sometimes be taken before going into another.† If it is admitted that an alleged prior user, if proved, would be fatal to the patent, the defendant may be allowed to call *[When issues are taken separately]*

---

* United Telephone Co. v. Mottishead, 1886, 3 R.P.C. 213.
† Richardson v. Castrey, 1887, 4 R.P.C. 265.

witnesses to prove such user before the rest of the case is gone into.*

Plaintiff for infringement must succeed on every point.

In order to be successful in an action for infringement the plaintiff must be successful on every point. From this it follows that the defendant needs to succeed on only a single point to be entitled to judgment.

Defendant in infringement must succeed on one point.

Now it might happen that a plaintiff who was entitled to succeed on every other point was unable to prove infringement; and the Court might say that since the defendant had succeeded on that ground, the other issues did not affect the result of the action, and need not be considered; this would, however, be very hard on a patentee, whose chief attention had been devoted to the issue of validity so as to get the validity of his patent established; since if the Court did not decide this issue, he would lose this advantage because he had failed in an entirely different direction. The same would apply equally to the decision of an appeal, and to avoid this hardship the Court of Appeal have decided that, even when an appeal could be dismissed on one point, the parties have a right to have every issue decided between them, and that where two points have been argued at full length in the Court below and decided, the Court of Appeal will hear and give a decision on both points in order to decide the litigation as far as possible.†

Court of Appeal will decide on every point if required.

---

* Badham v. Bird, 1888, 5 R.P.C. 238.
† Parkinson v. Simon, 1894, C.A., 11 R.P.C. 493.

Shorthand Note.

If the trial is likely to last more than one day, or if an appeal is at all probable, it is advisable to have a shorthand note of the evidence taken. The cost of this is very usually shared by the parties, but by agreement they may be made costs in the cause; unless this latter course be adopted they will not be allowed on taxation as between party and party.

CHAPTER XIX.

JUDGMENT IN INFRINGEMENT ACTION.

If the plaintiff succeeds in an action for infringement he is entitled to judgment for—

Injunction.
(1) "A perpetual injunction to restrain the defendant, his servants and agents, from infringing the letters patent during the remainder of the term."

This may extend to restraining the sale after the patent has expired of articles made during the term of the patent.* If the patent has expired, an injunction will be required only when the defendant has made a number of articles before the expiration of the patent for sale afterwards.

Damages or an account of profits.
(2) "Damages or an account of the profits made by the defendant through his infringements."

The plaintiff must choose one or the other alternative, he cannot have both,† and it is often very difficult to see which is likely to bring him the largest amount, since the damage suffered by the plaintiff is an entirely different matter from the profits made by the defendant.

Assessment of damages.
If the plaintiff chooses to have damages, they may be assessed by the Court, or possibly the

---

* Crossley v. Beverley, 1829, 1 R. & M. 166 n., 1 W.P.C. 106.

† De Vitre v. Betts, 1873, L.R., 6 H.L. 319; 21 W.R. 705; Siddell v. Vickers, 1892, 9 R.P.C. 162.

plaintiff may be entitled to apply at the trial to have them assessed by a jury ;* but as a rule the Court orders an inquiry to be taken of the amount of the damage suffered by the plaintiff, and the judgment will be for the amount so found.

When the plaintiff is a manufacturer, the usual measure of damages is the total profit the plaintiff would have made if he had supplied the infringing articles himself ;† but where an article is made partly by infringing and partly by other machinery the damages may be less than if the whole of the machinery was made in infringement to the plaintiff's patent rights.‡ When a complete article consists partly of a patented and partly of an unpatented part, and the parts are separate and obtainable separately, allowance should be made in respect of the unpatented part.§ *Measure of damages.*

Where the plaintiff would, but for the defendant's competition, have had a practical monopoly of manufacture of the patented article, loss to the plaintiffs caused by their having to lower their prices owing to competition by the defendant may be taken into account.‖ *Where patentee does not grant licenses.*

Lowering of prices may be considered.

As a general rule, a patentee can rightly claim

* American Braided Wire v. Thomson, 1888, C.A., 5 R.P.C. 696.

† Boyd v. The Tootal Broadhurst Lee Co., Ltd., 1894, 11 R.P.C. 175.

‡ United Horse Nail Co. v. Stewart and Co., 1887, 4 R.P.C. 130, 13 App. Cas. 401.

§ United Telephone v. Walker, 1887, 4 R.P.C. 63.

‖ The American Braided Wire Co. v. Thomson and Co., 1890, C.A., 7 R.P.C. 152.

Litigation may increase amount claimed, except when licenses are granted to all on fixed terms.

from an infringer who litigates more than he would be prepared to accept from a licensee,* but when a patentee both manufactures himself and licenses others on fixed terms, he can recover in damages only the amount which he would have received for royalties; and, if he has accepted this amount as royalty from the users of infringing machines, he cannot recover anything as damages from the manufacturers.†

Damages from purchaser and from manufacturer.

On the other hand, the fact that damages have been recovered against the manufacturer of infringing goods does not affect the amount of damages recoverable against a purchaser from him.‡

Account of profits in lieu of damages.

Instead of claiming damages the plaintiff may in a way adopt the acts of the defendant as those of his agent, and make the defendant account to him for all the profits which he has made by his infringements.

Costs of account.

In this case the Court will order an account to be taken, and as a general rule there will be judgment for the amount of profit so found together with the costs of taking the account; but if it seems probable that the amount found due on taking an account will be trifling the costs may be left to the discretion of the referee to whom the taking of the account is entrusted.§

Account of profits often advisable.

It is often to the patentee's advantage to adopt this course, since the profit direct and indirect

---

* Penn v. Bibby, 1866, L.R. 3 Eq. 308.
† Penn v. Jack, 1867, L.R. 5 Eq. 81.
‡ United Telephone v. Walker, 1887, 4 R.P.C. 63.
§ Shaw v. Jones, 1889, 6 R.P.C. 328.

made by the defendant may be much in excess of any damage which the plaintiff has suffered; indeed, the profits may be considerable when the damage is practically *nil*.

When the defendant both manufactures and sells the infringing articles, there is not, as a rule, much difficulty in ascertaining his profits.

When the infringement is by user of an infringing machine only, the proper course is to compare the profits arising when the infringing machine is used with those which would have resulted had the infringement not taken place.* Of course, where no other machine would do the work of the patented machine the plaintiff is entitled to the whole profit made by its use; but when the work could be done in other ways the plaintiff is entitled only to the increased profit arising from the use of his invention over what the defendants would have made if they had used what they could use in the absence of the plaintiff's invention.

When the infringing machine has been introduced into an existing manufacture the defendants must disclose their profits before and after its introduction.†

Whether damages or profits be chosen the defendant must make a full disclosure of all the articles made or sold, and of the prices obtained; he must also disclose the names and addresses of purchasers of infringing machines.‡

---

* Siddell *v.* Vickers, 1892, C.A., 9 R.P.C. 152.
† Siddell *v.* Vickers, 1889, 6 R.P.C. 464.
‡ Murray *v.* Clayton, 1872, L.R., 15 Eq. 115.

When an account of profits is taken, the amount found due is not due by way of damages, but rather as money had and received for the use of the plaintiff; and when an infringer is bankrupt a patentee may prove in the bankruptcy for profits which he is entitled to recover from the infringer.*

The Court may also order—

> (3) "The delivery up on oath by the defendant to the plaintiff, or the destruction of all infringing machines in the defendant's possession."

The value of infringing machines so ordered to be given up must not be considered in assessing the damages, or set off against the amount awarded for damages.†

When part only of a machine infringes, the infringing parts only need be delivered up.‡

Instead of being delivered up, the infringing articles are sometimes ordered to be marked so as to prevent their being sold by the defendant.§

---

* Watson v. Holliday, 1882, 20 Ch.D. 780.

† United Telephone v. Walker, 1887, 4 R.P.C. 63.

‡ Edison Bell Phonograph Corporation, Ltd., v. Smith and Young, 1894, C.A., 11 R.P.C. 389.

§ Westinghouse v. Lancashire Rail Co., 1884, 1 R.P.C. 253.

CHAPTER XX.

CERTIFICATE OF VALIDITY.

The Act of 1883 provides that—

"In an action for infringement of a patent, the Court or a judge may certify that the validity of the patent came in question; and if the Court or judge so certifies, then, in any subsequent action for infringement, the plaintiff in that action, on obtaining a final order or judgment in his favour, shall have his full costs, charges, and expenses, as between solicitor and client, unless the Court or judge trying the action certifies that he ought not to have the same." *Sect. 31. Effect of certificate of validity on costs.*

This shows that it is a very great advantage to a patentee to win an action on his patent, and get a certificate of validity, since he is then in a position of great advantage as against all other infringers. *Advantage of having a certificate.*

It will be noticed that the section applies only to an action for infringement, and it is doubtful whether a valid certificate can be given in an action for threats.* *No certificate in action for threats.*

As a general rule, where a certificate of validity has been given, a second one will not be given in a subsequent action;† but if the grounds on *Only one certificate of validity granted.*

---

* Crampton v. The Patents Investment Co., Limited, 1888, 5 R.P.C. 404.

† Edison and Swan Electric Light Co. v. Holland, 1889, C.A., 6 R.P.C. 287.

which validity was disputed in the second action were substantially different from those which had failed in the first action, a second certificate may be granted.*

Grant of certificate not appealable. The granting or withholding of a certificate of validity is in the discretion of the Court or judge, and from it there is no appeal.†

Validity need not be upheld. In order to obtain a certificate of validity it is not necessary that the validity should be upheld by the Court; it may be equally given when the *Validity need not be decided.* patent is declared invalid.‡ Nor is it necessary that the question of validity should be decided at all. A certificate can be given when after a contest the parties come to terms of settlement, and it may be a term of settlement that a certificate should be applied for.§

Certificate when defendant does not appear. A certificate has been granted even when the validity was not contested in court, when the issue had been raised in the defence, but the defendant failed to appear at the trial to support it.‖

What actions are affected by certificate of validity. The rule as to costs applies only to a subsequent action,—that is, to an action commenced after the certificate is given:¶ it applies even where in the subsequent action the validity is not put in question;** but when the defendant admitted in-

---

* Otto v. Steel, 1886, 3 R.P.C. 120.
† Haslam v. Hall, 1888, C.A., 5 R.P.C. 144.
‡ Ibid., 1888, 5 R.P.C. 27.
§ Delta Metal v. Maxim Nordenfelt Co., 1891, 8 R.P.C. 247.
‖ Haydock v. Bradbury, 1887, 4 R.P.C. 74; Edison Bell Phonograph v. Edison Phonograph, 1894, 11 R.P.C. 33.
¶ Automatic Weighing v. International Hygienic Soc., 1889, 6 R.P.C. 480.
** United Telephone v. Patterson, 1889, 6 R.P.C. 140.

fringement, and did not dispute validity, but had offered the plaintiff less than the amount of the judgment, which was for less than the amount claimed, the plaintiff was not allowed his full costs.* *When only issue is as to amount of damage.*

The rule as to costs applies unless the Court or the judge trying the action certifies that it ought not to apply ; so that whenever the plaintiff having a certificate of validity is successful, application should be made to the judge on behalf of the defendant for a certificate to deprive the plaintiff of solicitor and client costs. When he has obtained a certificate of validity, the plaintiff should in any subsequent action give the defendant notice of the fact, as it is likely to have considerable weight in inducing a submission ; it is as well also to mention it in the statement of claim, and to claim costs as between solicitor and client. *Rule as to costs applies unless it is ordered otherwise.*
Notice of certificate of validity should be given.

* Boyd v. The Tootal Broadhurst Lee Co., Limited, 1894, 11 R.P.C. 185 (Lanc. Ct. case).

CHAPTER XXI.

COSTS.

Costs of action follow event.

IN an action for infringement or threats, and in a petition for revocation, the successful party is, unless deprived thereof by the judge, entitled to the general costs of the action or petition.

Costs of issues may be set off.

Where, however, there are several issues to be decided, the costs of each separate issue may, if separable from the general costs of the action, be made to follow the event of the issue, and be set off against the costs awarded to the other party.

When costs of issue of infringement may be set off.

Thus a plaintiff unsuccessful in the action, but proving infringement, will be allowed the costs of that issue;* but this is only true when that issue can be distinguished from the rest of the case.†

The Court of Appeal has laid down that—

"There can be no infringement of a bad patent. If a man brings an action upon a patent which is bad, but is put to heaps of costs with reference to some part of the case, and certain issues which are unnecessary, by the defendant, we may apportion the costs and give the plaintiff the costs of those issues without infringement, because those costs have been improperly and unnecessarily incurred." ‡

---

* Badische Anilin Fabrik v. Levinstein, 1885, C.A., 2 R.P.C. 143; 29 Ch. D. 420.

† Guilbert-Martin v. Kerr, 1887. 4 R.P.C. 18.

‡ Blakey & Co. v. Latham & Co., 1889, C.A., 6 R.P.C. 190.

In this case the plaintiff was refused the costs of the issue of infringement.

Where the defendants were successful on in-fringement, but had pleaded that if they had infringed, the patent was bad, and the question of validity was not fought out, the plaintiffs were given the costs of all issues but that of infringement.* *When costs of other issues set off.*

"On taxation of costs regard shall be had to the particulars delivered by the plaintiff and by the defendant; and they respectively shall not be allowed any costs in respect of any particular delivered by them, unless the same is certified by the Court or a judge to have been proven, or to have been reasonable and proper, without regard to the general costs of the case." *Costs of particulars. Act 1883, sect 29 (6).*

In consequence of this it is necessary that both the plaintiff and defendant should ask the judge at the trial to certify that their particulars are reasonable and proper, or if proved, that they have been proved; but where the defendant is not called on to prove any particulars of objections, the judge will probably refuse a certificate as to their being reasonable and proper.† *Certificate as to particulars should always be applied for.*

On account of this the plaintiff may sometimes be able to deprive the defendant of the costs of his particulars of objections by submitting at the trial to having the action dismissed without his being heard. *Costs of particulars of objections when action is dismissed without being heard.*

It was in one such case suggested that the question of costs, and of the certificate as to the particulars of objections, should be reserved until

---

* Tweedale v. Ashworth, 1892, H.L., 9 R.P.C. 121.
† Newsum v. Mann, 1890, 7 R.P.C. 310.

the matter had been before the Taxing Master;* but it was afterwards decided that as no certificate had been given by the judge at the trial, no costs of the particulars of objections could be allowed.†

Cost of particulars cannot be given afterwards.

It appears, therefore, that if a defendant who is successful at the trial of the action does not obtain his certificate at once, the omission cannot be afterwards made good.

Certificate as to some particulars only may be given.

The judge sometimes gives a certificate as to some only of the particulars of objections; and judges have frequently complained of the insertion of particulars which are really not applicable to the case, but are put in as general forms.

Where action discontinued.

In a case in the County Palatine Court of Lancaster it was said that where the plaintiff discontinued the action after the delivery of particulars of objections the Taxing Master should decide which particulars were reasonable,‡ but it has been now decided by the High Court that the operation of the rule as to costs of particulars is not confined to cases in which an action is brought to trial,§ so that when the plaintiff discontinues after delivery of the defence the defendant has to bear the cost of the particulars of objections.

Court of Appeal can give certificate.

If the defendant fails at the trial, he does not require any certificate as to his particulars, since

---

* Mandleberg v. Morley, 1894, 11 R.P.C. 1.
† Mandleberg v. Morley, 1895, 12 R.P.C. 35.
‡ Rothwell v. King, 1887, 4 R.P.C. 397 (Lanc. Ct. case).
§ Middleton v. Bradley, 1895, W.N. 123 (7).

he must have failed on every issue; but if he appeals against the judgment, and the Court of Appeal reverse the decision of the Court below, they can give a certificate that the particulars of objections are reasonable and proper.*

Scale of Costs.

The costs usually given in a patent action are the ordinary party and party costs, although the actual costs are probably, as a rule, far heavier than those of an ordinary action. It is an almost universal rule, and in many cases it is almost necessary, to have a shorthand note of the evidence taken, but the costs thereof will not be allowed to the successful party unless they have by agreement been made costs in the cause. In case of an appeal the Court of Appeal will allow the costs of a shorthand note and transcription of the judgment, but not of the evidence. Although the preparation of any patent action for trial probably involves more work and more expense than that of an ordinary action, it is very rarely that costs are given on the higher scale; the rule is that only ordinary costs shall be given, except in a case of unusual difficulty and skill—antiquarian research and things of that kind,† not usually experienced in a patent action. <small>Costs of shorthand notes not allowed. Note of judgment allowed on appeal. Costs on higher scale very rare.</small>

It is very seldom that the costs of three counsel <small>Cost of counsel not allowed.</small>

* Cole *v.* Saqui, 1889, C.A., 6 R.P.C. 41 ; 40 Ch. D. 132.
† Gadd *v.* Mayor, &c., of Manchester, 1892, C.A., 9 R.P.C. 535.

will be allowed; a third counsel, even in a long and intricate case, is usually treated as a luxury, for which the party retaining him must pay in any event.

<small>Scale of costs is wholly inadequate,</small>

It seems rather hard that the ordinary scale of costs, inadequate in any kind of action, should be so rigidly adhered to in a class of action in which the expense incurred is necessarily very heavy; it is impossible to get efficient witnesses for the meagre fees allowed on taxation, and the preparation of a case for trial often necessitates long and expensive consultations, for which no allowance at all is made. The result is that both parties often feel that it will be less onerous for them to put up with injustice than to enforce what they believe to be their just rights; the patentee allows infringement to pass unchecked, or accepts a lower royalty than he feels that he is entitled to, and the manufacturer pays royalties under what he believes to be an invalid patent, because each fears the unknown volume of extra costs which he will have to pay even if he is completely successful in asserting his rights.

<small>and often cause of injustice.</small>

CHAPTER XXII.

EXTENSION OF TERM OF LETTERS PATENT.

It has been seen that by the Statute of Limitations the time for which letters patent for an invention could be granted was absolutely limited to fourteen years; and this is so far still the limit that every patent is now granted for that term. It was found, however, that in some cases the term of fourteen years was not long enough to enable an inventor to get his invention introduced and to obtain a proper reward for his labour, and so in special cases Parliament extended the limit of time beyond the fourteen years. To attain this object a special Act of Parliament was formerly required, but it was thought better to simplify the process, and to allow the Crown to extend the term of a patent upon a report of the Judicial Committee of the Privy Council that the patentee has been inadequately remunerated by his patent. *The fourteen years limit is sometimes found too short. Extension was by special Act. Extension now by Privy Council when remuneration is inadequate.*

This is the only ground upon which a patent may be extended; and in order to obtain an extension the patentee will have to show that his invention was one of unusual merit, and that, through no fault of his, he has failed to secure proper remuneration, but not necessarily that if *Grounds for extension of term.*

the term be extended he will probably be able to do so.*

Extension as to part of patent.

A petition may be presented and an extension of the patent may be granted for part only of the invention originally protected.†

Procedure for obtaining Extension.

Patentee may petition for extension. Act 1883, sect. 25 (1).

"A patentee may, after advertising in manner directed by any rules made under this section his intention to do so, present a petition to Her Majesty in Council, praying that his patent may be extended for a further term; but such petition must be presented at least six months before the time limited for the expiration of the patent."

The limit of time applies only to patents granted under the Acts now in force, and a petition for the extension of a patent granted prior to the Act of 1883 may be presented at any time before its expiration.‡

A patentee here means a person for the time being entitled to the benefit of the patent; and it is only such a person who may present a petition for extension. If the petitioner be an assignee he must prove his title strictly;§ but there is no objection to an extension being granted to an assignee, whether a private person or a public company.‖

---

* Jones' Patent, 1840, 1 W.P.C. 579.

† Bodmer's Patent, 1853, 8 Moo. P.C.C. 282; Lee's Patent, 1856, 10 Moo. P.C.C. 226; Napier's Patent, 1881, L.R., 6 App. Cas. 174.

‡ Brandon's Patent, 1884, 1 R.P.C. 154.

§ Galloway's Patent, 1843, 1 W.P.C. 725.

‖ Houghton's Patent, 1871, L.R., 3 P.C. 461.

Where a patent is mortgaged the patentee will be required to extend the mortgage so as to cover the extended patent.*

There does not appear to have been any case in which one of several joint patentees has presented a petition for extension without joining his co-patentees, but there seems no reason, provided he can show what profits they have made, why such a petition would not be properly presented, and an extension granted to such joint patentee with due provision for preserving the rights of his co-patentees.

<small>A joint patentee can probably petition alone.</small>

When a patent has been once extended, no further extension can be granted.†

In a petition for extension the petitioner must not withhold anything which is material; the committee require that *uberrima fides* shall be shown by him, since the grant of an extension is entirely a matter of grace; and if the committee find that any material fact has been suppressed, they will dismiss the petition.‡

The Act of 1883 provides that—

<small>Act 1883, sect. 25 (6).</small>

"It shall be lawful for Her Majesty in Council to make, from time to time, rules of procedure and practice for regulating proceedings on such petitions, and subject thereto such proceedings shall be regulated according to the existing procedure and practice in patent matters of the Judicial Committee."

<small>Rules for procedure on petitions.</small>

No rules have as yet been made under this section, and consequently the rules made under

---

* Church's Patents, 1886, 3 R.P.C. 95.
† Goucher's Patent, 1865, 2 Moo. P.C.C. N.S. 532.
‡ Horsey's Patent, 1884, 1 R.P.C. 225; Clark's Patent, 1870, L.R., 3 P.C. 421.

the repealed Act of 1835 are those by which proceedings on petitions for extension are now regulated. They are as follows:

[Rules to be observed in proceedings for the extension of the term of letters patent before the Judicial Committee of the Privy Council under the Act of 5 & 6 Will. IV, c. 83 (repealed), intituled "An Act to amend the Law touching Letters Patent for Inventions."]

Notice by advertisement of intention to present petition.

"1. A party intending to apply by petition under section 2 of the said Act shall give public notice by advertising in the 'London Gazette' three times and in three London papers, and three times in some country papers published in the town where or near to which he carries on any manufacture of anything made according to his specification, or near to or in which he resides in case he carries on no such manufacture, or published in the county where he carries on such manufacture or where he lives, in case there shall not be any paper published in such town, that he intends to petition His Majesty under the said section, and shall in such advertisements state the object of such petition, and give notice of the day on which he intends to apply for a time to be fixed for hearing the matter of his petition (which day shall not be less than four weeks from the date of the publication of the last of the advertisements to be inserted in the 'London Gazette'), and that on or before such day notice must be given of any opposition intended to be made to the petition; and any person intending to oppose the said application shall lodge notice to that effect at the Council Office on or before such day so named in the said advertisement, and having lodged such notice shall be entitled to have from the petitioner four weeks' notice of the time appointed for the hearing."

Rule 1 applies only to petitions for confirmation of a patent which are now practically obsolete, but the advertisements directed are the same as those directed in section 4 of the Act which relates to petitions for extension.

"2. A party intending to apply by petition under section 4

EXTENSION OF TERM OF LETTERS PATENT. 205

of the said Act shall, in the advertisements directed to be published by the said section, give notice of the day on which he intends to apply for a time to be fixed for hearing the matter of his petition (which day shall not be less than four weeks from the date of the publication of the last of the advertisements to be inserted in the 'London Gazette'); and that on or before such day caveats must be entered, and any person intending to enter a caveat shall enter the same at the Council Office on or before such day so named in the said advertisements, and having entered such caveat shall be entitled to have from the petitioner four weeks' notice of the time appointed for the hearing.

"3. Petitions under Sections 2 and 4 of the said Act must be presented within one week from the insertion of the last of the advertisements required to be published in the 'London Gazette.' *Time for petition.*

"4. All petitions must be accompanied with affidavits of advertisements having been inserted according to the provisions Section 4 of the said Act, and the first and second of these rules and the matters in such affidavits may be disputed by the parties opposing upon the hearing of the petitions. *Affidavits as to advertisements.*

"5. All persons entering caveats under Section 4 of the said Act, shall respectively be entitled to be served with copies of petitions presented under the said section, and no application to fix a time for hearing shall be made without affidavit of such service. *Persons entitled to be served.*

"6. All parties served with petitions shall lodge at the Council Office within a fortnight after such service notice of the grounds of their objections to the granting of the prayers of such petitions. *Notice of grounds of objections.*

"7. Parties may have copies of all papers lodged in respect of any application under the said Act, at their own expense. *Copies of documents.*

"8. The Registrar of the Privy Council or other officer to whom it may be referred to tax the costs incurred in the matter of any petition presented under the said Act shall allow or disallow, in his discretion, all payments made to persons of science or skill examined as witnesses to matters of opinion chiefly. *Taxation of costs.*

"9. A party applying for an extension of a patent, under section 4 of the said Act, must lodge at the Council Office six printed *Papers required by Privy Council.*

copies of the specification, and also four copies of the balance-sheet of expenditure and receipts relating to the patent in question, which accounts are to be proved on oath before the Lords of the Committee at the hearing. In the event of the applicant's specification not having been printed, and if the expense of making six copies of any drawing therein contained or referred to would be considerable, the lodging of two copies only of such specification and drawing will be deemed sufficient.

Time for leaving papers.

"All copies mentioned in this rule must be lodged not less than one week before the day fixed for hearing the application.

Crown may oppose petition.

"The Judicial Committee will hear the Attorney-General or other Counsel on behalf of the Crown against granting any application made under either the second or fourth section of the said Act in case it shall be thought fit to oppose the same on such behalf."

It will be seen that the advertisement must give notice that any person may lodge a caveat against the petition within a certain time, and the Act provides that—

Caveats. Act 1883, sect. 25 (2).

"Any person may enter a caveat addressed to the Registrar of the Council at the Council Office, against the extension."

A caveat must be lodged in the name of the actual objector, not in that of a patent agent for him.*

Who will be heard on petition. Act 1883, sect. 25 (3).

"If Her Majesty shall be pleased to refer any such petition to the Judicial Committee of the Privy Council, the said committee shall proceed to consider the same, and the petitioner and any person who has entered a caveat shall be entitled to be heard by himself or by counsel on the petition."

As a rule not more than two counsel will be heard on behalf of any party entitled to be heard.

Grounds for decision. Sect. 25 (4).

"The Judicial Committee shall, in considering their decision, have regard to the nature and merits of the invention in

---

* Lowe's Patent, 1852, 8 Moo. P.C.C. 1.

relation to the public, to the profits made by the patentee as such, and to all the circumstances of the case."

The first thing which the Judicial Committee look at is the profit made by the patentee, and it is most essential that the accounts filed should be as perfect as possible. *Accounts must be perfect.*

The accounts should on the one side show all receipts in connection with the patent, and on the other all the expenditure, and in the latter may be included the cost of legal proceedings, the cost of the patent and of experiments, and the expense of bringing the invention into use.*

The accounts of the original patentee must of course be filed, and if he has sold his patent to a company for cash and shares, the accounts must show the profits made by the company.† The accounts must of course show all royalties received from licensees under the patent, and if there be a free licensee, the profits made by him compared with those made by royalty-paying licensees should be shown in the account,‡ and manufacturer's profit cannot be distinguished from patentee's profit.§ The ground for granting an extension being want of proper remuneration for the invention, the patentee must show what remuneration he has received for the invention independently of the English patent. For this purpose, if there be any foreign patents, accounts *Profits of company working patent.*
Profits of free licensee.
Profits of foreign patents must be stated.

---

* Galloway's Patent, 1843, 1 W.P.C. 725.
† Deacon's Patents, 1887, 4 R.P.C. 119.
‡ Thomas's Patents, 1892, 9 R.P.C. 367.
§ Muntz's Patents, 1846, 2 W.P.C. 121; Duncan and Wilson's Patents, 1884, 1 R.P.C. 257; Saxby's Patent, 1870, L.R., 3 P.C. 292.

of the profits in respect of them should be submitted to the Judicial Committee.*

If proper accounts are not filed in time, an adjournment will not be granted;† and if the accounts are not clear, evidence to explain them will not be allowed, but the petition will be dismissed with costs.‡

When there is any profit, the utmost accuracy is necessary; but when the accounts show a heavy loss, extreme accuracy is not required.§

Remuneration for patentee's time.

In estimating the patentee's profits the Judicial Committee will, where he has been personally engaged in developing his invention, and in superintending the manufacture of goods under it, make an allowance out of the net amount received by him for remuneration for the time so expended by him.∥ Thus, even when the patentee has received considerably more than a fair return for capital expended by him, he may be able to show that most of the balance would be absorbed in paying him at a fair rate for work done after the patent was granted.¶

In order to have a *primâ facie* case for extension the remuneration must appear to be decidedly inadequate; and where large profits are

---

* Newton's Patents, 1884, 9 App. Cas. 592, 1 R.P.C. 177; Johnson's Patent, 1871, L.R., 4 P.C. 75.

† Yates and Kellett's Patent, 1887, 4 R.P.C. 150.

‡ Lake's Patent, 1891, 8 R.P.C. 227.

§ Darby's Patent, 1891, 8 R.P.C. 380.

∥ Joy's Patent, 1893, 10 R.P.C. 89; Carr's Patent, 1873, L.R., 4 P.C. 539; Perkin's Patent, 1845, 2 W.P.C. 17.

¶ Livet's Patent, 1892, 9 R.P.C. 332; Hazeland's Patent, 1894, 11 R.P.C. 467.

shown the Judicial Committee will not go into the question of merit.*

When the accounts show that the patentee has not made very large profits the Judicial Committee will proceed to examine into the merits of the invention and into the other circumstances of the case. For this purpose the Judicial Committee assume that the patent is a valid one,† even though it may have been declared invalid in a court of first instance, against the judgment of which an appeal is pending.‡ Although the general question of validity will not be considered, evidence of anticipation by patents and by actual user is admissible.§ *When merits are considered. Validity assumed.*

In order to obtain prolongation the petitioner must show that there is exceptional merit in the invention,∥ and when a reasonable profit has resulted the committee will consider whether the benefit to the patentee is commensurate with that to the public.¶ *Exceptional merit must be shown.*

If the patentee has not made any profit from the patent, the only questions for the Judicial Committee to consider are those of the merit of the invention and the conduct of the patentee.

The patentee will also have to show that there is some considerable usefulness to the public** in *Utility must be shown.*

---

* Houghton's Patent, 1871, L.R., 3 P.C. 461.
† Heath's Patent, 1853, 2 W.P C. 247; Hill's Patent, 1863, 1 Moo. P.C.C., N.S. 258.
‡ Lane Fox's Patent, 1892, 9 R.P.C. 411.
§ Duncan Stewart's Patent, 1885, 3 R.P.C. 7.
∥ Beanland's Patent, 1887, 4 R.P.C. 489.
¶ Derosne's Patent, 1844, 2 W.P.C. 1.
** Woodcroft's Patent, 1846, 2 W.P.C. 31.

the invention, and on the question of utility the fact that the invention has not been brought into extensive public use might lead the Judicial Committee to infer that it was not useful ;* to remove this inference the patentee should be prepared to show that the invention is not from its nature easily brought into public use.†

<small>Invention not brought into use.</small>
As a rule, if the invention has not been brought into public use at all, this fact will go very strongly against any extension being granted, since the inference is that if not used for fourteen years the invention cannot be of any value.‡

<small>Extension of patent not brought into use.</small>
If, however, the patentee can show that the invention is of such limited applicability that it has hardly had a fair chance of being used, and that there is every prospect that if the term be extended it will get into use, the Judicial Committee may grant the extension.§

The consideration of utility by the Judicial Committee is not at all connected with validity; the following quotation will make this clear:

<small>Utility considered in relation to merit.</small>
"Their Lordships do not propose in this case to go into any question with reference to the novelty or utility of this invention. In point of fact, it is not the practice of this tribunal to decide upon the novelty or utility of a patent; and although

---

* Simister's Patent, 1842, 1 W.P.C. 723; Napier's Patent, 1861, 13 Moo. P.C.C. 543.

† Semet and Solway's Patent, 1895, A.C. 78, 12 R.P.C. 10.

‡ Wright's Patent, 1839, 1 W.P.C. 576; Roper's Patent, 1887, 4 R.P.C. 201; Allan's Patent, 1867, L.R., 1 P.C. 507.

§ Roper's Patent, 1887, 4 R.P.C. 201; Stoney's Patent, 1888, 5 R.P.C. 518; Southby's Patent, 1891, 8 R.P.C. 433; Bakewell's Patent, 1852, 15 Moo. P.C.C. 385.

they would of course abstain in any case from prolonging a patent which was manifestly bad, yet, in one point of view, they are in the habit, in taking into account that which may be termed the question of utility, to consider not that amount of utility which would be necessary to support a patent, but that kind of utility which might more properly be described as merit."*

The Judicial Committee must also consider all the circumstances of the case, and in this connection they will look at what the patentee has done in endeavouring to get the patent worked. It will go against him if he has slept on his rights for a long time, either by allowing infringements to go unchecked, or by not endeavouring to get the invention worked till a large part of his time had expired.† *Effect of unchecked infringement.*

An agreement giving one party an exclusive right to use the invention will be treated with disfavour;‡ and if an extension be granted, an exclusive licensee may be required to renounce all claim under his license before the extension is registered.§ *Effect of exclusive license.*

When there are foreign patents, whether granted before or after the English patent, the fact that they have lapsed does not affect the discretion of the Judicial Committee in recommending an extension; ‖ but if, at the date of the application for a patent in this country, the invention was well *Lapsed foreign patents do not affect extension.*

---

* Saxby's Patent, L.R., 1870, 3 P.C. 294; Cockling's Patent, 1885, 2 R.P.C. 151.
† Pettit Smith's Patent, 1850, 7 Moo. P.C.C. 133.
‡ Darby's Patent, 1891, 8 R.P.C. 384.
§ Shone's Patent, 1892, 9 R.P.C. 438.
‖ Semet and Solvay's Patent [1895], A.C. 78.

known abroad, the importer is unlikely to obtain any extension.*

<small>Act 1883, sect. 25 (5). How patent is extended.</small>
"If the Judicial Committee report that the patentee has been inadequately remunerated by his patent, it shall be lawful for Her Majesty in Council to extend the term of the patent for a further term not exceeding seven, or in exceptional cases fourteen years; or to order the grant of a new patent for the term therein mentioned, and containing any restrictions, conditions, and provisions that the Judicial Committee may think fit."

When the extension is granted to some party other than the original patentee, the Judicial Committee sometimes make it a condition that some benefit should be reserved to him † or to his family,‡ unless he has been already remunerated.§

It is not unusual to impose terms as to the granting of licenses to any persons who may care to apply for them,‖ and to make other conditions for the working of the patent, so as to protect the public and parties other than the patentee from hardship or injustice.¶

<small>Assessor may be called in Act 1883, Sect. 28 (2). (3).</small>
"The Judicial Committee of the Privy Council may, if they see fit, in any proceeding before them, call in the aid of an assessor.

"The remuneration, if any, to be paid to an assessor under this section shall be determined by the Judicial Committee, and be paid in the same manner as the other expenses of the execution of this Act."

---

* Claridge's Patent, 1851, 7 Moo. P.C.C. 394.
† Hardy's Patent, 1849, 6 Moo. P.C.C. 441.
‡ Herbert's Patent, 1867, L.R., 1 P.C. 399.
§ Bodmer's Patent, 1849, 6 Moo. P.C.C. 468.
‖ Lyon's Patent, 1894, 11 R.P.C. 537; Mallet's Patent, 1866, L.R., 1 P.C. 308.
¶ Normandy's Patent, 1855, 9 Moo. P.C.C. 452.

"The costs of all parties of and incident to such proceedings shall be in the discretion of the Judicial Committee; and the orders of the committee respecting costs shall be enforceable as if they were orders of a division of the High Court of Justice."

<small>Costs.
Act 1883, sect. 25 (7).</small>

No rule can be laid down as to costs in petitions for extension; in each case the Judicial Committee will consider all the circumstances of the case, and one case is no guide to what will be done in another. If the petition is abandoned the petitioner will have to pay the opponent's costs.*

Council Office Fees.

ON PETITIONS TO THE QUEEN IN COUNCIL.

	£	s.	d.
Entering	1	1	0
Setting down petition	0	10	0
Summons	0	10	0
Committee Report	1	10	0
Order of Her Majesty in Council	3	2	6
Committee Order	1	12	6
Lodging affidavit	1	1	0
Lodging petition	1	1	0
Searching books for information for parties	0	10	0
Committee references	2	2	0
Lodging caveat	1	1	0
Subpœna to witness	0	10	0
Fee for taxation petitions	1	1	0

* Morgan Brown's Patent, 1886, 3 R.P.C. 212.

CHAPTER XXIII.

OFFENCES.

Act 1883, sect. 105. Penalty on falsely representing articles to be patented.
"(1) ANY person who represents that any article sold by him is a patented article, when no patent has been granted for the same, shall be liable for every offence on summary conviction to a fine not exceeding five pounds.

"(2) A person shall be deemed, for the purposes of this enactment, to represent that an article is patented if he sells the article with the word 'patent,' 'patented,' or any word or words expressing or implying that a patent has been obtained for the article stamped, engraved, or impressed on, or otherwise applied to the article.

If patent has lapsed.
If a patent has been granted, but has lapsed before the time at which the representation is made, this will be sufficient to avoid the penalty.*

Act 1883, sect. 93. Falsification of register.
"If any person makes or causes to be made a false entry in any register kept under this Act, or a writing falsely purporting to be a copy of an entry in any such register, or produces or tenders or causes to be produced or tendered in evidence any such writing, knowing the entry or writing to be false, he shall be guilty of a misdemeanor."

Using the title of patent agent. Act 1888, sect. 1 (1).
"After the 1st day of July, 1889, a person shall not be entitled to describe himself as a patent agent, whether by advertisement, by description on his place of business, by any document issued by him, or otherwise, unless he is registered as a patent agent in pursuance of this Act."

---

* Myers v. Baker, 1858, 3 H. & N. 802; Cheavin v. Walker, 1876, 5 Ch. D. 850; The Leather Cloth Co. v. The American Cloth Co., 1865, 11 H.L.C. 523.

"If any person knowingly describes himself as a patent agent in contravention of this section, he shall be liable on summary conviction to a fine not exceeding £20." *Sect. 1 (4).*

A person applying for a patent as agent for another does not thereby describe himself as a patent agent.*

"In Scotland any offence under this Act declared to be punishable on summary conviction may be prosecuted in the Sheriff Court." *Act 1883, sect. 108. Summary proceedings in Scotland.*

"In the application of this Act to Ireland, 'summary conviction' means a conviction under the Summary Jurisdiction Acts, that is to say, with reference to the Dublin Metropolitan Police District the Acts regulating the duties of justices of the peace and of the police for such district, and elsewhere in Ireland the Petty Sessions (Ireland) Act, 1851, and any Act amending it." *Act 1883, sect. 117. In Ireland.*

"Any offence under this Act committed in the Isle of Man which would in England be punishable on summary conviction may be prosecuted, and any fine in respect thereof recovered at the instance of any person aggrieved, in the manner in which offences punishable on summary conviction may for the time being be prosecuted." *Act 1883, sect. 112 (c). In Isle of Man.*

"The punishment for a misdemeanor under this Act in the Isle of Man shall be imprisonment for any term not exceeding two years, with or without hard labour, and with or without a fine not exceeding one hundred pounds, at the discretion of the Court." *Act 1883, sect. 112 (b). Misdemeanor in Isle of Man.*

---

* Graham v. Fanta, 1892, 9 R.P.C. 164 (Div. Ct.).

CHAPTER XXIV.

REGISTER OF PATENTS.

<small>Act 1883, sect. 23.</small>

"THERE shall be kept at the Patent Office a book called the Register of Patents, wherein shall be entered the names and addresses of grantees of patents, notifications of assignments and of transmission of patents, of licenses under patents, and such other matters affecting the validity or proprietorship of patents as may from time to time be prescribed.

"The Register of Patents shall be *primâ facie* evidence of any matters by this Act directed or authorised to be inserted therein.

"Copies of deeds, licenses, and any other documents affecting the proprietorship in any letters patent or in any license thereunder must be supplied to the Comptroller in the prescribed manner for filing in the Patent Office."

The actual proprietorship must in general be affected by a document that is entered on the register; a letter agreeing to give an exclusive license on terms of royalties to be agreed on is not a document that can be entered on the register.*

<small>Patent Rules 67. Entry of grant.</small>

"Upon the sealing of a patent the Comptroller shall cause to be entered in the Register of Patents the name, address, and description of the patentee as the grantee thereof, and the title of the invention."

---

* Fletcher's Patent, 1893, 10 R.P.C. 252.

"Upon the issue of a certificate of payment under Rule 48, the Comptroller shall cause to be entered in the Register of Patents a record of the amount and date of payment of the fee on such certificate." *Patent Rules 75. Entry of payment of fees on issue of certificate.*

"If a patentee fails to make any prescribed payment within the prescribed time, or any enlargement thereof duly granted, such failure shall be duly entered in the register." *Patent Rules 76. Entry of failure to pay fees.*

"Where a person becomes entitled by assignment, transmission, or other operation of law to a patent, the Comptroller shall, on request, and on proof of title to his satisfaction, cause the name of such person to be entered as proprietor of the patent in the Register of Patents. The person for the time being entered in the Register of Patents as proprietor of a patent shall, subject to the provisions of this Act and any rights appearing from such register to be vested in any other person, have power absolutely to assign, grant licenses as to, or otherwise deal with the same, and to give effectual receipts for any consideration for such assignment, license, or dealing. Provided that any equities in respect of such patent may be enforced in like manner as in respect of any other personal property." *Act 1883, sect. 87. Registration of assignments, &c.*

But although it is provided that—

"There shall not be entered in any register kept under this Act, or be receivable by the Comptroller, any notice of any trust expressed, implied, or constructive," *No notice of trust on register. Act 1883, sect. 85.*

it has been decided that an equitable assignment of a patent can be entered in the register.* *Equitable assignment.*

"Where a person becomes entitled to a patent or to any share or interest therein by assignment, either throughout the United Kingdom and the Isle of Man, or for any place or places therein, or by transmission or other operation of law, a request for the entry of his name in the register as such complete or partial proprietor of the patent, or of such share or interest therein, as the case may be, shall be addressed to the Comptroller, and left at the Patent Office." *Patent Rules 68. Request for entry of subsequent proprietorship.*

---

* Stewart v. Casey, 1892, C.A., 9 R.P.C. 9.

218   LAW OF PATENTS.

P. 261.

Such request must be made on Patent Form L, which must bear a stamp for 10s.

Change of address.
P. 267.

The address of a proprietor is also entered, and in case of an alteration being required application must be made on Patent Form R, bearing a stamp for 5s.

Patent Rule 73. Body corporate.
Patent Rules 69. Signature of request.

"A body corporate may be registered as proprietor by its corporate name."

"Such request shall in the case of individuals be made and signed by the person requiring to be registered as proprietor, or by his agent duly authorised to the satisfaction of the Comptroller, and in the case of a body corporate by their agent authorised in like manner.

Patent Rules 70. Particulars to be stated in request.

"Every such request shall state the name, address, and description of the person claiming to be entitled to the patent or to any share or interest therein, as the case may be (hereinafter called the claimant), and the particulars of the assignment, transmission, or other operation of law, by virtue of which he requires to be entered in the register as proprietor, so as to show the manner in which, and the person or persons to whom, the patent, or such share or interest therein as aforesaid, has been assigned or transmitted.

Patent Rules 71. Production of documents of title and other proof.

"Every assignment and every other document containing, giving effect to, or being evidence of the transmission of a patent or affecting the proprietorship thereof as claimed by such request, except such documents as are matters of record, shall be produced to the Comptroller, together with the request above prescribed, and such other proof of title as he may require for his satisfaction.

"As to a document which is a matter of record, an official or certified copy thereof shall in like manner be produced to the Comptroller.

Patent Rules 72. Copies for Patent Office.

"There shall also be left with the request an examined copy of the assignment or other document above required to be produced.

"As to a document which is a matter of record, an official or certified copy shall be left with the request in lieu of an examined copy.

"Where an order has been made by Her Majesty in Council for the extension of a patent for a further term, or for the grant of a new patent, or where an order has been made by the Court for the revocation of a patent or the rectification of the register under section 90 of the Act of 1883, or otherwise affecting the validity or proprietorship of the patent, the person in whose favour such order has been made shall forthwith leave at the Patent Office an office copy of such order. The register shall thereupon be rectified, or the purport of such order shall otherwise be duly entered in the register, as the case may be." Patent Rules 74. Entry of orders of the Privy Council or of the Court.

An application for the entry of an Order of the Privy Council in the Register must be made on Patent Form S, and must bear a stamp for 10s. P. 268.

"If any rectification of a register under this Act is required in pursuance of any proceeding in a court in Scotland or Ireland, a copy of the order, decree, or other authority for the rectification shall be served on the Comptroller, and he shall rectify the register accordingly." Scotch or Irish Order, how registered. Act 1883, sect. 111 (2).

"An attested copy of every license granted under a patent shall be left at the Patent Office by the licensee, with a request that a notification thereof may be entered in the register. The licensee shall cause the accuracy of such copy to be certified as the Comptroller may direct, and the original license shall at the same time be produced and left at the Patent Office if required for further verification." Patent Rules 77. Entry of licenses.

A request to enter a notification of a license must be made on Patent Form M, and must bear a stamp for 10s. P. 262.

"Every register kept under this Act shall at all convenient times be open to the inspection of the public, subject to the provisions of this Act and such regulations as may be prescribed; and certified copies, sealed with the seal of the Patent Office, Act 1883, sect. 88. Register to be open to public.

of any entry in any such register shall be given to any person requiring the same on payment of the prescribed fee."

The fee for each inspection is 1s.

<small>Patent Rules 78. Hours of inspection of register.</small>

"The Register of Patents shall be open to the inspection of the public on every week-day between the hours of ten and four, except on the days and at the times following:

- "(*a*) Christmas Day, Good Friday, the day observed as Her Majesty's birthday, days observed as days of public fast or thanksgiving, and days observed as holidays at the Bank of England; or
- "(*b*) Days which may from time to time be notified by a placard posted in a conspicuous place at the Patent Office;
- "(*c*) Times when the register is required for any purpose of official use."

<small>Act 1883, sect. 89. Sealed copies are evidence.</small>

"Printed or written copies or extracts, purporting to be certified by the Comptroller and sealed with the seal of the Patent Office, of or from patents, specifications, disclaimers, and other documents in the Patent Office, and of or from registers and other books kept there, shall be admitted in evidence in all courts in Her Majesty's dominions, and in all proceedings, without further proof or production of the originals."

<small>Patent Rules 79. Certified copies of documents.</small>

"Certified copies of any entry in the register, or certified copies of, or extracts from, patents, specifications, disclaimers, affidavits, statutory declarations, and other public documents in the Patent Office, or of or from registers and other books kept there, may be furnished by the Comptroller on payment of the prescribed fee."

The fee for office copies is 4*d*. per 100 words, and the cost of drawings according to agreement. The cost of a printed specification is 8*d*. There is a fee of 1*s*. for certifying an office copy or specification, &c.

<small>Certificate as to entry in register. Act 1883, sect. 96.</small>

"A certificate purporting to be under the hand of the Comptroller as to any entry, matter, or thing which he is authorised by this Act, or any general rules made thereunder, to make or do, shall be *primâ facie* evidence of the entry having been made and of the contents thereof, and of the matter or thing having been done or left undone."

The fee for a certificate from the Comptroller is 5s.; it is given on Patent Form Q. P. 266.

"The Comptroller may, on request in writing, accompanied by the prescribed fee,— Clerical errors may be corrected. Act 1883, sect. 91.
  "(*a*) Correct any clerical error in or in connection with an application for a patent; or
  "(*b*) Correct any clerical error in the name, style, or address of the registered proprietor of a patent."

An application to the Comptroller to correct a clerical error must be made on Patent Form P, which must bear a stamp for 5s. or £1, according as the application is made before or after the patent is sealed. P. 265.

"The Court may, on the application of any person aggrieved by the omission without sufficient cause of the name of any person or of any other particulars from any register kept under this Act, or by any entry made without sufficient cause in any such register, make such order for making, expunging, or varying the entry, as the Court thinks fit; or the Court may refuse the application; and in either case may make such order with respect to the costs of the proceedings as the Court thinks fit. Correction of register by the Court. Act 1883, sect. 90.

"The Court may, in any proceeding under this section, decide any question that it may be necessary or expedient to decide for the rectification of a register, and may direct an issue to be tried for the decision of any question of fact, and may award damages to the party aggrieved.

"Any order of the Court rectifying a register shall direct that due notice of the rectification be given to the Comptroller."

The Court here means the High Court or other court having jurisdiction in patent matters. See p. 133

Act 1883, sect. 93. Falsification of register a misdemeanor.

"If any person makes or causes to be made a false entry in any register kept under this Act, or a writing falsely purporting to be a copy of an entry in any such register, or produces or tenders or causes to be produced or tendered in evidence any such writing, knowing the entry or writing to be false, he shall be guilty of a misdemeanor."

CHAPTER XXV.

MISCELLANEOUS.

Warlike Inventions.

"(1) THE inventor of any improvement in instruments or munitions of war, his executors, administrators, or assigns (who are in this section comprised in the expression the inventor), may (either for or without valuable consideration) assign to Her Majesty's Principal Secretary of State for the War Department (hereinafter referred to as the Secretary of State), on behalf of Her Majesty, all the benefit of the invention, and of any patent obtained or to be obtained for the same; and the Secretary of State may be a party to the assignment. Act 1883, sect. 44. Assignment to Secretary for War of certain inventions.

"(2) The assignment shall effectually vest the benefit of the invention and patent in the Secretary of State for the time being on behalf of Her Majesty, and all covenants and agreements therein contained for keeping the invention secret and otherwise shall be valid and effectual (notwithstanding any want of valuable consideration), and may be enforced accordingly by the Secretary of State for the time being.

"(3) Where any such assignment has been made to the Secretary of State, he may at any time before the application for a patent for the invention, or before publication of the specification or specifications, certify to the Comptroller his opinion that, in the interest of the public service, the particulars of the invention and of the manner in which it is to be performed should be kept secret. Secretary for War may prevent publication of specifications.

"(4) If the Secretary of State so certifies, the application and specification or specifications with the drawings (if any), and any amendment of the specification or specifications, and any copies of such documents and drawings, shall, instead of Specifications, &c., kept in sealed packet.

being left in the ordinary manner at the Patent Office, be delivered to the Comptroller in a packet sealed by authority of the Secretary of State.

"(5) Such packet shall, until the expiration of the term or extended term during which a patent for the invention may be in force, be kept sealed by the Comptroller, and shall not be opened save under the authority of an order of the Secretary of State, or of the law officers.

"(6) Such sealed packet shall be delivered at any time during the continuance of the patent to any person authorised by writing under the hand of the Secretary of State to receive the same, and shall, if returned to the Comptroller, be again kept sealed by him.

"(7) On the expiration of the term or extended term of the patent, such sealed packet shall be delivered to any person authorised by writing under the hand of the Secretary of State to receive it.

"(8) Where the Secretary of State certifies as aforesaid, after an application for a patent has been left at the Patent Office, but before the publication of the specification or specifications, the application, specification, or specifications, with the drawings (if any), shall be forthwith placed in a packet sealed by authority of the Comptroller, and such packet shall be subject to the foregoing provisions respecting a packet sealed by authority of the Secretary of State.

No revocation of patent not published.

"(9) No proceeding by petition or otherwise shall lie for revocation of a patent granted for an invention in relation to which the Secretary of State has certified as aforesaid.

No copies allowed.

"(10) No copy of any specification or other document or drawing, by this section required to be placed in a sealed packet, shall in any manner whatever be published or open to the inspection of the public, but save as in this section otherwise directed, the provisions of this part of this Act shall apply in respect of any such invention and patent as aforesaid.

May be published at any subsequent time.

"(11) The Secretary of State may, at any time by writing under his hand, waive the benefit of this section with respect to any particular invention, and the specifications, documents, and drawings shall be thenceforth kept and dealt with in the ordinary way.

"(12) The communication of any invention for any improvement in instruments or munitions of war to the Secretary of State, or to any person or persons authorised by him to investigate the same or the merits thereof, shall not, nor shall anything done for the purposes of the investigation, be deemed use or publication of such invention so as to prejudice the grant or validity of any patent for the same." *(Communication of invention to Secretary for War is not a publication.)*

Patents existing prior to Act 1883.

(1) The provisions of this Act relating to applications for patents and proceedings thereon shall have effect in respect only of applications made after the commencement of this Act. *(Act 1883, sect. 45.)*

"(2) Every patent granted before the commencement of this Act, or on an application then pending, shall remain unaffected by the provisions of this Act relating to patents binding the Crown, and to compulsory licenses. *(Provisions respecting patents prior in date.)*

"(3) In all other respects (including the amount and time of payment of fees) this Act shall extend to all patents granted before the commencement of this Act, or on applications then pending, in substitution for such enactments as would have applied thereto if this Act had not been passed.

"(4) All instruments relating to patents granted before the commencement of this Act required to be left or filed in the Great Seal Patent Office shall be deemed to be so left or filed if left or filed before or after the commencement of this Act in the Patent Office."

Postal Communications.

"(1) Any application, notice, or other document authorised or required to be left, made, or given at the Patent Office or to the Comptroller, or to any other person under this Act, may be sent by a prepaid letter through the post; and if so sent shall be deemed to have been left, made, or given respectively at the time when the letter containing the same would be delivered in the ordinary course of post. *(Act 1883, sect. 97.)*

"(2) In proving such service or sending, it shall be sufficient to prove that the letter was properly addressed and put into the post."

Excluded Days.

Act 1883, sect. 98.

"Whenever the last day fixed by this Act, or by any rule for the time being in force, for leaving any document or paying any fee at the Patent Office shall fall on Christmas Day, Good Friday, or on a Saturday or Sunday, or any day observed as a holiday at the Bank of England, or any day observed as a day of public fast or thanksgiving, herein referred to as excluded days, it shall be lawful to leave such document or to pay such fee on the day next following such excluded day, or days if two or more of them occur consecutively."

Person incapacitated from doing Anything.

Act 1883, sect. 99.

"If any person is, by reason of infancy, lunacy, or other inability, incapable of making any declaration or doing anything required or permitted by this Act or by any rules made under the authority of this Act, then the guardian or committee (if any) of such incapable person, or if there be none, any person appointed by any Court or judge possessing jurisdiction in respect of the property of incapable persons, upon the petition of any person on behalf of such incapable person, or of any other person interested in the making such declaration or doing such thing, may make such declaration or a declaration as nearly corresponding thereto as circumstances permit, and do such thing in the name and on behalf of such incapable person, and all acts done by such substitute shall for the purposes of this Act be as effectual as if done by the person for whom he is substituted."

Fraudulent Applications.

Act 1883, sect. 35.

"A patent granted to the true and first inventor shall not be invalidated by an application in fraud of him, or by provisional protection obtained thereon, or by any use or publication of the invention subsequent to that fraudulent application during the period of provisional protection."

Power to dispense with Evidence, &c.

Patent Rules 80.

"Where, under these rules, any person is required to do any act or thing, or to sign any document, or to make any declaration on behalf of himself or of any body corporate, or any document or evidence is required to be produced to or left with the Comptroller or at the Patent Office, and it is shown to the satisfaction of the Comptroller that from any reasonable cause such person is unable to do such act or thing, or to sign such document or make such declaration, or that such document or evidence cannot be produced or left as aforesaid, it shall be lawful for the Comptroller, with the sanction of the Board of Trade, and upon the production of such other evidence, and subject to such terms as they may think fit, to dispense with any such act or thing, document, declaration, or evidence."

"Where any discretionary power is by this Act given to the Comptroller, he shall not exercise that power adversely to the applicant for a patent, or for amendment of a specification, without (if so required within the prescribed time by the applicant) giving the applicant an opportunity of being heard personally or by his agent. *Act 1883, sect. 94. Discretionary power of Comptroller.*

"The Comptroller may, in any case of doubt or difficulty arising in the administration of any of the provisions of this Act, apply to either of the law officers for directions in the matter." *Act 1883, sect. 95. Difficulties in administration.*

"The Comptroller shall, before the first day of June in every year, cause a report respecting the execution by or under him of this Act to be laid before both Houses of Parliament, and therein shall include for the year to which each report relates all general rules made in that year under or for the purposes of this Act, and an account of all fees, salaries, and allowances and other money received and paid under this Act." *Annual reports of Comptroller. Act 1883, sect. 102.*

Ireland and the Isle of Man.

"All parties shall, notwithstanding anything in this Act, have in Ireland their remedies under, or in respect of, a patent as if the same had been granted to extend to Ireland only." *Act 1883, sect. 110. Reservation of remedies in Ireland.*

"This Act shall extend to the Isle of Man, and— *Act 1883, sect. 112 (1).*

"Nothing in this Act shall affect the jurisdiction of the courts in the Isle of Man, in proceedings for infringement, or in any action or proceeding respecting a patent, competent to those courts."

Patent Museum, South Kensington.

Patent Office Circular, p. 8.

"This Museum was in 1883 placed under the management of the Department of Science and Art. It no longer forms a separate section, but has been incorporated with the general Science Collections of the South Kensington Museum. All communications relating thereto should be addressed to the Secretary, Science and Art Department, South Kensington, London, S.W. The Science Collections are open to the public *free* daily, from 10 a.m. to 4, 5, or 6 p.m., according to the season. A number of the models may be seen in motion from 11 a.m. to the hour of closing. Entrance—Exhibition Road."

Models for Patent Museum. Act 1883, sect. 42.

"The Department of Science and Art may at any time require a patentee to furnish them with a model of his invention on payment to the patentee of the cost of the manufacture of the model; the amount to be settled in case of dispute by the Board of Trade."

Act. 1883, sect. 100. Documents sent to British capitals.

"Copies of all specifications, drawings, and amendments left at the Patent Office after the commencement of this Act, printed for and sealed with the seal of the Patent Office, shall be transmitted to the Edinburgh Museum of Science and Art, and to the Enrolments Office of the Chancery Division in Ireland, and to the Rolls Office in the Isle of Man, within twenty-one days after the same shall respectively have been accepted or allowed at the Patent Office; and certified copies of or extracts from any such documents shall be given to any person requiring the same on payment of the prescribed fee; and any such copy or extract shall be admitted in evidence in all courts in Scotland and Ireland and in the Isle of Man without further proof or production of the originals."

Patent Office Publications.

See p. 5. Patent Office Circular, p. 8.

"These may be consulted daily at the Free Public Library in the Patent Office; at the Science and Art Department, South Kensington; and at a large number of Free Libraries. They are also on sale at the Patent Office Sale Branch, 25, Southampton Buildings, Chancery Lane, W.C.

"Specifications and other publications will be forwarded by post from the Patent Office on receipt of the price and of the postage when such is charged. *Sums amounting to* 1s. *or more must be remitted by Postal or Post Office Order payable to Sir Reader Lack.* Postage stamps sent in payment of any amount exceeding 11*d.* will be returned. Cheques will not be accepted.

"In ordering specifications the name of the Patentee, the No. of Patent, and year in which applied for must be given. These particulars can be obtained by searching the Indexes of Patents and (for recent specifications) the illustrated Official Journal. The Indexes and the Journals can be referred to at the places named in the List 'A' following, and at the Patent Office Library. The price of each specification is 8*d.*, which includes postage in the United Kingdom.*

"Printed specifications or other publications cannot be returned by the purchasers unless a wrong number has been supplied through an error on the part of the Patent Office."

List of Places receiving Donations of Patent Office Works.

A.—*Places in the United Kingdom receiving a complete set of the publications of the Patent Office, including the Specifications, on condition that they shall be daily accessible to the public, for reference or for copying, free of all charge.*

Belfast (*Free Library*).
†Birmingham (*Central Library, Reference Department, Eden Place*).
Bolton-le-Moors (*Public Library, Exchange Buildings*).
Bradford, Yorkshire (*Free Library, Darley Street*).
Brighton (*Free Library*).
†Bristol (*Free Library, King Street*).
†Cardiff (*Free Library and Museum*) *from* 1871.
Carlisle (*Public Free Library, Tullie House*).
Derby (*Free Library and Museum*).
Dublin (*National Library of Ireland, Kildare Street*).

---

* For form of postal application see p. 251.
† This Library has also received since 1893 a set of Specifications of United States Patents.

†Dundee (*Public Library, Albert Institute*).
†Glasgow (*Stirling's Library, Miller Street*).
Halifax (*Public Library, Akroyd Park*).
Horwich (*Mechanics' Institute*).
Huddersfield (*Corporation Offices*).
†Hull (*Mechanics' Institute, George Street*).
Ipswich (*Museum Library, Museum Street*).
Keighley (*Mechanics' Institute, North Street*).
Kidderminster (*Free Library*).
†Leeds (*Public Library*).
Leicester (*Free Library, Wellington Street*).
Liverpool (*Free Library, William Brown Street*).
London (*British Museum*).
  ,, (*Free Library, London Street, Bethnal Green*) from 1881.
†Manchester (*Free Library, King Street*).
Newcastle-upon-Tyne (*Public Library, New Bridge Street*).
Newport, Monmouth (*Free Library*).
Nottingham (*Free Public Libraries*).
Oldham (*Free Library, Union Street*).
Plymouth (*Free Library*).
Preston (*Dr. Shepherd's Library, Cross Street*).
Rochdale (*Free Library, Town Hall*).
Salford (*Free Library, Peel Park*).
†Sheffield (*Free Library, Surrey Street*).
Stockport (*Central Free Library*).
Swansea (*Free Library*).
Wolverhampton (*Free Library*).

B.—*Public Offices, &c., in the United Kingdom, and British Colonies and Foreign States receiving a complete set of the publications of the Patent Office.*

Public Offices, &c.

Department of Science and Art, South Kensington.
†Museum of Science and Art, Edinburgh.
Public Record Office, Dublin.

---

† This Library has also received since 1893 a set of Specifications of United States Patents.

British Colonies, &c.

Canada—Patent Office, Ottawa.
  Council of Arts and Manufactures of Quebec, Montreal.
  Public Library, Toronto.
India—Patent Office, Imperial Secretariat, Calcutta.
  Patent Office, Secretariat, Bombay.
  Patent Office, Secretariat, Madras.
New South Wales—Patent Office, Sydney.
New Zealand—Patent Office, Wellington.
Queensland—Patent Office, Brisbane.
South Australia—Colonial Institute, Adelaide.
   Patent Office, Adelaide (*from* 1878).
Tasmania—General Register Office, Hobart.
Victoria—Patent Office, Melbourne.
  Public Library, Melbourne.

Foreign States.

Austria—Polytechnic University, Vienna.
Belgium—Ministère Directeur l'Industrie, Brussels.
  Musée de l'Industrie, Palais du Midi, Brussels.
Denmark—Patent Office, Copenhagen (*from* 1893).
France—Bibliothèque Nationale, Paris.
  Bureau de la Propriété Industrielle, Ministère du Commerce, Paris (*from* 1876).
  Conservatoire des Arts et Métiers, Paris.
Germany—Kaiserliches Patentamt, Berlin.
  Kaiserliches Statistiche amt, Berlin.
  Baden—Polytechnic School, Carlsruhe (*from* 1876).
  Bavaria—Polytechische Verein, Munich.
  Prussia—Königliche Bibliothek, Berlin.
   Polytechnische Schule, Hanover.
  Saxony—Polytechnische Schule, Dresden.
  Mulhouse—Société Industrielle.
Italy—Ufficio delle Privative, Rome.
  Royal Institution for the Encouragement of Science, Naples (*from* 1852).
Japan—Patent Office, Tokio (*from* 1884).
Norway—Patent Office, Christiania (*from* 1884).

Russia—Bibliothèque Impériale, St. Petersburg.
        Polytechnic School, Riga.
Spain—Madrid.
Sweden—Patent Office, Stockholm.
United States—Patent Office, Washington, D.C.
        Astor Library, New York, N.Y.
        State Library, Albany, N.Y.
        Franklin Institute, Philadelphia, Pa.
        Free Public Library, Boston, Mass.
        Public Library, Cincinnati, Ohio.
        Free Public Library, Chicago, Ill.
        Peabody Institute, Baltimore, Md.
        Cornell University, Ithaca, N.Y.
        Mercantile Library, St. Louis, Mo.
        Mechanics' Institute, San Francisco, Cal.
        Historical Society, Madison, Wis.

CHAPTER XXVI.

INTERNATIONAL AND COLONIAL ARRANGEMENTS.

"If her Majesty is pleased to make any arrangements with the Government or Governments of any foreign state or states for mutual protection of inventions, then any person who has applied for protection for any invention in any such state shall be entitled to a patent for his invention under this Act in priority to other applicants; and such patent shall have the same date as the date of the application in such foreign state. Act 1883, sect. 103 (1). International arrangements for protection of inventions.

"Provided that his application is made within seven months from his applying for protection in the foreign state with which the arrangement is in force.

"Provided that nothing in this section contained shall entitle the patentee to recover damages for infringements happening prior to the date of the actual acceptance of his complete specification."

"Where it is made to appear to Her Majesty that the Legislature of any British possession has made satisfactory provision for the protection of inventions patented in this country, it shall be lawful for Her Majesty from time to time, by Order in Council, to apply the provisions of the last preceding section, with such variations or additions (if any) as to Her Majesty in Council may seem fit, to such British possession. Act 1883, sect. 104. Provision for Colonies and India.

"An Order in Council under this Act shall, from a date to be mentioned for the purpose in the Order, take effect as if its provisions had been contained in this Act; but it shall be lawful for her Majesty in Council to revoke any Order in Council made under this Act.

"'British possession' means any territory or place situate Act 1883, sect. 117.

Definition of British possession. within her Majesty's dominious, and not being or forming part of the United Kingdom, or of the Channel Islands, or of the Isle of Man, and all territories and places under one Legislature, as hereinafter defined, are deemed to be one British possession for the purposes of this Act:

"'Legislature' includes any person or persons who exercise legislative authority in the British possession; and where there are local Legislatures as well as a central Legislature, means the central Legislature only."

Patent Office Circular, p. 8. "Under this power Great Britain has joined in an International Convention for the protection of inventions, which now exists between the following States:

Belgium.	New Zealand.
Brazil.	Norway.
Curaçoa and Surinam.	Portugal.
Denmark.	Queensland.
East Indian Colonies of the Netherlands.	Santo Domingo.
	Servia.
France.	Spain.
Great Britain.	Sweden.
Guatemala.	Switzerland.
Italy.	Tunis.
Netherlands.	United States.

"Similar arrangements, for the mutual protection of inventions, have been made between Great Britian on the one side, and each of the following States and Colonies on the other:

Ecuador (Designs and Trade Marks only).	Paraguay.
	Roumania (Designs and Trade Marks only).
Greece (Designs and Trade Marks only).	Tasmania.
Mexico.	Uruguay.

Act 1883, sect. 103 (2). "The publication in the United Kingdom or the Isle of Man during the period aforesaid of any description of the invention, or the use therein during such period of the invention, shall not invalidate the patent which may be granted for the invention.

Act 1883, sect. 103 (3). "The application for the grant of a patent under this section must be made in the same manner as an ordinary application under this Act."

Where the foreign state in which the first patent was taken out became a member subsequently to the date of that patent but before that of the application here, the International Convention was held to apply.* State joining Convention after date of first patent.

An appeal lies to the law officer with regard to an application under the International Convention.

"The provisions of this section shall apply only in the case of those foreign states with respect to which Her Majesty shall from time to time by Order in Council declare them to be applicable, and so long only in the case of each state as the Order in Council shall continue in force with respect to that state." Act 1883, sect. 103 (4). Limitation of international arrangements.

"The term 'foreign application' shall mean an application by any person for protection of his invention in a foreign state or British possession to which by any Order of Her Majesty in Council for the time being in force the provisions of section 103 of the Patents, Designs, and Trade Marks Act, 1883, have been declared applicable. Definition of foreign application. Patent Rule 24.

"An application in the United Kingdom for a patent for any invention in respect of which a foreign application has been made shall contain a declaration that such foreign application has been made, and shall specify all the foreign states or British possessions in which foreign applications have been made, and the official date or dates thereof respectively. The application must be made within seven months from the date of the first foreign application, and must be signed by the person or persons by whom such first foreign application was made. If such person, or any of such persons, be dead, the application must be signed by the legal personal representative of such dead person, as well as by the other applicants, if any." Patent Rule 25. Who may apply under international arrangements.

A foreign patentee must elect whether he will apply under the International Convention, or risk

---

* *Re* Main's Patent, 1890, 7 R.P.C. 13.

having his patent invalidated by a prior publication in England of his prior foreign patent.*

Only the foreign patentee himself, or his legal personal representative, can take advantage of the International Convention; a patent to an agent for him can only be granted as of the date of application as on "an application for a communication from abroad."†

<small>Patent Rule 26. Form of application, p. 247.</small>

"The application in the United Kingdom shall be made in the Form A2 in the second schedule to these rules, and in addition to the specification, provisional or complete, left with such application must be accompanied by—

<small>Copies of foreign specification to accompany application.</small>

"(1) A copy or copies of the specification, and drawings or documents corresponding thereto, filed or deposited by the applicant in the Patent Office of the Foreign State or British Possession in respect of the first foreign application duly certified by the official chief or head of the Patent Office of such Foreign State or British Possessions as aforesaid, or otherwise verified to the satisfaction of the Comptroller.

<small>Declaration of identity of inventions.</small>

"(2) A statutory declaration as to the identity of the invention in respect of which the application is made with the invention in respect of which the said first foreign application was made, and if the specification or document corresponding thereto be in a foreign language, a translation thereof shall be annexed to and verified by such statutory declaration.

<small>Patent Rules 27. Date of foreign application to be entered on Register.</small>

"On receipt of such application, together with the prescribed specification and the other document or documents accompanying the same, required by the last preceding rule, and with such other proof (if any) as the Comptroller may require of or relating to such foreign application, or of the official date thereof, the Comptroller shall make an entry of the applications

---

* The British Tanning Co., Limited, v. Groth, 1891, 8 R.P.C. 121.

† Shallenberger's application, 1889, 6 R.P.C. 550.

in both countries and of the official dates of such applications respectively.

"All further proceedings in connection with such application shall be taken within the times and in the manner prescribed by the Acts or rules for ordinary applications." Patent Rule 28.

Such further proceedings include any act within the discretion or jurisdiction of the Comptroller, and consequent appeals to the law officer.*

"The patent shall be entered in the Register of Patents as dated of the date on which the first foreign application was made, and the payment of renewal fees and the expiration of the patent shall be reckoned as from the date of the first foreign application." Date of patent. Patent Rule 29.

The chief points in the International Convention are—

(1) The right of priority obtained by a person who first applies for a patent in this country is seven months. Art. IV.

(2) The importation by the patentee into the country where the patent has been granted of objects manufactured in any other state belonging to the Union does not entail forfeiture; but the patentee must work his patent in conformity with the laws of the country into which he so imports articles when any working in such country is required in order to keep a patent in force. Importation. Art. V.

(3) Temporary protection is given to patentable inventions for articles exhibited at official or officially recognised International Exhibitions. Art. XI.

"An International Office, in connection with the Convention, has been established at Berne, which publishes a monthly International Office and periodical.

---

* *Re* Main's Patent, 1890, 7 R.P.C. 13.

periodical, entitled 'La Propriété Industrielle.' The yearly subscription (including postage) for all countries within the Postal Union is 5 francs 60 centimes, and should be forwarded by money order to M. S. Collin, Imprimeur, Berne."

List of Fees payable on and in connection with Letters Patent.

Up to Sealing.

		£ s. d.	£ s. d.
1.	On application for provisional protection	1 0 0	
2.	On filing complete specification	3 0 0	
			4 0 0

Or—

3.	On filing complete specification with first application		4 0 0
4.	On appeal from Comptroller to Law Officer. By appellant		3 0 0

5.	On notice of opposition to grant of patent. By opponent		0 10 0
6.	On hearing by Comptroller. By applicant and by opponent respectively		1 0 0

On application to amend specification:

7.	Up to sealing. By applicant		1 10 0
8.	After sealing. By patentee		3 0 0
9.	On notice of opposition to amendment. By opponent		0 10 0
10.	On hearing by Comptroller. By applicant and by opponent respectively		1 0 0
11.	On application to amend specification during action or proceeding. By patentee		3 0 0

12.	On application to the Board of Trade for a compulsory license. By person applying		5 0 0
13.	On opposition to grant of compulsory license. By patentee		5 0 0

		£	s.	d.
	On certificate of renewal:			
14.	Before the expiration of the 4th year from the date of the patent and in respect of the 5th year	5	0	0
15.	Before the expiration of the 5th year from the date of the patent and in respect of the 6th year	6	0	0
16.	Before the expiration of the 6th year from the date of the patent and in respect of the 7th year	7	0	0
17.	Before the expiration of the 7th year from the date of the patent and in respect of the 8th year	8	0	0
18.	Before the expiration of the 8th year from the date of the patent and in respect of the 9th year	9	0	0
19.	Before the expiration of the 9th year from the date of the patent and in respect of the 10th year	10	0	0
20.	Before the expiration of the 10th year from the date of the patent and in respect of the 11th year	11	0	0
21.	Before the expiration of the 11th year from the date of the patent and in respect of the 12th year	12	0	0
22.	Before the expiration of the 12th year from the date of the patent and in respect of the 13th year	13	0	0
23.	Before the expiration of the 13th year from the date of the patent and in respect of the 14th year	14	0	0
	On enlargement of time for payment of renewal fees:			
24.	Not exceeding one month	1	0	0
25.	,, two months	3	0	0
26	,, three months	5	0	0

LIST OF FEES.

		£	s.	d.
27.	For every entry of an assignment, transmission, agreement, license, or extension of patent	0	10	0
28.	For duplicate of letters patent . each	2	0	0
29.	On notice to Comptroller of intended exhibition of a patent under Section 39	0	10	0
30.	Search or inspection fee . . each	0	1	0
31.	For office copies . . every 100 words (but never less than one shilling).	0	0	4
32.	For office copies of drawings, cost according to agreement.			
33.	For certifying office copies, MSS. or printed, each	0	1	0
33A.	On postal request for printed copy specification	0	0	8
34.	On request to Comptroller to correct a clerical error:			
	up to sealing	0	5	0
	after sealing	1	0	0
35.	For certificate of Comptroller under Section 96	0	5	0
36.	For altering address in register	0	5	0
37.	For enlargement of time for filing complete specification, not exceeding one month	2	0	0
38.	For enlargement of time for acceptance of complete specification:			
	Not exceeding one month	2	0	0
	,, two months	4	0	0
	,, three months	6	0	0

PATENT FORMS.

			PAGE
A.—	Form of Application for Patent	. .	243
A1.—	,, ,, ,, communicated from abroad		245
A2.—	,, ,, under international convention	.	247
B.—	,, Provisional Specification	. .	249
C.—	,, Complete ,,	. .	250
C1.—	,, Postal Request for printed copy of specification (for use in the United Kingdom only)	. . . .	251
D.—	,, Opposition to Grant of Patent	. .	252
E.—	,, Application for Hearing by Comptroller	.	253
F.—	,, ,, to amend Specification or Drawings		254
G.—	,, Opposition to Amendment of Specification or Drawings	. . .	255
H.—	,, Application for Compulsory Grant of License	. . . .	256
H1.—	,, Petition for Compulsory Grant of Licenses		257
I.—	,, Opposition to Compulsory Grant of License	. . .	258
J.—	,, Application for Certificate of Payment or Renewal	. . .	259
K.—	,, Application for Enlargement of Time for Payment of Renewal Fee	. .	260
L.—	,, Request to enter Name upon the Register of Patents	. . .	261
M.—	,, Request to enter Notification of License in Register	. . .	262
N.—	,, Application for Duplicate of Letters Patent		263
O.—	,, Notice of Intended Exhibition of Unpatented Invention	. .	264
P.—	,, Request for Correction of Clerical Error	.	265
Q.—	,, Certificate of Comptroller	. .	266
R.—	,, Notice for Alteration of an Address in Register	. . .	267
S.—	,, Application for Entry of Order of Privy Council in Register	. .	268
T.—	,, Appeal to Law Officer	. .	269
U.—	,, Application for Extension of Time for leaving a complete Specification	.	270
V.—	,, Application for Extension of Time for acceptance of complete Specification	.	271

| PATENT |

**PATENTS, DESIGNS, AND TRADE MARKS ACTS,
1883 TO 1888.**

Form **A.**

To be accompanied by two copies of Form B or of Form C.

―――

APPLICATION FOR PATENT.

―――

(a) Here insert name and full address and calling of applicant or applicants.

(b) Here insert title of invention.

(c) In the case of more than one applicant, state whether all, or if not, who is or are the inventor or inventors.

(*a*)

                                                                                              do hereby declare that   in possession of an invention the title of which is (*b*)

that (*c*)   the true and first inventor   thereof; and that the same is not in use by any other person or persons to the best of   knowledge and belief; and   humbly pray that a Patent may be granted to   for the said invention.

Dated   day of   18

(*d*)

(d) To be signed by applicant or applicants. In the case of a firm, each member of the firm must sign.

NOTE.—Where application is made through an agent (Rule 8), the authorisation on the back (if used) should be signed by the applicant or applicants.

*To the Comptroller,
Patent Office,* 25, *Southampton Buildings,
Chancery Lane, London, W.C.*

For the convenience of applicants, suggested forms of authorisation to an agent and statement of address respectively are printed below.

---

(1) *Where application is made through an Agent (Rule 8).*

---

                hereby appoint
of
to act as   agent in respect of the within application for a Patent, and request that all notices, requisitions, and communications relating thereto may be sent to such agent at the above address.

                   day of   18

                       *

* To be signed by applicant or applicants.

---

(2) *Where application is made without an Agent (Rule 9).*

---

                hereby request that all notices, requisitions, and communications in respect of the within application may sent to   at

                   day of

† To be signed by applicant or applicants.

PATENT.

PATENTS, DESIGNS, AND TRADE MARKS ACTS, 1883 TO 1888.

Form **A 1**.

(To be accompanied by two copies of Form B *or of Form* C.)

APPLICATION FOR PATENT FOR INVENTIONS COMMUNICATED FROM ABROAD.

(*a*) Here insert name, full address, and calling of applicant.

I (*a*)   of   in the county of   do hereby declare that I am in possession of an invention the title of which is (*b*)

(*b*) Here insert title of invention.

(*c*) Here insert name, address, and calling of communicant.

which invention has been communicated to me by (*c*), that I claim to be the true and first inventor thereof; and that the same is not in use within the United Kingdom of Great Britain and Ireland and the Isle of Man by any other person or persons to the best of my knowledge and belief; and I humbly pray that a Patent may be granted to me for the said invention.

Dated   day of   18

(*d*) To be signed by applicant or applicants.

(*d*)

NOTE.—Where application is made through an agent (Rule 8) the authorisation on the back (if used) should be signed by the applicant or applicants.

To the Comptroller,
  Patent Office, 25, Southampton Buildings,
    Chancery Lane, London, W.C.

For the convenience of applicants, suggested forms of authorisation to an agent and statement of address respectively are printed below.

---

(1) *Where application is made through an Agent (Rule 8).*

---

     hereby appoint
of
to act as   agent in respect of the within application for a patent, and request that all notices, requisitions, and communications relating thereto may be sent to such agent at the above address.

         day of   18

* *To be signed by applicant or applicants.*

   *

---

(2) *Where application is made without an Agent (Rule 9).*

---

     hereby request that all notices, requisitions, and communications in respect of the within application may be sent to

       at

       day of   18

† *To be signed by applicant or applicants.*

   †

| Patent. |

PATENTS, DESIGNS, AND TRADE MARKS ACTS, 1883 TO 1888.

Form A 2.

APPLICATION FOR PATENT UNDER INTERNATIONAL AND COLONIAL ARRANGEMENTS.

(a) Here insert name, full address, and calling of applicant, or of each of the applicants.

(a)

(b) Here insert title of invention.

do hereby declare that I (or we) have made foreign applications for protection of my (or our) invention of (b)

(c) Here insert the names of each Foreign State followed by the official date of the application in each respectively.

in the following Foreign States, and on the following official dates, viz. (c)

(d) Here insert the names of each British Possession followed by the official date of the application in each respectively.

and in the following British possessions and on the following official dates, viz. (d)

(e) Here insert the official date of the earliest foreign application.

That the said invention was not in use within the United Kingdom of Great Britain and Ireland and the Isle of Man by any other person or persons before the (e) to the best of   knowledge, information, and belief, and humbly pray that a patent may be granted to   for the said invention in priority to other applicants, and that such patent shall have the date (*f*)

(*f*) Here insert the official date of the earliest foreign application.

(*g*)

(*g*) Signature of applicant or of each of applicants.

To the Comptroller,
  Patent Office, 25, *Southampton Buildings,*
    Chancery Lane, London, W.C.

To be issued with Form **A**, **A 1**, or **A 2**.

PATENTS, DESIGNS, AND TRADE MARKS ACTS, 1883 TO 1888.

Form B.

PROVISIONAL SPECIFICATION.
(To be furnished in Duplicate.)

(*a*) Here insert title as in declaration.

    (*a*)

(*b*) Here insert name, full address, and calling of applicant or applicants as in declaration.

    (*b*)

do hereby declare the nature of this invention to be as follows : (*c*)

(*c*) Here insert short description of invention.

NOTE.—No stamp is required on this document, which must form the commencement of the Provisional Specification ; the continuation to be upon wide-ruled foolscap paper (but on one side only) with a margin of two inches on left hand of paper. The Provisional Specification and the " Duplicate " thereof must be signed by the applicant or his agent on the last sheet, the date being first inserted as follows :

    " Dated this   day of   18 ."

To the Comptroller,
    Patent Office, 25 *Southampton Buildings,*
      Chancery Lane, London, W.C.

(Obverse.)

PATENTS FORM C 1.

To the Comptroller-General.

Please send one copy of Specification No.   Year

to

(Name in full)

(Address)

PATENTS,
7½d.

(Reverse.)

½d.

The Comptroller-General,

Patent Office,

25, *Southampton Buildings,*

London, W.C.

PATENT FORMS. 251

PATENTS, DESIGNS, AND TRADE MARKS ACTS, 1883 TO 1888.

> Where provisional specification has been left, quote No. and date.
> No. ....
> Date ....

Form C.

PATENT.

COMPLETE SPECIFICATION.

(To be furnished in Duplicate—one unstamped.)

(a) Here insert title as in declaration.

(a)

(b) Here insert name, full address, and calling of applicant or applicants as in declaration.

(b)

do hereby declare the nature of this invention and in what manner the same is to be performed, to be particularly described and ascertained in and by the following statement:

(c) Here insert full description of invention, which must end with a distinct statement of claim or claims in the following form: "Having now particularly described and ascertained the nature of my said invention, and in what manner the same is to be performed, I declare that what I claim is

(c)

NOTE.—This document must form the commencement of the complete specification; the continuation to be upon wide-ruled foolscap paper (but on one side only) with a margin of two inches on left hand of paper. The complete specification and the "Duplicate" thereof must be signed by the applicant, or his agent, on the last sheet, the date being first inserted as follows:

"Dated this   day of   18 ."

Here 1.
state 2.
distinctly 3
the features of novelty claimed.

To the Comptroller,
    Patent Office, 25, Southampton Buildings,
        Chancery Lane, London, W.C.

PATENTS, DESIGNS, AND TRADE MARKS ACTS, 1883 TO 1888.

D.

PATENT.

FORM OF OPPOSITION TO GRANT OF PATENT.

[To be accompanied by an unstamped copy.]

* Here state name and full address.

*I hereby give notice of my intention to oppose the grant of letters patent upon application No.   of   , applied for by

† Here state upon which of the grounds of opposition permitted by section 11 of the Act the grant is opposed.

upon the ground†

‡ Here insert signature of opponent.

(Signed)‡

To the Comptroller,
   Patent Office, 25, Southampton Buildings,
      Chancery Lane, London, W.C.

PATENTS, DESIGNS, AND TRADE MARKS ACTS, 1883 TO 1888.

Form E.

PATENT.

FORM OF APPLICATION FOR HEARING BY THE COMPTROLLER.

IN CASES OF REFUSAL TO ACCEPT, OPPOSITION, OR APPLICATIONS FOR AMENDMENTS, &C.

SIR,

                        of (*a*)

(a) Here insert address.

hereby apply to be heard in reference to

and request that I may receive due notice of the day fixed for the hearing.

                Sir,
        Your obedient Servant,

To the Comptroller,
    Patent Office, 25, *Southampton Buildings,*
      Chancery Lane, London, W.C.

PATENTS, DESIGNS, AND TRADE MARKS ACTS.
1883 TO 1888.

Form F.

| PATENT. | FORM OF APPLICATION FOR AMENDMENT OF SPECIFICATION OR DRAWINGS. |

* Here state name and full address of applicant or patentee.

*

seek leave to amend the specification of Letters Patent No.   of 188 , as shown in red ink in the copy of the original specification hereunto annexed

† Here state reasons for seeking amendment; and where the applicant is not the patentee, state what interest he possesses in the letters patent.

My reasons for making this amendment are as follows : †

‡ To be signed by applicant.

(Signed) ‡

To the Comptroller,
    Patent Office, 25, Southampton Buildings,
        Chancery Lane, London, W.C.

PATENTS, DESIGNS, AND TRADE MARKS ACTS, 1883 TO 1888.

Form G.

| PATENT. |

FORM OF OPPOSITION TO AMENDMENT OF SPECIFICATION OR DRAWINGS.

[*To be accompanied by an unstamped copy.*]

* Here state name and full address of opponent.

*

† Here state reason of opposition.

hereby give notice of objection to the proposed amendment of the specification or drawings of Letters Patent No.   of 188   for the following reason : †

(Signed)

To the Comptroller,
    Patent Office, 25, Southampton Buildings,
        Chancery Lane, London, W.C.

PATENTS, DESIGNS, AND TRADE MARKS ACTS, 1883 TO 1888.

Form H.

| PATENT. | FORM OF APPLICATION FOR COMPULSORY GRANT OF LICENSE. |

[To be accompanied by an unstamped copy.]

* Here state name and full address of applicant.

*

† Here state name and address of patentee, and number and date of his patent.

hereby request you to bring to the notice of the Board of Trade the accompanying petition for the grant of a license to me by †

(Signed)

NOTE.—The petition must clearly set forth the facts of the case, and be accompanied by an examined copy thereof. See form next page.

To the Comptroller,
    Patent Office, 25, Southampton Buildings,
        Chancery Lane, London, W.C.

PATENTS, DESIGNS, AND TRADE MARKS ACTS, 1883 TO 1888.

Form H 1.

FORM OF PETITION FOR COMPULSORY GRANT OF LICENSES.

To the LORDS of the COMMITTEE of PRIVY COUNCIL for TRADE.

THE PETITION of (a)   of   in the county of   , being a person interested in the matter of this petition as hereinafter described :—

(a) Here insert name, full address, and description.

SHEWETH as follows :—

1. A patent dated   No.   was duly granted to   for an invention of (b)

(b) Here insert title of invention.

2. The nature of my interest in the matter of this petition is as follows :—(c)

(c) Here state fully the nature of petitioner's interest.

3. (d)

(d) Here state in detail the circumstances of the case under section 22 of the said Act, and show that it arises by reason of the default of the patentee to grant licenses on reasonable terms. The statement of the case should also show as far as possible that the terms of the proposed order are just and reasonable. The paragraphs should be numbered consecutively.

Having regard to the circumstances above stated, the petitioner alleges that by reason of the aforesaid default of the patentee to grant licenses on reasonable terms (e)

(e) Here state the ground or grounds on which relief is claimed in the language of section 22, subsections (a), (b), or (c), as the case may be.

Your petitioner therefore prays that an order may be made by the Board of Trade (f)

(f) Here state the purport and effect of the proposed order and the terms as to the amount of royalties, security for payment, or otherwise, upon which the petitioner claims to be entitled to the relief in question.

or that the petitioner may have such other relief in the premises as the Board of Trade may deem just.

17

Patent.

PATENTS, DESIGNS, AND TRADE MARKS ACTS, 1883 to 1888.

Form I.

FORM OF OPPOSITION TO COMPULSORY GRANT OF LICENSE.

* Here state name and full address.

*

hereby give notice of objection to the application of

for the compulsory grant of a License under Patent No. of 188 .

(Signed)

To the Comptroller,
    Patent Office, 25, *Southampton Buildings,*
        Chancery Lane, London, W.C.

PATENTS, DESIGNS, AND TRADE MARKS ACTS, 1883 TO 1888.

Form J.

APPLICATION FOR CERTIFICATE OF PAYMENT OR RENEWAL.

* Here insert name of patentee.

† Here insert name and full address.

        hereby transmit the fee prescribed for the continuation in force of*   Patent No.   of 18   for a further period of

        Name†

        Address

To the Comptroller,
    Patent Office, 25, Southampton Buildings,
      Chancery Lane, London, W.C.

(This part of the Form to be filled in at the Patent Office.)

PATENT.

CERTIFICATE OF PAYMENT OR RENEWAL.

Letters Patent No.   , of 188 .

                                              18 .

    This is to certify that   did this day of   18   , make the prescribed payment of £   in respect of a period of   from   and that by virtue of such payment the rights of the patentee remain in force.*

* See section 17 of the Patents, Designs, and Trade Marks Act, 1883.

Patent Office, London.

                                                                     (Seal.)

PATENT. PATENTS, DESIGNS, AND TRADE MARKS ACTS, 1883 TO 1888.

Form K.

FORM OF APPLICATION FOR ENLARGEMENT OF TIME FOR PAYMENT OF RENEWAL FEE.

SIR,

  I HEREBY apply for an enlargement of time for   month   in which to make the payment of £   upon my patent, No.   of 188 .

  The circumstances in which the payment was omitted are as follows (a) :—

(a) See Rule 49.

            I am,
              Sir,
                Your obedient Servant,

(b)

(b) Here insert full address to which receipt is to be sent.

    To the Comptroller,
      Patent Office, 25, Southampton Buildings,
        Chancery Lane, London, W.C.

| PATENT. |

PATENTS, DESIGNS, AND TRADE MARKS ACTS, 1883 TO 1888.

Form L.

FORM OF REQUEST TO ENTER NAME UPON THE REGISTER OF PATENTS.

(a) *Or* We. Here insert name, full address, and description.
(b) My *or* our.
(c) *Or* names.
(d) I *or* we.
(e) Here insert the nature of the claim.
(f) Here give name and address, &c., of Patentee or Patentees.
(g) Here insert title of the invention.
(h) Here specify the particulars of such document, giving its date, and the parties to the same, and showing how the claim here made is substantiated.
(i) Here insert the nature of the document.
(j) Where any document which is a matter of record is required to be left, a certified or official copy in lieu of an attested copy must be left.

I (a)

hereby request that you will enter (b)   name (c) in the Register of Patents :—

(d)   claim to be entitled (e) of the Patent No.   of 188 , granted to (f)

for (g)

by virtue of (h)

And in proof whereof I transmit the accompanying (i) with an attested copy thereof (j)

                I am,
                  Sir,
                  Your obedient Servant,

To the Comptroller,
     Patent Office, 25, Southampton Buildings,
         Chancery Lane, London, W.C.

| PATENT. |

PATENTS, DESIGNS, AND TRADE MARKS ACTS, 1883 TO 1888.

Form M.

FORM OF REQUEST TO ENTER NOTIFICATION OF LICENSE IN THE REGISTER OF PATENTS.

Sir,

    I hereby transmit an attested copy of a license granted to me by

under Patent No.   of 188 , as well as the original license for verification, and I have to request that a notification thereof may be entered in the Register.

                I am,
                  Sir,
                    Your obedient Servant,

(*a*)

(*a*) Here insert full address.

To the Comptroller,
    Patent Office, 25, Southampton Buildings,
        Chancery Lane, London, W.C.

PATENT FORMS.

[PATENT.]

PATENTS, DESIGNS, AND TRADE MARKS ACTS, 1883 TO 1888.

Form **N.**

APPLICATION FOR DUPLICATE OF PATENT.

Date

Sir,

    I REGRET to have to inform you that the letters patent

[* Here insert date, No., name, and full address of Patentee.]
dated*   No.

granted to

[† Here insert title of invention.]
for an invention of†

[‡ Here insert the word "destroyed" or "lost," as the case may be.]
have been‡

    I beg therefore to apply for the issue of a duplicate of such letters patent.§

[§ Here state interest possessed by applicant in the letters patent.]

    [Signature of Applicant.]

To the Comptroller,
    Patent Office, 25, Southampton Buildings,
        Chancery Lane, London, W.C.

[Patent.]

PATENTS, DESIGNS, AND TRADE MARKS ACTS, 1883 TO 1888

Form O.

NOTICE OF INTENDED EXHIBITION OF AN UNPATENTED INVENTION.

---

* Here state name and full address of applicant.

*

       hereby give notice of my intention to exhibit a ‡   of   at the

† State "opened" or "is to open."

Exhibition, which†   of   18 , under the provisions of the Patents, Designs, and Trade Marks Act of 1883.

‡ Insert brief description of invention, with drawings if necessary.

‡   herewith enclose

(Signed)

To the Comptroller,
   Patent Office, 25, Southampton Buildings,
      Chancery Lane, London, W.C.

PATENT FORMS.

| PATENT. |

PATENTS, DESIGNS, AND TRADE MARKS ACTS, 1883 TO 1888.

Form P.

FORM OF REQUEST FOR CORRECTION OF CLERICAL ERROR.

SIR,

(*a*) Or errors.   I HEREBY request that the following clerical error (*a*)

(*b*) Here state whether in application, specification, or register.

in the (*b*) No.   of 18   , may be corrected in the manner shown in red ink in the certified copy of the original (*b*)

hereunto annexed.

Signature

Full Address

To the Comptroller,
 Patent Office, 25, Southampton Buildings,
  Chancery Lane, London, W.C.

| PATENT. | **PATENTS, DESIGNS, AND TRADE MARKS ACTS, 1883 TO 1888.**

Form **Q.**

CERTIFICATE OF COMPTROLLER-GENERAL.

        Patent Office,
         London,
             18

  I,   , Comptroller-General of Patents, Designs, and Trade Marks, hereby certify

To *

* Here insert name and full address of person requiring the information.

PATENTS, DESIGNS, AND TRADE MARKS ACTS, 1883 TO 1888.

[Patent.]

Form R.

FORM OF NOTICE FOR ALTERATION OF AN ADDRESS IN REGISTER.

SIR,

(*a*) Here state name or names and full address of applicant or applicants.

(*a*) hereby request that address now upon the Register may be altered as follows

(*b*) Here insert full address.

(*b*)

Sir,
Your obedient Servant,

To the Comptroller,
   Patent Office, 25, Southampton Buildings,
      Chancery Lane, London, W.C.

PATENT.

PATENTS, DESIGNS, AND TRADE MARKS ACTS, 1883 TO 1888.

Form S.

FORM OF APPLICATION FOR ENTRY OF ORDER OF PRIVY COUNCIL IN REGISTER.

(*a*) Here state name and full address of applicant.

(*a*)

(*b*) Here state the purport of the order.

hereby transmit an office copy of an Order in Council with reference to (*b*)

Sir,
Your obedient Servant,

To the Comptroller,
Patent Office, 25, Southampton Buildings,
Chancery Lane, London, W.C.

PATENTS, DESIGNS, AND TRADE MARKS ACTS, 1883 TO 1888.

[Patent]

Form T.

Form of Appeal to Law Officer.

(a) Here insert name and full address of appellant.

I, (a)   of (a)

hereby give notice of my intention to appeal to the Law Officer from (b)

(b) Here insert "the decision" or "that part of the decision," as the case may be.

of the Comptroller of the   day of
18   , whereby he (c)

(c) Here insert "refused (or allowed) application for patent," or "refused (or allowed) application for leave to amend patent," or otherwise, as the case may be.

No. (d)   of the year 18   (d)

Signature

Date

(d) Insert number and year.

N.B.—This notice has to be sent to the Comptroller-General at the Patent Office, London, W.C., and a copy of same to the Law Officers' Clerk at Room 549, Royal Courts of Justice, London.

PATENT.

PATENTS, DESIGNS, AND TRADE MARKS ACTS, 1883 TO 1888.

Form U.

FORM OF APPLICATION FOR EXTENSION OF TIME FOR LEAVING A COMPLETE SPECIFICATION.

SIR,

    hereby apply for extension of time for one month in which to leave a complete specification upon application.

      dated

The circumstances in and grounds upon which this extension is applied for are as follows (*a*) :—

(*a*) See Rule 50.

      Sir,
    Your obedient Servant,
    (*b*)

(*b*) To be signed by applicant or applicants, or his or their agent.

To the Comptroller,
  Patent Office, 25, Southampton Buildings,
    Chancery Lane, London, W.C.

| Patent. | **PATENTS, DESIGNS, AND TRADE MARKS ACTS,**
1883 TO 1888.

Form **V.**

FORM OF APPLICATION FOR EXTENSION OF TIME FOR ACCEPTANCE OF A COMPLETE SPECIFICATION.

SIR,
              hereby apply for extension of time for month for the acceptance of the complete specification upon application No.   dated

    The circumstances in and grounds upon which this extension is applied for are as follows (*a*) :

(*a*) See Rule 50.

                              Sir,
                    Your obedient Servant,
                          (*b*)

(*b*) To be signed by applicant or applicants, or his or their agent.

To the Comptroller,
    Patent Office, 25, Southampton Buildings,
        Chancery Lane, London, W.C.

Forms are not supplied by the Patent Office, but can be purchased on personal application at the Inland Revenue Office, Royal Courts of Justice (Room No. 6), or at a few days' notice at any money order office in the United Kingdom upon prepayment of the value of the stamp.

If it should not be convenient to apply in person in either of the ways specified, the stamped forms can be ordered by post from the Controller of Stamps, Room 7, Inland Revenue Office, Somerset House, London, W.C. In that case a banker's draft or a money or postal order payable to the Commissioners of Inland Revenue and crossed Bank of England, for the value of the stamp and for the cost of postage and registration, must be forwarded to Somerset House with the application for the form.

Forms A, B, C, and C 1 are, however, *usually kept on sale* at the undermentioned places:

The Inland Revenue Office, Royal Courts of Justice (Room No. 6).

The following post offices:

London General Post Office, E.C.
Post office, 195, Whitechapel Road, E.
    ,,   239, Borough High Street, S.E.
    ,,   Charing Cross, W.C.
    ,,   Lombard Street, E.C.
    ,,   28, Eversholt Street, Camden Town, N.W.
    ,,   12, Parliament Street, S.W.; and at the following chief post offices:

In England and Wales.
Accrington.
Altrincham.
Ashton-under-Lyne.
Barnsley.
Barrow-in-Furness.
Bath.
Bedford.
Beverley.
Birkenhead.
Birmingham.
Blackburn.
Bolton.
Bradford.
Brighton.
Bristol.
Bromsgrove.
Burnley.
Burslem.
Burton-on-Trent.
Bury.
Cambridge.
Cardiff.
Carlisle.

PATENT FORMS. 273

England and Wales—continued.
  Chatham.
  Chester.
  Clitheroe.
  Congleton.
  Coventry.
  Crewe.
  Croydon.
  Darlaston.
  Derby.
  Dewsbury.
  Doncaster.
  Dorchester.
  Driffield.
  Droitwich.
  Dudley.
  Durham.
  Exeter.
  Gateshead.
  Goole.
  Greenwich.
  Guildford.
  Halifax.
  Hartlepool.
  Huddersfield.
  Hull.
  Ipswich.
  Keighley.
  Kendal.
  Kidderminster.
  Knaresborough.
  Knutsford.
  Lancaster.
  Leamington.
  Leeds.
  Leicester.
  Lichfield.
  Lincoln.

  Liverpool.
  Macclesfield.
  Manchester.
  Middlesborough.
  Nantwich.
  Newcastle.
  Newport (Mon.).
  Northallerton.
  Northampton.
  Nottingham.
  Nuneaton.
  Oldbury.
  Oldham.
  Patrington.
  Plymouth.
  Pontefract.
  Portsmouth.
  Prescot.
  Preston.
  Reading.
  Redditch.
  Richmond (Yorks).
  Ripon.
  Rochdale.
  Rotherham.
  Rugby.
  St. Helens.
  Salford.
  Scarborough.
  Sedgeley.
  Sheffield.
  Southampton.
  Stafford.
  Stalybridge.
  Stockport.
  Stoke-on-Trent.
  Stourbridge.
  Stourport.
  Sunderland.

England and Wales—continued.
  Swansea.
  Tamworth.
  Truro.
  Tunstall.
  Wakefield.
  Walsall.
  Warrington.
  Wednesbury.
  West Bromwich.
  Whitby.
  Widnes.
  Wigan.
  Wolverhampton.
  Wolverton.
  Woolwich.
  Worcester.
  York.

In Scotland.
  Aberdeen.
  Dumbarton.
  Dundee.
  Edinburgh.
  Glasgow.
  Greenock.
  Inverness.
  Lanark.
  Leith.
  Paisley.
  Perth.
  Renfrew.

In Ireland.
  Belfast.
  Cork.
  Dublin.
  Dundalk.
  Galway.
  Limerick.
  Londonderry.
  Waterford.
  Wexford.

APPENDIX.

REGISTER OF PATENT AGENTS RULES, 1889.

For the purpose of giving effect to the provisions of the Patents, Designs, and Trade Marks Act, 1888, relating to the registration of patent agents, the Board of Trade, by virtue of the provisions of the said Act, hereby make the following Rules:—

1. A Register shall be kept by the Institute of Patent Agents, subject to the provisions of these Rules and to the Orders of the Board of Trade, for the registration of patent agents in pursuance of the Act. *Register to be kept. See p. 285.*

2. The Register shall contain in one list all patent agents who are registered under the Act and these Rules. *Contents of Register.*

Such list shall be made out alphabetically, according to the surnames of the registered persons, and shall also contain the full name of each registered person, with his address, the date of registration, and a mention of any honours, memberships, or other additions to the name of the registered person which the Council of the Institute may consider worthy of mention in the Register. The Register shall be in the Form 1, in Appendix A, with such variations as may be required.

3. The Institute shall cause a correct copy of the Register to be, once every year, printed, under their direction, and published and placed on sale. Such correct copy shall, in the year 1889, be printed and published at as early a date as is possible, and in every year subsequent to the year 1889, shall be printed and published on the 31st day of January. A copy of the Register for the time being purporting to be so printed and published shall be admissible as evidence of all *Printed copies to be published annually, and to be evidence of contents of Register. See p. 286.*

matters stated therein, and the absence of the name of any person from the Register shall be evidence, until the contrary is made to appear, that such person is not registered in pursuance of the Act.

Registrar. See p. 285.

4. The Institute shall appoint a Registrar, who shall keep the Register in accordance with the provisions of the Act, and these Rules, and subject thereto, shall act under the directions of the Institute, and the Board of Trade.

Registration of persons who were patent agents prior to the passing of this Act.

5. A person who is desirous of being registered in pursuance of the Act, on the ground that prior to the passing of the Act he had been bonâ fide practising as a patent agent, shall produce or transmit to the Board of Trade a statutory declaration in the Form 2 in Appendix A.; provided that the Board of Trade may in any case in which they shall think fit, require further or other proof that the person had, prior to the passing of the Act been bonâ fide practising as a patent agent. Upon the receipt of such statutory declaration or of such further or other proof to their satisfaction as the case may be, the Board of Trade shall transmit to the Registrar a certificate that the person therein named is entitled to be registered in pursuance of the Act, and the Registrar shall on the receipt of such certificate cause the name of such person to be entered in the Register.

Final qualifying examination for registration.

6. Subject to the provisions of the Act in favour of every person who proves to the satisfaction of the Board of Trade that prior to the passing of the Act he had been bonâ fide practising as a patent agent, no person shall be entitled to be registered as a patent agent unless he has passed, and produces or transmits to the Registrar a certificate under the seal of the Institute that he has passed such final examination as to his knowledge of patent law and practice, and of the duties of a patent agent as the Institute shall from time to time prescribe.

Exemption of pupils and assistants from preliminary examination.

7. Any person who has been for at least seven consecutive years continuously engaged as a pupil or assistant to one or more registered patent agents, and any person for the time being entitled to practise as a Solicitor of the Supreme Court of Judicature in England or Ireland, or as a law agent before

the Court of Session in Scotland, shall be entitled to be registered without passing any examination other than the final examination provided for in the last preceding Rule. The Registrar shall before registering the name of any such person as a patent agent (in addition to the final examination certificate) require proof satisfactory to the Registrar that such person has been for at least seven consecutive years continuously engaged as such pupil or assistant, or is entitled to practise as such Solicitor or Law Agent.

8. Any person who is not qualified under Rule 7 must, in order to be entitled to present himself for the final qualifying examination, be— *Qualifications of persons generally for registration.*

> A person who has passed one of the preliminary examinations mentioned in Appendix B., or such other examination as the Institute shall, with the approval of the Board of Trade, by regulation prescribe.

9. The Institute shall hold at least once in the year commencing with the first day of July, 1889, and in every other succeeding year, a final qualifying examination, which shall be the final qualifying examination required under Rules 6 and 7; and the Institute shall, subject to these Rules, have the entire management and control of all such examinations, and may from time to time make regulations with respect to all or any of the following matters, that is to say, *Final qualifying examinations to be held by the Institute.*

> (a.) The subjects for, and the mode of examination of candidates;
> (b.) The times and places of the examinations, and the notices to be given of examinations;
> (c.) The certificates to be given to persons of their having passed the examinations;
> (d.) The appointment and removal of examiners, and the remuneration, by fees or otherwise, of the examiners so appointed; and
> (e.) Any other matter or thing as to which the Institute may think it necessary to make regulations for the purpose of carrying out this Rule.

10. The Registrar shall from time to time insert in the *Corrections of names and*

Register any alteration which may come to his knowledge in the name or address of any person registered.

addresses in Register.

11. The Registrar shall erase from the Register the name of any registered person who is dead.

Erasure of names of deceased persons.

12. The Registrar may erase from the Register the name of any registered person who has ceased to practise as a patent agent, but not (save as hereinafter provided) without the consent of that person. For the purposes of this Rule the Registrar may send by post to a registered person to his registered address a notice inquiring whether or not he has ceased to practise or has changed his residence, and if the Registrar does not within three months after sending the notice receive an answer thereto from the said person, he may, within fourteen days after the expiration of the three months, send him by post to his registered address another notice referring to the first notice, and stating that no answer has been received by the Registrar; and if the Registrar either before the second notice is sent receives the first notice back from the dead letter office of the Postmaster-General, or receives the second notice back from that office, or does not within three months after sending the second notice receive any answer thereto from the said person, that person shall, for the purposes of this Rule, be deemed to have ceased to practise, and his name may be erased accordingly.

Erasure of names of persons who have ceased to practise.

13. If any registered person shall not, within one month from the day on which his annual registration fee becomes payable, pay such fee, the Registrar may send to such registered person to his registered address a notice requiring him, on or before a date to be named in the notice, to pay his annual registration fee; and if such registered patent agent shall not within one month from the day named in such notice pay the registration fee so due from him, the Registrar may erase his name from the Register: Provided that the name of a person erased from the Register under this rule may be restored to the Register by direction of the Institute or the Board of Trade on payment by such person of the fee or fees due from him, together with such further sum of money, not exceeding in

Erasure of name for non-payment of fees.

amount the annual registration fee, as the Institute or the Board of Trade (as the case may be) may in each particular case direct.

14. In the execution of his duties the Registrar shall, subject to these Rules, in each case act on such evidence as appears to him sufficient. *Registrar to act on evidence.*

15. The Board of Trade may order the Registrar to erase from the Register any entry therein which is proved to their satisfaction to have been incorrectly or fraudulently inserted. *Erasure of incorrect or fraudulent entries.*

16. If any registered person shall be convicted in Her Majesty's dominions or elsewhere of an offence which, if committed in England, would be a felony or misdemeanor, or after due inquiry, is proved to the satisfaction of the Board of Trade to have been guilty of disgraceful professional conduct, or having been entitled to practise as a Solicitor or Law Agent shall have ceased to be entitled, the Board of Trade may order the Registrar to erase from the Register the name of such person. Provided that no person shall be adjudged by the Board of Trade to have been guilty of disgraceful professional conduct unless such person has received notice of, and had an opportunity of defending himself from, any charge brought against him. *Erasure of names of persons convicted of crimes, and persons found guilty of disgraceful conduct.*

17.—(1.) Where the Board of Trade direct the erasure from the Register of a name of any person, or any other entry, the name of the person or the entry shall not be again entered in the Register, except by order of the Board of Trade. *Restoration of erased name.*

(2.) The Board of Trade may in any case in which they think fit restore to the Register any name or entry erased therefrom either without fee, or on payment of such fee, not exceeding the registration fee, as the Board of Trade may from time to time fix, and the Registrar shall restore the name accordingly.

(3.) The name of any person erased from the Register at the request or with the consent of such person shall, unless it might, if not so erased, have been erased by order of the Board of Trade, be restored to the Register by the Registrar on his application and on payment of such fee, not exceeding the registration fee, as the Institute shall from time to time fix.

Inquiry by Board of Trade before erasure of name from Register.

18. For the purpose of exercising in any case the powers of erasing from and of restoring to the Register the name of a person, or an entry, the Board of Trade may appoint a committee consisting of such persons as they shall think fit. Every application to the Board of Trade for the erasure from, or restoration to, the Register of the name of any patent agent shall be referred for hearing and inquiry to the committee, who shall report thereon to the Board of Trade, and a report of the committee shall be conclusive as to the facts for the purpose of the exercise of the said powers by the Board of Trade.

Appeal to Board of Trade.

19. Any person aggrieved by any order, direction, or refusal of the Institute or Registrar may appeal to the Board of Trade.

Notice of appeal.

20. A person who intends to appeal to the Board of Trade under these rules (in these Rules referred to as the appellant) shall, within fourteen days from the date of the making or giving of the order, direction, or refusal complained of, leave at the office of the Institute a notice in writing signed by him of such his intention.

Case on appeal.

21. The notice of intention to appeal shall be accompanied by a statement in writing of the grounds of the appeal, and of the case of the appellant in support thereof.

Transmission of notice of appeal to Board of Trade.

22. The appellant shall also immediately after leaving his notice of appeal at the Institute send by post a copy thereof with a copy of the appellant's case in support thereof addressed to the Secretary of the Board of Trade, 7, Whitehall Gardens, London.

Directions as to hearing of appeal.

23. The Board of Trade may thereupon give such directions (if any) as they may think fit for the purpose of the hearing of the appeal.

Notice of hearing of appeal.

25. Seven days' notice, or such shorter notice as the Board of Trade may in any particular case direct, of the time and place appointed for the hearing of the appeal shall be given to the appellant and the Institute and the Registrar.

Hearing and decision of appeal.

24. The appeal may be heard by the President, a Secretary, or an Assistant Secretary to the Board of Trade, and the decision and order thereon of the President, Secretary, or Assistant

Secretary, as the case may be, shall be the decision of the Board of Trade on such appeal. On the appeal such decision may be given or order made in reference to the subject-matter of the appeal as the case may require.

26. The fees set forth in Appendix C. to these Rules shall be paid in respect of the several matters, and at the times and in the manner therein mentioned. The Board of Trade may from time to time, by orders signed by the Secretary of the Board of Trade, alter any of, or add to, the fees payable under these Rules. Fees.

27. Any regulation made by the Institute under these Rules may be altered or revoked by a subsequent regulation. Copies of all regulations made by the Institute under these rules shall, within twenty-eight days of the date of their being made, be transmitted to the Board of Trade, and if within twenty-eight days after a copy of any regulation has been so transmitted, the Board of Trade by an order signify their disapproval thereof, such regulation shall be of no force or effect; and if, after any regulation under these Rules has come into force, the Board of Trade signify in manner aforesaid their disapproval thereof, such regulation shall immediately cease to be of any force or effect. Alteration of regulations.

28. The Institute shall once in every year in the month of December transmit to the Board of Trade a report stating the number of applications for registration which have been made in the preceding year, the nature and results of the final examinations which have been held, and the amount of fees received by the Institute under these Rules, and such other matters in relation to the provisions of these Rules, as the Board of Trade may from time to time, by notice signed by the Secretary of the Board of Trade and addressed to the Institute, require. Report to Board of Trade.

29. In these Rules, unless the context otherwise requires— Definitions.

"The Act" means the Patents, Designs, and Trade Marks Act, 1888.

"The Institute" means the Institute of Patent Agents acting through the Council for the time being.

"The Registrar" means the Registrar appointed under these Rules.

"Registered patent agent" means any agent for obtaining patents in the United Kingdom whose name is registered under the Act and these Rules.

Commencement. 30. These rules shall commence and come into operation on the 12th day of June, 1889, but at any time after the making thereof any appointment or regulations may be made and things done for the purpose of bringing these Rules into operation on the said day.

Title. 31. These Rules may be cited as the Register of Patent Agents Rules, 1889.

By the Board of Trade,

COURTENAY BOYLE,
Assistant Secretary, Railway Department.

The 11th day of June, 1889.

APPENDIX A.

Form 1.

Form of Register.

Name.	Designation.	Address.	Date of Registration.

Form 2.

*Form of Statutory Declaration.

Register of Patent Agents Rules, 1889.

I, A.B. [*insert full name, and in the case of a member of a firm add,* "a member of the firm of   "], of

* A printed form of his declaration for use of applicants is now also on sale.

, in the county of
, Patent Agent, do solemnly and sincerely declare as follows:

1. That prior to the 24th December, 1888, I had been bonâ fide practising in the United Kingdom as a patent agent.

2. That I acted as patent agent in obtaining the following patents:—

[*Give the official numbers and dates of some patents for the United Kingdom in the obtaining of which the declarant acted as patent agent.*]

3. That I desire to be registered as a patent agent in pursuance of the said Act.

And I make this solemn declaration conscientiously believing the same to be true and by virtue of the provisions of the Statutory Declarations Act, 1835.

Declared at

APPENDIX B.

Particulars of Preliminary Examinations.

1. The Matriculation Examination at any University in England, Scotland, or Ireland. See p. 286.

2. The Oxford or Cambridge Middle Class Senior Local Examinations.

3. The Examinations of the Civil Service Commissioners for admission to the Civil Service.

APPENDIX C.

Fees.

Nature of Fee.	When to be paid.	To whom to be paid.	Amount.
			£ s. d.
For registration of name of patent agent who had been bonâ fide in practice prior to the passing of the Act.	On application and before registration.	To the Registrar at the Institute.	5 5 0
For registration of name of any person other than as above.	Do. do.	Do. do.	5 5 0
Annual Fee to be paid by every registered patent agent.	On or before November 30th of each year, in respect of the year commencing January 1st following.	Do. do.	3 3 0
On entry of a candidate for the final qualifying examination.	At time of entering name.	Do. do.	2 2 0

REGISTER OF PATENT AGENTS RULES, 1891.

WHEREAS by the Register of Patent Agents Rules, 1889, it is provided, amongst other things, that the Register of Patent Agents established by the said Rules shall be kept, and certain duties in reference thereto and to the examination and registration of and otherwise in relation to Patent Agents shall be performed, by the Institute of Patent Agents referred to in the said Rules:

And whereas the said Institute of Patent Agents has been dissolved and ceased to exist, and in place thereof the Chartered Institute of Patent Agents has, by Royal Charter dated the 11th day of August, 1891, been incorporated:

Now, THEREFORE, for the purpose of giving effect to the provisions of the Patents, Designs, and Trade Marks Act, 1888, relating to the registration of Patent Agents, the Board of Trade, by virtue of the provisions of the said Act, hereby make the following rules:—

1. From and after the commencement of these Rules all the duties and powers of the Institute of Patent Agents under the Register of Patent Agents Rules, 1889 (hereafter in the present Rules referred to as "the Rules of 1889"), shall be transferred to and vested in the Chartered Institute of Patent Agents, and the Rules of 1889 shall, where applicable, and save so far as they are altered by the present Rules, have effect, with the following modifications:— *Transfer of powers and duties of Institute of Patent Agents to Chartered Institute.*

    (1.) For the words "The Institute of Patent Agents" there shall be substituted the words "The Chartered Institute of Patent Agents."

(2.) The Registrar shall be the person who, for the purposes of the duties of the Registrar under the Rules of 1889 and the present Rules, shall be continued in office or appointed by the Chartered Institute of Patent Agents.

Saving rights, privileges, acts, appointments, and regulations under Rules of 1889.

2. Nothing contained in the present Rules shall affect any right, privilege, obligation, or liability acquired, accrued, or incurred, any act done, or appointment or regulation made under the Rules of 1889; and any regulation made by the Institute of Patent Agents under the Rules of 1889 prior to the commencement of the present Rules shall be subject to alteration and revocation by subsequent regulations to be made by the Chartered Institute of Patent Agents under Rule 27 of the Rules of 1889, as amended by the present Rules.

Publication of register.

3. So much of Rule 3 of the Rules of 1889 as provides that the correct copy of the Register therein referred to shall be printed and published in every year subsequent to the year 1889 on the 31st day of January is hereby annulled, and instead thereof the following Rule shall have effect:—

In the month of February in each year, and at such other times as the Chartered Institute of Patent Agents may think desirable, the said Chartered Institute shall cause a correct copy of the register to be printed under their direction and placed on sale.

Alteration of Appendix B.

4. Instead of Appendix B. to the Rules of 1889 there shall be substituted the Appendix to the present Rules, which may be cited as Appendix B.

Commencement and citation.

5. The present Rules shall commence and come into operation on the 19th day of November 1891, and, together with the Rules of 1889, may be cited as the Register of Patent Agents Rules, 1889 to 1891.

By the Board of Trade,

COURTENAY BOYLE,
Assistant Secretary.

Dated the 18th day of November, 1891.

APPENDIX B.

Particulars of Preliminary Examinations.

1. The Matriculation examination at any University in England, Scotland, or Ireland.

2. The Oxford or Cambridge Middle Class Senior Local Examinations.

3. The first public examination before Moderators at Oxford.

4. The previous examination at Cambridge.

5. The examination in Arts for the second year at Durham.

6. The examination for first-class certificate of the College of Preceptors (40 and 41 Vict. c. 25. s. 10).

7. The examination resulting in the obtaining of a Whitworth Scholarship.

INDEX.

	PAGE
ACCEPTANCE OF SPECIFICATION,	
amendment before	109
effect of	53, 54
extension of time for	56
how advertised	52, 57
time for, limited	56
ACTION	
for infringement, *see* INFRINGEMENT.	
for threats, *see* THREATS.	
to support threats	165
ACTIONS,	
consolidation of	150
pending, what are	108
ADDRESS,	
alteration of, on Register	218
change of, how notified	46
notified on application form	45
of applicant or agent required	45
AGENT	
Custom House, not liable for infringement	138
for foreign inventor	38
form of appointment of	45
importer need not be an	38
may improve the invention	38
may sign specification	47
penalty for using description patent agent	122
signature as, does not incur penalty	123
who may act as, in patent matters	122

	PAGE
AGENTS,	
patent, who are	122, 282
Chartered Institute of	283
register of	275
AGREEMENT for license, enforceable	100
AMBIGUITY	
evidence to explain, may be given	144
in specification avoids patent	71
may be removed by amendment	106
AMENDMENT OF SPECIFICATION,	
appeal against refusal of leave for	113
appeal to law officer on	111
applicant for, may be required to explain	112
application for	109
before acceptance	50, 109
discretion of Comptroller as to	112
effect of, on damages	114
law officer's decision final	112
leave for, when given, unquestionable	113
limitation on refusal to allow	112
may invalidate patent	114
must not enlarge claim	107
of doubtful effect is allowed	107
opposition to	110
pending action, costs of	109
pending action for infringement	108
pending action for threats does not affect	108
pending appeal does not affect	108
pending revocation petition	159
procedure, when allowed	113
second application for, no appeal against refusal of leave for	113
when complete for purpose of action	114
who may apply for	107

ANTICIPATION,

by publication must be complete	31
by sale of patented article	29
invalidates patent	27
what constitutes	26

APPEAL,

all issues may be decided on	186
certificate of particulars given on	199
judgment reversed on, by consent	13
pending, does not affect amendment	108
to law officer, see LAW OFFICER.	

APPLICANT FOR PATENT

dying before patent sealed	59
later may withdraw	52
must not conceal anything of value	69
who may be	33

APPLICATION FOR PATENT

by post, when deemed received	49
by representative of deceased inventor	59
by whom signed	44
completion of	54
comprising several inventions, how dealt with	51
effect of acceptance of	53
forms of	44
how numbered	49
joint, advantages of a	37
lost in post	49
more than one for the same invention	52
referred to an examiner	50
representations in	9
through agent	44
under international convention, how made	236
usually granted unless opposed	12
where to be sent	46

INDEX.

	PAGE
ASSIGNEE	
of patent becomes patentee	92
of profits of patent, rights of	94
ASSIGNMENT, equitable, registration of	217
ASSIGNOR	
may not dispute validity	145
of patent does not warrant its validity	92
ASSISTANTS	
inventor may employ	40
may even improve an invention	40
BANKRUPTCY OF INFRINGER, proof for profits admissible in	192
CARRIERS of infringing articles may be sued	138
CERTIFICATE	
as to particulars	197
by Comptroller of any Act	220
of particulars may be given on appeal	199
of payment of renewal fees	89
of validity	193
as a rule only one granted	193
effect of on costs	194
grant of, discretionary	194
in action for threats	170
when action is settled	194
when patent is held bad	194
CERTIFIED COPIES of records in Patent Office	220
CLAIMING CLAUSE, form of	74
CLAIMS,	
absence of, does not void patent	74
amendment must not enlarge	107
complete specification must end with	73
must all be valid	76
CLERICAL ERRORS, how corrected	106

COLONIAL ARRANGEMENTS . 233

COMBINATION,
new parts in, need not be distinguished . . 75
of old parts may be invention . . 23
test of novelty of 25
when infringed by use of an equivalent . 129

COMPANY
may apply for patent . . . 36
may be registered as owner of patent . . 218

COMPTROLLER 3
absent, deputy for 4
appeal against, no costs allowed in . . 113
appeal from the discretion of . . 52, 56
discretion of, as to amendments . . 112
    how exercised 51
    to refuse patent, limited . . . 11
may require explanations . . . 51

CONSIDERATION for grant of patent . 69

CONSOLIDATION OF ACTIONS . . 150

COPIES
certified by Patent Office . . . 220
Office, of records 220
sealed, of specifications, &c. . . . 220

COPYRIGHT, a subject for, is not an invention . 16

CORPORATION,
a, may apply for letters patent . . 36
may be registered as owner of patent . . 218

COSTS
before law officer, recovery of . . 119
follow the event 196
granted on unopposed revocation petition . 158
how affected by certificate of validity . . 194
may be awarded by law officer . . 119
of abortive appeal to law officer . . 117

INDEX.

	PAGE
COSTS (*continued*)—	
of amendment pending action	109
of issues, when set off	196
of obtaining Attorney General's *fiat* allowed only by consent	156
of particulars	197
when action is discontinued	198
when action is dismissed unheard	197
of shorthand notes	199
on higher scale rarely allowed	199
COUNSEL, employment of, in patent matters	123
CROWN,	
the, bound by letters patent	96
need not admit validity	96
not bound by recitals in grant	10
not compelled to grant patent	10
procedure for infringement against	96
terms of user of invention by	96
CUSTOM-HOUSE AGENTS not liable for holding infringements	138
DAMAGES,	
for infringement, how assessed	188
measure of, in action for threats	170
none claimable during enlargement of time for renewal	89
undertaking as to, on grant of injunction	141
DAYS NOT RECKONED as last days for doing anything	226
DECLARATIONS, statutory, how made	82
DEFENDANT,	
may be estopped from disputing validity	145
out of jurisdiction	138
procedure by, on motion for interim injunction	140
who may be made, in patent action	138

	PAGE
DELIVERY up of infringing articles	192
DESIGN, a, is not an invention	16
DIRECTORS liable for infringement by their Company	138

DISCLAIMERS,
amendment by	107
when action pending	108
object of	75
special and general	85

DISCLAIMING clauses	74

DISCOVERY
in action for infringement	149
in petition for revocation	158
not necessarily invention	16
of equivalent may be invention	22

DRAWINGS
accompanying specifications, rules for	47
supplement the letterpress	68

EQUIVALENT,
discovery of an, is invention	22
substitution of a known, not invention	22
substitution of an, when infringement	128

ERRORS, clerical, how corrected	221
ESTOPPEL from disputing validity	145

EVIDENCE
as to meaning of specification allowed	178
before Comptroller, form of	82
before Law Officer	118
how dispensed with	226
in a patent action	184
of infringement subsequent to writ	143
of public knowledge	176
on petition for extension	207

INDEX.

	PAGE
EXAMINATION OF SPECIFICATIONS, scope of	50

EXAMINERS,
- applications referred to 50
- complete specifications referred to . . 56
- reports of, confidential 57

EXHIBITION, notice to Comptroller of intended . 34

EXHIBITIONS,
- industrial, inventions protected at . . 33
- international, inventions protected at . 34

EXTENSION OF TERM, see LETTERS PATENT

FEES FOR KEEPING UP PATENT,
- certificate of payment of 89
- enlargement of time for payment of . . 89
- enlargement of time for payment not a matter of right 89
- how paid 88
- payable in advance 89
- payable in connection with letters patent . 239

FOREIGN PATENTEE alone can apply under international convention 236

FOREIGN RESPONDENT, notice to, in revocation petition 157

FOREIGN VESSELS, use of invention on . 98

FORM
- of claiming clauses of complete specification . 74
- of grant of letters patent 7

FORMS,
- how altered 5
- patent . . . . . 243 *seqq*.
  - how obtainable . . . 272
- some, of particulars of objections . . 173

INDEX.

IMPORTER,
    an, is an inventor 37
    of infringing article liable . . . 133

IMPORTERS, classes of . . 38

IMPROVEMENT, in patent for, new parts must be
    distinguished from old . . . 75

IMPROVEMENTS, letters patent for . . 21

INFRINGEMENT,
    admitted, damages on . . . 143
    after issue of writ, evidence of . . 143
    amendment pending action for . . 108
    by importation . . . 133
    by manufacture only . . . 132
    by sale of component parts of article . 131
    by *user* only 132
    is a question of fact . . . 131
    no action for, before sealing of patent . 136
    patentee must not incite to . . 133
    penalties of . . . 94, 125
    profits of, recoverable in bankruptcy . 192
    test of 130
    threatened, action to restrain . 95, 126
    what constitutes . . . 126

INFRINGEMENT ACTION,
    accounts of profits in . . . 190
    a defence in action for threats . . 165
    amendment of particulars in . . 148
    certificate of validity in . . 193
    damages in, how assessed . . 188
    defence in 143
    defendant alleging trade secret . 149
    defendant in 138
    defendant pleading license cannot question
        validity 146

INDEX.

INFRINGEMENT ACTION (*continued*)—

	PAGE
delivery up of infringements	192
discovery in	149
evidence in support of particulars alone allowed	148
expert witnesses in	184
form of defence in	147
in what court brought	135
inspection of defendant's works, when allowed	148
inspection of plaintiff's works, when allowed	149
interrogatories in	149
issues in, when taken separately	185
judgment in	188
jury unusual in	182
models required in	184
names of customers not disclosed before judgment	150
names of purchasers must be disclosed after judgment	191
one of several defendants estopped	147
particulars of breaches in	141
particulars of objections required in	147
pending, threats allowable while	167
plaintiff in	136
plaintiff's title usually admitted in an	184
profits recoverable in bankruptcy	192
statement of claim in	141
to restrain threatened infringement	137
triable at Assizes	177
triable with assessor	182
trial of, in Scotland	183
what constitutes diligence in bringing	166
when validity indisputable	145

INFRINGING ARTICLES may be ordered to be delivered up 192

INJUNCTION, INTERIM, . . . 139
    granted on default of defendant . . 140

INDEX. 299

INJUNCTION, INTERIM (*continued*)—   PAGE
   granted when validity allowed . . 140
   not granted, if strongly resisted . . 140
   plaintiff obtaining, undertakes in damages . 141
   withheld, on undertaking by defendant . 141

INSPECTION
   in actions for infringement . . . 148
   of anticipating machines, only by consent . 175

INTERNATIONAL
   arrangements 233
      application under, how made . . 236
      patent under, how dated . . 237
      who may apply for patent under . . 235
      with what countries existing . . 234
   convention, provisions of . . . 237
   exhibitions, inventions protected at . . 34
   office for patents 237
   periodical for patents . . . 237

INTERROGATORIES
   in action for infringement . . . 149
   in petition for revocation . . . 158

INVALIDITY may be cured by amendments . 106

INVENTION
   a question of fact 26
   communicated, when patentable . . 38
   defined by complete specification . . 67
   disclosure of, by applicant . . . 6
   each requires separate patent . . . 50
   illegal or immoral, no patent for . . 11
   may be application of knowledge . . 40
   may consist in re-discovery . . . 42
   may be suggested by another . . . 39
   must be fully disclosed . . . 69
   slight, often valuable . . . 13
   what constitutes an 22
   what is an 2

INVENTOR,

	PAGE
application by representative of deceased	36
dying before taking out a patent	3, 59
foreign agent for	38
includes importer	37
may employ assistants	40
must have exercised ingenuity	39

INVENTORS, rival, which gets patent . . 41

IRELAND,

actions in	135
offences how punishable in	215
official documents of Patent Office in	228
reservations as to	227

ISLE OF MAN,

official documents of Patent Office in	228
reservations as to	227

ISSUES,

all are usually tried together	185
costs of, when set off	196
Court of Appeal will decide all	186

JOINT OWNER

can sue for infringement	136
petition for extension by	203
powers of, to grant licenses	100

JOURNAL,

International, for patents	237
official, of Patent Office	6

LAW OFFICER,

appeal to, as to part of decision of Comptroller	116
from discretion of Comptroller	52, 56
notice of hearing of	117
costs before, on abortive appeal	117
decision of, final	115
documentary evidence before	119

INDEX.

LAW OFFICER (*continued*)—
    may award costs 119
    may employ experts in cases of opposition . 118
    may order witnesses to attend . . 118
    may take evidence *vivâ voce* . . . 118
    notice of appeal to, to whom sent . . 116
    procedure on appeals to . . . 115
    proceedings before, notice by post in . . 120
    time for appealing to . . . 115
    whom the, must hear . . . 117

LAW OFFICERS may make rules for procedure . 120

LEGAL PROCEEDINGS, none begun before sealing 58

LETTERS PATENT,
    amendment may invalidate . . . 114
    area affected by 91
    assignment of, in whole or in part . . 91
    benefits of, may pass to non-owners . . 94
    bind the Crown 96
    corporations may apply for . . . 36
    cover one invention only . . . 50
    date of 58
    dated prior to 1883, provisions as to . . 225
    determine unless fees are paid . . 87
    extension of term of, grounds for . . 201
        how obtained 201
        for part of 202
    extension of, granted only once . . 203
    for imported invention good . . . 18
    for improvements 21
    form of grant of 7
    grant of, an act of grace . . . 10
    grant of, is formal 43
    granted for combination . . . 23
    granted on application in due form . . 11
    how applicable to foreign vessels . . 98
    how numbered 49

	PAGE
LETTERS PATENT (*continued*)—	
lost, replaceable	58
profits of, rights of assignee of	94
refusable in some cases	11
refused for immoral invention	43
several persons may jointly apply for	35
subject of, must be new within the realm	18
must be useful	17
term of	87
when sealed	58
who may apply for	35
LIBRARY OF PATENT OFFICE	5
LICENSE UNDER LETTERS PATENT	99
agreement for, enforceable	100
consideration for	101
compulsory grant of	104
covering several patents	103
granted by joint owner	100
grant of, does not warrant validity	101
licensee may repudiate	102
may be equivalent to assignment	103
not necessarily assignable	102
not under seal, enforceable	99
plea of abandonment of, not notice thereof	146
registration of	219
when revocable by patentee	101
LICENSEE	
cannot sue alone for infringement	103, 137
entitled to have specification construed	144
estoppel of, does not bind partner	146
may give evidence as to ambiguity in specification	144
may not dispute licensor's title	144
may not dispute validity	101, 146
may repudiate license	146
may show that licensor's title has expired	144
usually covenants not to dispute validity	102

LICENSOR
does not indemnify against infringement of earlier patent	101
does not warrant validity	101
not bound to keep up patent	102

MACHINE, use of the word, in title . . 62

MANUFACTURE, what is a . . 15

MANUFACTURER
and user may be sued together	139
may defend as third party	139

MASTER PATENT
is liberally construed	20
what is a	19

MISTAKES in specification, effect of . . 73

MODELS
of inventions for Patent Museum	228
required in action	184

MONOPOLIES,
advantages of	1
in ancient times	1
limited to fourteen years	2
Statute of	2

MONOPOLY,
conditions usually imposed on grantee of a	1
grant of, an act of grace	1

MORTGAGOR of patent can sue for infringement . 137

NAMES
of customers, interrogatories not allowed as to	150
of purchasers of infringements must be disclosed after judgment	191

NOTICE

	PAGE
of appeal to Law Officer	115
of intention to petition for extension	204
of opposition to grant of patent	77
of opposition to amendment	110
of opposition to extension	205
of refusal of grant by Comptroller	51
of restrictions must be given to purchaser	93
of revocation petition to foreign respondent	157
to Comptroller of intention to exhibit	34

NOVELTY

need not imply invention	22
want of, invalidates patent	27

OFFICIAL JOURNAL

6

OPPOSITION

to amendment	110
to grant of patent, appeal to law officer in	77, 84
Comptroller's decision to be notified	84
disclaimer may be ordered in	85
evidence before Comptroller	82
first ground of, *obtained from opponent*	78
grounds for	77
notice of hearing by Comptroller	83
notice of, how given	77
notice of, to applicant	77
opponent restricted to grounds stated in his notice	83
second ground of, *prior patent*	79
second ground, who may oppose on	79
time for leaving evidence	83
third ground of, *a subsequent application*	81
when likely to succeed	84
who will be heard in	80
law officer may employ experts	77, 118

PARTICULARS,
 certificate as to 197
 costs of 197
  when action is discontinued . . 198
  when action is dismissed unheard . . 197
 of breaches in infringement action . . 141
 of objections, forms of . . . 173
  should omit weak ones . . . 172
  should specify claims attacked . . 171
  to validity . . . 147, 171

PATENT, *see* LETTERS PATENT.
 a bad, often valuable . . . 12
 a bad, needs skilful management . . 13
 action, Court of Appeal can decide all issues in . 186
  issues in a 178
  trial of 177
  trial of, procedure in . . . 183
 agents 122
 agents, register of 275
 agents' rules 275
 for a principle is void . . . 16
 forms, how obtainable . . . 272
  list of, and forms of . . 242 *seqq.*
 increased in value by litigation . . 12
 Museum 228
 Office 3
  circular 121
  library 5
  publications of 6
  publications, how obtainable . . 228
  publications, where copies may be seen . 229
  seal 4
  when open 5

PATENTEE,
 definition of 87
 joint, rights of 93

PATENTEE (*continued*)—

	PAGE
must supply Public Services	96
rights of a	91

PENALTIES,

how enforced in Ireland	215
in Isle of Man	215
in Scotland	215

PENALTY

for falsifying register	214
for representing unpatented article as patent	214
for using title 'Patent Agent'	214

PERSONS incapacitated, provisions as to . 226

PETITION FOR EXTENSION OF TERM OF PATENT,

accounts of profits required	207
by assignee	212
caveats against	206
costs in, how taxed	205
costs of, when abandoned	213
costs of, how recoverable	212
Crown may oppose	206
documents required in, by Privy Council	205
effect of unchecked infringement on	211
exceptional merit required	209
fees in connection with	213
imperfect accounts may be fatal	208
importer not likely to succeed	211
invention not brought into public use	210
lapsed foreign patents do not affect	211
may be granted conditionally	212
must not withhold anything	203
notice of intention to present	204
opposition to	205
profits must be decidedly inadequate	208
profits of foreign patents must be shown	207

PETITION FOR EXTENSION OF TERM OF
    PATENT (*continued*)—
    registration of order on . . . 219
    remuneration allowed for patentee's time . 208
    rules for procedure in . . 203 *seqq*.
    time for presentation of . . . 202
    utility considered only as affecting merit . 210
    utility to public must be shown . . 209
    validity of patent assumed on . . 209
    what Judicial Committee consider in . 206
    where there is an exclusive license . . 211
    who may present . . . 202, 203

PETITION FOR REVOCATION, *see* REVOCATION.

PLACES where patent office publications may be seen 229

PLAINTIFF in action for infringement . . 136

POSTAL,
    applications when deemed received . . 49
    communications to the Patent Office . . 225

PRINCIPLE, patent cannot be granted for a 16, 20

PRIOR PUBLICATION
    anticipates patent 27
    what is 30

PRIOR USER
    need not be continuous . . . 29
    what is 27

PROCESS, new, may be invention . . 23

PROFESSIONAL ASSISTANCE in patent matters 121

PROVISIONAL PROTECTION, what is . . 53

PUBLICATION
    at exhibition before application . . 33
    foreign, may anticipate patent . . 32
    of invention, what constitutes . . 27
    prior, must be complete . . . 32
    proof of prior 32

INDEX.

	PAGE
PUBLICATIONS of Patent Office	6

PUBLIC KNOWLEDGE,
- how proved . . . 176
- limits invention . . 22

RECITALS,
- if untrue, avoid patent . . 10
- in grant, binding on applicant . 10
- not binding on Crown . . 10

REGISTER
- of patents 216
  - alteration of address on . . 218
  - certified copies of, how obtained . 220
  - equitable assignment, enterable on . 217
  - inspection of, by the public . 219
  - licenses entered in . . 219
  - no notice of trust allowed in . 217
  - penalty for falsifying . . 214
  - rectification of, by the Court . 219, 221
  - request to make entry in, how made . 218
  - sealed copy of, is evidence . 220
- of patent agents rules . . 275

REPORTS
- by Comptroller to Parliament . 227
- of examiners, confidential . 57

REPRESENTATIVES
- of deceased applicant may continue application 59
- of deceased inventor may apply for patent . 3

REVOCATION OF LETTERS PATENT,
- for fraud, re-grant of patent on . 155
- forms of proceedings for obtaining . 153
- grounds for . . . 154
- petition for, amendment after judgment . 159
  - amendment of specification in . 159
  - amendment pending . . 108
  - Attorney-General's *fiat* as to . 155

REVOCATION OF LETTERS PATENT (continued)—

	PAGE
costs in, follow event	159
defendant opens in, on trial	158
expert witnesses in	184
general procedure in	158
is not a matter *inter partes*	157
judgment in	159
jury in, unusual	182
jury in, when fraud alleged	158
may be tried at Assizes	158
notice to foreign respondent	157
opposed, usually tried as witness action	158
particulars of objections in	157
security not given by foreign respondent	158
triable at Assizes	177
triable with assessor	182
unopposed, granted with costs	158
who may present	154

ROYALTIES for working patent . . . 101

RULES,
    effect of 5
    for patent procedure, how made . . 4
    to be laid before Parliament . . . 5

SALE,
    conditional, of patented articles, restrictions on . 92
    may be subject to restrictions on use . . 133
    of article may void subsequent patent . . 29

SCOTLAND,
    actions in 135
    offences, how punishable in . . . 215
    official documents of Patent Office in . 228

SEAL of Patent Office 4

SEARCHES 122

SERVANTS,
    independent inventions of, protected . . 41
    may improve an invention for master . . 40

SHORTHAND NOTES, cost of . . . 187

SPECIFICATION,
    acceptance of, how advertised . . 52, 57
    ambiguity in, avoids patent . . . 71
    amendment of, before acceptance . 50, 109
        pending petition for revocation . . 159
            action for infringement . . 108
            appeal does not affect . . 108
            action for threats does not affect . 108
    certified copies of 220
    complete, extension of time for leaving . 55
        how prepared 55
        how to be left 54
        may describe method different from that in the provisional . . . 66
        may describe things unclaimed . . 67
        may embody improvements . 54, 66
        may be narrower than provisional . 67
        must describe same invention as the provisional 65
        nature of 65
        protection by acceptance of . . 54
        referred to examiner . . . 56
        requirements of . . . 68
        signed by some applicants only . . 55
    construction of . . . 126, 178
        benevolent 180
        forms a precedent . . . 179
    copies of, how obtainable . . . 57
    how prepared for filing . . . 46
    how signed 47
    may assume what is of common knowledge . 69
    may be signed by anyone as agent . . 123
    may be supplemented by drawings . . 68

SPECIFICATION (*continued*)—

misleading, avoids patent	71
mistakes in, effect of	73
must accompany application	46
must not be equivocal	71
must not leave need for experiments	70
need describe one method only	72
need not state chemical nature of a product	72
often settled by counsel	124
provisional, description of	63
nothing outside can be protected	65
protects by acceptance	53
should be in general terms	64
title of, choice of	60
to what class of persons addressed	69
when open to public inspection	57
when printed	57
where copies of, may be seen	229
STATEMENT OF CLAIM in infringement action	141
STATUTORY DECLARATIONS, how made	82

SUBORDINATE INTEGERS

are protected	23
how claimed	76

TEST ACTION 151

THREATS,

action for restraining	163
and counter-action must deal with similar infringements	166
certificate of validity in	170, 193
counter-action need not succeed	167
counter-action need not test validity	165
damages in	170
does not affect amendment	108
interim injunction in	169
infringement action a defence in	165
particulars required in	168
procedure on trial of	170

INDEX.

THREATS (*continued*)—

validity may be questioned in	169
when stayed because of infringement action	170
conditions under which allowable	165
issue as to	182
limitation of	163
of action may be effective	95
summary of law as to	168
value of	160
what constitute	163

TITLE

of specification, choice of	60
too general, may avoid patent	61

USER

alone may be infringement	132
may be restricted on sale	132
of invention, what constitutes prior	28

UTILITY,

a question of fact	18
how much is required for patent	17
necessary to support patent	17
necessary for extension of patent	209
no relation to commercial success	18

VALIDITY,

certificate of	13
licensee may not dispute	101
no examination as to, by Patent Office	44
not warranted on sale of patent	92
by licensor	101
objections to, mostly questions of fact	181

WARLIKE INVENTIONS, special provisions as to 223 *seqq.*

WRIT in an action for infringement . 137

PRINTED BY ADLARD AND SON,
BARTHOLOMEW CLOSE, E.C., AND 20, HANOVER SQUARE, W.

www.ingramcontent.com/pod-product-compliance
Lightning Source LLC
Chambersburg PA
CBHW031858220426
43663CB00006B/675